# CONTAGION

# Studies in Continental Thought

**John Sallis, general editor**

# CONTAGION

## Sexuality, Disease, and Death in German Idealism and Romanticism

DAVID FARRELL KRELL

INDIANA UNIVERSITY PRESS

*Bloomington & Indianapolis*

The paper used in this publication meets the minimum requirements of American National Standard for Information Sciences—Permanence of Paper for Printed Library Materials, ANSI Z39.48-1984.

Manufactured in the United States of America

**Library of Congress Cataloging-in-Publication Data**
Krell, David Farrell.
    Contagion : sexuality, disease, and death in German idealism and romanticism / David Farrell Krell.
      p.    cm. — (Studies in Continental thought)
    Includes bibliographical references and index.
    ISBN 0-253-33371-7 (alk. paper). — ISBN 0-253-21170-0 (pbk. : alk. paper)
    1. Philosophy of nature—Germany—History—18th century.   2. Philosophy of nature—Germany—History—19th century.   3. Novalis, 1772–1801—Contributions in philosophy of nature.   4. Schelling, Friedrich Wilhelm Joseph von, 1775–1854—Contributions in philosophy of nature.   5. Hegel, Georg Wilhelm Friedrich, 1770–1831—Contributions in philosophy of nature.   I. Title.
II. Series.
B2748.N35K74   1998
113'.092'243—dc21                            96-37764

1  2  3  4  5  03  02  01  00  99  98

*For my students at DePaul University
from 1993 through 1996,
who were carriers.*

*Among all* poisons, *the* soul *is the most potent.*

—*NOVALIS*, DAS ALLGEMEINE BROUILLON, 2: 706

*Every substance can become a poison. For only through
the activity of an organism does a substance become poisonous.*

—*SCHELLING*, ERSTER ENTWURF, 73

*The living is something fixed and determined in-and-for-itself.
Whatever it touches chemically on the outside is immediately
transformed by this contact. . . . The living immediately poisons
this other, transforms it, as spirit does when it intuits something,
transforming it and making it its own. For that something
is* its *representation.*

—*HEGEL*, ENZYKLOPÄDIE, 9: 402-403

# CONTENTS

# PREFACE

The present book began as a lecture course given at the Collegium Phaeno-menologicum in Perugia in 1996. The program, directed by Walter Brogan, was devoted to the general topic, "The Forces of Nature in German Idealism." During the third and final week, I presented some texts in the philosophies of nature of Friedrich von Hardenberg (Novalis, 1772–1801), Friedrich Wilhelm Joseph von Schelling (1775–1854), and Georg Wilhelm Friedrich Hegel (1770–1831). These materials, from the years 1798 to 1806, pertain to the "early periods" of Schelling and Hegel, whereas Novalis died before any such convenient distinctions could be made. My course, "*Con-tagium:* Dire Forces of Nature in Novalis, Schelling, and Hegel," was designed to continue the work begun in the two earlier courses that summer, the first on the forces of nature in Kant's third *Critique*, taught by Rodolphe Gasché, the second on the role of nature in Hölderlin's poems, fictions, dramas, and essays, taught by Françoise Dastur. Yet I had no illusions about the fact that my restriction of the general topic to the *dire* or *baneful* forces of nature was controversial; indeed, such a restriction contradicted the general sense we have about the forces of nature in German Idealism and Romanticism, which seem anything but dire.

The lecture course focused on the interwoven accounts of sexuality, disease, and death in these three thinkers. The word *contagium*, somewhere between "contact" and "contagion," I had first found in Schelling, who was quoting William Harvey. It seemed best suited to name the painful proxim-ity of eros, *morbus*, and thanatos in all three thinkers. The course was, and is, part of a larger project, one that has been in the planning stages for decades now, under the working title, *Eggs and Lips: Toward a History of Genitality.* I have no idea at this point whether the larger project—which extends from the Presocratics, Plato, and Aristotle, through Hegel, Freud, and Ferenczi, to Bataille, Foucault, Irigaray, and Derrida—will ever be realized, and I have decided to publish this fragment of it, which manifests, I hope, a certain unity of range and conception all its own.

My thanks to Walter Brogan for his kind invitation to teach at the Collegium, and to Kevin Miles, who threatened me gently with all the dire forces of nature if I did not accept Walter Brogan's generous invitation. Thanks also to Peg Birmingham, who made it possible for me to attend the Collegium, and who over the years has been such a discerning friend and stimulating interlocutor, especially in matters of pleasure and politics. My gratitude to Janet Rabinowitch, my first editor and a friend for many years now, to Anna Vaughn, who read an early draft of the book and offered astute criticisms and apposite suggestions, to David Thomas, who amassed all the research materials for the book, and to the helpful staff of the John T. Richardson Library at DePaul. Finally, my gratitude to the Deutscher Akademischer Austauschdienst and the University Research Council at DePaul for making possible my study visit to the University of Freiburg in 1996.

*In der Strobelhütte*, St. Ulrich

# CONTAGION

CONTAGION

## INTRODUCTION

$\mathcal{W}$ord is that the German Idealists and Romantics were dreamy folk whose hearts leapt up when they beheld a rainbow in the sky. So they were. Yet in their own estimation the leap was always as much a result of a nervous disturbance in the heart muscle as of euphoria. For the so-called Romantics and Idealists in Germany at the end of the eighteenth century, *all* the forces of nature were *dire* forces. Or, to put it somewhat less trenchantly, whatever the *beneficent* powers of nature might be, they could not be separated from the baneful ones. The solar flame toward which the sunflower and the human eye turned as toward their hope was the same fire that scorched and blinded. Forces of nature as *dire* forces? The point, as Colonel T. E. Lawrence would later say, is not minding that they hurt.

One of the differences between us and the German Romantics and Idealists is that they knew a great deal about nature and the sciences of nature. Whereas philosophers today are generally failed mathematicians or humanists who left chemistry and physics far behind after secondary school, philosophers like Novalis, Schelling, and Hegel were themselves in intimate contact with, or were themselves, practicing chemists, biologists, physicists, and physicians. What astonishes us when we study the scientific notebooks and theoretical treatises of these thinkers is their vast learning and our own considerable ignorance. We had thought—indeed, we had been taught—that because science progresses inexorably we ourselves would progress right along with it without having to lift a finger or a phial. We took retorts to be clever replies to clever objections, we took mineral deposits to be lodes of metaphors, we took flowers to be pleasant—but still we thought we would wax in age, wisdom, and scientific know-how, one-third of which came true. The Romantics were less romantic.

Heidegger says somewhere that German Idealism never went into decline; rather, he says, those who followed in its wake were simply not up to it. One hopes that Heidegger is simply being his usual sardonic, chastising self. Alas, he is right. The more we study German thought and science in the 1790s, the more shocking our own dearth of knowledge becomes to us, and the more embarrassing the limits of our own range of inquiry—our hyperspecializations—seem to us. How impoverished our scientific imagination appears to be, in spite of all those wonderful nature programs on public television that our forebears never had a chance to watch.

And it is not simply our ignorance that troubles us. It is also our loss of heart, our inability to inquire in any sustained way into fields we take to have become too specialized and too technical for us. We have surrendered so much to the technocrats! Besides, we are so busy making speeches about ethics and politics these days, so busy being righteous and engaged and correct, that we have no time to do philosophy, especially philosophy of nature, much less to muse on the mysteries of the universe in pond or tree or sex. Finally, I suspect that our loss of heart runs deeper: secretly we feel betrayed by nature nowadays, at least apart from the politically correct lip-service we pay to the wilderness. For the wilderness within ourselves we have lost our love. The sexes look upon one another either as sources of fatal infection or as instigators of subjugation and humiliation—subjects for further speeches and litigations. The world the of Jena Romantics and Idealists is not a world of innocents, to be sure, and certainly not of naïfs, but it does manifest more energy and more courage than we today can muster. Such energy and courage enable these thinkers to face the quandary that is at the heart of the present book, the conundrum that might be put this way: Nature is the source of the life that is in us, the giver of all the gifts we enjoy; yet among those gifts is the *Gift* of contagion, infection, illness, and eventual death. The forces of nature are simultaneously life-giving and death-dealing, and no act of thought or achievement of poetry can obscure what in later history, the history of our own time, will be called *lifedeath*, the fatal imbrication in nature of birthing and dying.

In the three parts of the present book, I argue that the responses to nature in the thought of Novalis, Schelling, and Hegel are infinitely complicated by their recognition of the *dire forces* of nature. The infinite complication expresses itself in a certain *ambivalence* in the response to nature of these thinkers. When does such ambivalence first assume the importance I am claiming it already has in Novalis, Schelling, and Hegel? I do not know. I hesitate to wield the vast epochal rubrics of *Enlightenment* and *Romanticism*, or to make any claims on the basis of these colossal distinctions. And it may be that one can find traces of such ambivalence in every Judaeo-Christian writer of the past two millennia in the West. Yet it seems to me that one can find early forms of a specifically modern ambivalence in both Goethe and Kant. Before we turn to the younger generation of Jena romantics and philosophers in the 1790s, we might therefore take a look at two works published at the outset of that decade, both in 1790, namely, Goethe's *Metamorphosis of Plants* and Kant's *Critique of Judgment*. Understandably, our treatment of Kant's massive work will take more time and concentration than our perusal of Goethe's graceful pamphlet.

## HOPES AND TANGLES: GOETHE AND KANT

An early text copied out by Goethe *(Die Natur,* ca. 1780) expresses in its antiphonal form—in the intense dialectic of its every assertion and counterassertion—the ambivalence Goethe feels toward nature:

> Nature! We are surrounded and embraced by her—without being able to exit from her or to enter into her more deeply. Unasked and unwarned, we are taken up into the circuitry of her dance; she has her way with us, until we grow weary and sink from her arms. . . .
>
> We live in the midst of her and are foreign to her. She speaks to us ceaselessly and does not betray her secret to us. We work our endless effects on her, yet have no dominion over her.
>
> She seems to have invested all her hopes in individuality, and she cares nothing for the individuals. Always she builds, always she destroys, and we have no access to her workshop.
>
> She lives in a profusion of children, and their mother, where is she? —
>
> She squirts her creatures out of nothingness, and does not tell them where they came from and where they are going. Their task is to run; *hers* is to know the orbit.[1]

Goethe's ambivalence has not resolved itself a decade later, by the time of his *Metamorphose der Pflanzen,* even if the skeptical antiphon has in the meantime been muted. For, in spite of the paean to nature in *Metamorphosis of Plants,* something like a sense of the dire forces of nature lies concealed there—especially at the beginning and at the end of the treatise.[2] Near the outset of the work (§§3–8), Goethe explains that he will interpret only the *regular, progressive* development of plants, the development that is based on internal principles of modification. Yet there is also, he says, a *regressive, irregular* development that merits attention, although for the moment he is excluding it from his purview. Further, Goethe explains that he will pay no heed to the *accidental* or *merely contingent* aspects of plant growth and reproduction; his example is pollination through contact by insects.

Yet why are insects more contingent than the winds, winds more contingent than the variegated pistils and stamens themselves? How is contingency or accident related to irregularity, hence to regression? What precisely is the nature of an accident, and the accident of a nature?

Even the regular, progressive action of stamens and pistil, which is subsequent to the development of stem, node, leaf, calyx, and flower in the plant, is mysterious in its necessitous course. Early in the *Metamorphosis of Plants*, Goethe describes the *anastomosis* or branching of veins and arteries in the leaf. *Anastomosis* means "to supply with a mouth," in the sense of the mouth of a river, or delta. The leaf of the plant supplies a mouth for the purpose of plant nourishment, a *second* mouth, inasmuch as the root system, supported and nursed by the earth, is the plant's first mouth. The second mouth, the mouth of anastomosis, completes the process of plant growth by exposing the leaf's most refined liquids to the action of the sun and the gases of the air—the gases, essences, or spirits of the air, one might say. When the expansive, nourishing anastomosis reaches a certain point, a powerful contraction ensues. The plant stops growing. Its life suddenly becomes more luxurious and more complex. Pollen from the stamens of one plant engages in a "spiritual anastomosis" (§63) with the pistil of another. Pollen, or, rather, the rarefied liquid that according to Goethe is contained within each minuscule kernel of *Blütenstaub* (literally, "blossom dust"), "communicates its influences" to the pistil *(seine Einflüsse mitteilt)*. As we shall soon hear, Kant too in 1790 speaks of sexual contact—this time among humans—in terms of a *mitteilen*, a communicating. He does not specify it as a *geistige* anastomosis, however, inasmuch as he is in a hurry to get to the presumably more spiritual moral law. The generation of thinkers who pored over Goethe's *Metamorphose der Pflanzen* and Kant's *Kritik der Urteilskraft* must have wondered why the regular, progressive growth and reproduction of plants (and also of humans?) culminates in this uncanny "communication," which is either contingently or necessarily spiritual. They also must have wondered why Kant was in such haste to abandon what Goethe had identified as eminently spiritual, as though communication were a kind of contagion.

Near the end of his inquiry (§§107–11), Goethe writes some strange paragraphs—oddly telescoped, elliptical, belated—on his choice of the annual rather than the perennial plant for his demonstrations. The more typical example of metamorphosis, he says, would have been Linnaeus's six-year cycle in the growth and development of trees; it is only for heuristic purposes that he has chosen to show the principles of expansion and contraction at work in a plant that lasts only one season. Goethe does not explain why the six-year cycle prevails in plant life, nor does he muse at any length on this invasion of *time* into his theme. No one could say that time is a purely dire force in the life of plants, of course, since plants burgeon in time. Yet no one could ignore the fact that plants that live but a single season have a different biological fate than those that awaken and renew themselves each spring, those whose wintry death is only "relative."

In a later work, from the year 1824, Goethe has much to say about "relative death" and the absolute absence of "absolute death" in nature (1: 424). Yet it is the constancy of this dire relative of relative death—absolute demise—that shadows and haunts Goethe's otherwise inspiring and inspired philosophy and science of nature. For is not death always absolute for the *individual* that undergoes it in each case, whether wildflower or human being? Are not all of nature's hopes invested in the individuals she invariably consigns to demise? And is not absolute death somehow coiled at the very heart of life and love, whether in a rose or in a rose by any other name? "She seems to have invested all her hopes in individuality, and she cares nothing for the individuals." Goethe's later *Wahlverwandtschaften (Elective Affinities)*, composed in 1808–1809, was to show that the chemistry of love could be deadly, that even a landscaped nature was never truly domesticated, never truly deprived of its daimonic force, and that human nature in particular resisted trimming and taming.

The generation of young thinkers and poets who watched the great man grow old knew that Goethe—the inveterate observer and collector, the great lover of nature—was never unaware of the baneful forces of nature. His relationship with Schiller had begun with an argument, for the man of high moral ideals had found

Goethe's *Metamorphosis of Plants* too empirical. Yet even though Schiller might idealize nature and turn it into a morality play, Goethe always felt constrained to report on what transpired under his hands and before his eyes. What transpired was not always what the moralizing human beings might have wanted.

It is of course impossible to overestimate the impact of Kant's *Critique of Judgment* on all the thinkers and writers of Kant's own and the later generations. It goes without saying that the generation immediately after Kant inherited the task that his third and final *Critique* had undertaken but only partly fulfilled—that of a comprehensive systematic synthesis of the realms of knowledge, morality, and feeling. The integrative function of judgment among the faculties, and of the feelings of pleasure and pain among the human responses to beauty and purposiveness, were Kant's great hopes for such a synthesis—and not only his. Yet the *play* of the faculties and the *upsurgence* of feelings forced the discipline of science to keep company with the vagaries of taste and liking and compelled reason to dwell somewhere between sensuous necessity and suprasensuous freedom. What a tangle of problems Kant and the next generation had to confront! Nature herself, however, as Kant informed them all in the preface to the first edition of the *Critique of Judgment*, is responsible for that "tangle," responsible for the unavoidable obscurity in what he is trying to accomplish.[3]

Why does nature involve us in such tangles? This apparently straightforward question is one of the many that rose to confront Kant's first readers. We cannot hope to respond to such a question—which is not at all straightforward—here. However, let us examine quite briefly the figure of nature in the third *Critique*, focusing on its baneful or more problematic side. That figure plays a major role, not only in the Analytic of Teleological Judgment, as we would expect, but also in the Analytic of the Beautiful, the Analytic of the Sublime, and the Doctrine of Method. It may be that a look at the dire aspect of nature will enable us to see something behind or beneath the tangles and the obscurity that trouble Kant and his young followers.

Kant is aware that purposiveness is a special transitional figure or mediator between the concepts of nature and freedom (xxxiv). Moreover, purposiveness is bound up with the feeling of pleasure. Negative pleasure, which is not quite yet pain, is bound up with something like a recalcitrant purposiveness in nature, somewhere between the appropriateness and inappropriateness of nature; negative pleasure emerges on a scene where limits and boundaries are difficult to determine—especially the boundary between nature's measuring up to, or failing to measure up to, what the human mind demands of it. No doubt, the Analytic of the Sublime is the privileged place of such negative pleasure and recalcitrant purposiveness. It is also the privileged place for a discussion of nature's dire forces, and so we shall now turn to it.

In the transition from the beautiful to the sublime (*KU*, §23), Kant distinguishes between the outright delight we take in the beautiful, our liking for the beautiful that grants us "directly" a feeling of the "furtherance of life," and the more complex response we have to the sublime. The feeling of the sublime is a pleasure that arises "only indirectly," by means of a "momentary inhibition of the life-forces," followed by a sudden "outpouring" or "ejaculation" of such forces, all the stronger for their having been dammed up or contained (*KU*, 75). Whereas the imagination seems to be "at play" when confronting the beautiful, it is seriously engaged and challenged by the sublime. Schelling will pay considerable attention to this inhibition (*Hemmung*) of the forces of life and nature—to the point where one might say that Schelling's philosophy of nature, from start to finish, is an engagement with inhibitive sublimity. For Kant, however, the sublime only *seems* to have nature as its object. Indeed, it seems to have as its object the most recalcitrant and obstreperous aspects of nature, those that resist every attribution of purposiveness, those that seem utterly inappropriate to our imagination and utterly beyond our powers of depiction, those that seem to do our faculties violence (*KU*, 76). Yet it is this *seeming*, above all, that Kant places at the center of his analysis. For the only proper object of the sublime is the human heart of hearts, the mind of man, the famous untranslatable *Gemüt*. Sublimity arises from ideas of reason, not from the realm of nature as such. Nevertheless, the violent face of nature, nature experienced as Chaos, nature "in its wildest, most unbridled disorder and devastation," the dire forces of nature *call forth* this experience in our heart of hearts (*KU*, 78). The more counterpurposive nature appears to us in its storms at sea or blizzards in the mountains, and the more "aorgically" it rages (as Hölderlin will soon say), the more revelatory it is of an "altogether independent purposiveness in us" (ibid.). Sublimity, according to Kant, is in fact an experience of nature's *withdrawal* or *evanescence* before the power of the human mind. Kant does concede that this spectacle of nature's putative obeisance or complaisance before the mind of man is best observed from some point of safety, a refuge from the dire natural forces that otherwise would destroy us. Ahab waxes eloquent on the planks of the *Pequod* but has less to say once the whirring line has bound him to the sounding white whale. Kant, like Melville, waxes eloquent at the writing desk.

What Kant pursues in his Analytic of the Sublime is the "expansive" movement of the human heart or mind, the *Erweiterung* or dilation of the imagination and the heart, which seem to imitate the first movement in the metamorphosis of plants—the movement of growth, outward expansion, and reach. Yet the sense of recoil, of a kind of contraction in the face of a violent nature, is also always present there. In terms of the rhetoric of the Analytic of the Sublime, recoil and contraction are in fact the more prominent aspects of Kant's own text. From its secure purchase, at its safe remove, and after an inhibition that may in fact be more than momentary, the (Kantian) human heart opens in diastole to the sublimity of its self— a sublimity that Kant will soon be able to steer in the predictable directions of the noumenal human being and the moral law. In the context of the dire forces of nature, however, let us dwell for more than a moment on the momentary inhibition of pleasure; let us dwell upon the recalcitrance, the measurelessness, the inappropriateness, the destructive violence of chaotic nature. Let us dwell on Kant's best moments at the writing desk.

One should seek examples of sublimity not in "natural things" such as plants or animals, things whose very concept implies purposiveness, but in "raw nature" itself (*KU*, 89). Again, however, nature should not be so raw that it touches us directly with "actual danger"; rather, raw nature should show us its magnificent—albeit not magnanimous—side, the side of its grandeur, the side that manifests its "suprasensuous substrate" (*KU*, 94). Raw nature seemingly yields to ideas of reason—ideas not of purposiveness but of something, as Wordsworth will say, "far more deeply interfused." Such yielding waits upon a reversal of the usual way we perceive the putative sublime, a reversal of that *Subreption* by which objects of nature surreptitiously seize our attention, whereas our attention should be focused precisely on our own powers of attention. Kant describes the usual usurpation by objects of nature in terms of the following rhetorical question: "And at all events, who would wish to call *sublime* those shapeless masses of mountain rock piled on top of one another in wild disarray, with their icy pyramids, or the gloomy, surging sea, etc.?" (*KU*, 95). The answer to the rhetorical question *who?* is, of course, *everyone*, inasmuch as the subreption would otherwise pose no threat to the analysis of sublimity. It is the surreptitious claim on our attention of a savage and monstrous nature that Kant's entire analysis must try to expose and overcome. Yet it cannot repudiate that claim by *fiat*. Indeed, wild nature continues to assert itself in Kant's text, not so much surreptitiously as boldly—with the keenest rhetorical flourishes. Surely, the generation after Kant must have mused on the maneuver or trope of subreption, wondering about its power to fascinate as they admired the Kantian prose evoked by it. And they must also have noted that the principal figure of speech in Kant's descriptions of (sublime) nature is *prosopopoeia*, personification, as though the text itself were surreptitiously restoring the rights of the human person (or the human *persona*) against nature's natural subreption; as though, in other words, the primal subreption by nature were itself a rhetorical turn. Subreption by nature? Or by Kant? Kant writes:

> Boldly overhanging cliffs, menacing us, as it were *[gleichsam drohende]*, thunderclouds towering high in the sky, sweeping over us with lightning and crackling thunder, volcanoes in all their destructive violence, hurricanes with the devastation they leave in their wake, the boundless ocean stirred to indignation *[in Empörung gesetzt]*, the high waterfall of a mighty stream: all these kinds of things transform our capacity to resist them— when that capacity is compared to their might—into puny insignificance. Yet the sight of them becomes all the more attractive as it grows increasingly frightful, though only when we find our way to safety; and we readily call these objects *sublime*, because they augment our psychic strength *[die Seelenstärke]* beyond its customary modicum, and they enable us to discover in ourselves a capacity to resist that is of an altogether different kind, one that encourages us to measure ourselves against the backdrop of the seeming omnipotence of nature. (*KU*, 104)

Hegel will be particularly happy to make this discovery and to submit to Kant's guidance even as he criticizes his guide and master. He will be relieved to find that "our physical impotence" (*KU*, 105) is outmatched by the impotence of nature herself. He will be reassured to see nature swooning before a vigilant, confident spirit. Novalis and Schelling will be more likely to worry about the subreption involved in this happy discovery, the putative discovery of "another, non-sensuous standard" by which the human spirit, safely ensconced, proves to its own satisfaction that it is indomitable. When Kant celebrates the felicitous discovery of a sublimity that is ultimately *gemütlich* ("Herein is truth" [*KU*, 106]), hailing it as "a major moment for the critique of judgment" (*KU*, 112), all three thinkers would doubtless like to affirm it. Yet they, especially Novalis and Schelling, are troubled by the contagious nature of this "surreption." While they can sense in themselves the expansion of spirit that accompanies the view of a storm at sea, "as an abyss that threatens to swallow everything" (*KU*, 119), and while they would like to make the leap to the moral law on the basis of that very expansion, they are perhaps troubled by Kant's obsession with power *(Macht, Gewalt)* and his waxing militancy—his approbation of war and of warlike *virtù* and his diatribes against "the melting affects," "the tyranny of the sensuous," and "enthusiasm." Kant goes so far as to say that enthusiasm is a "debilitating illness" (*KU*, 126), even though he himself calls natural beauty a source of "voluptuosity of the spirit" (*KU*, 168), and even though his most telling affirmation of sublimity occurs in a reference to the goddess of the Temple of Isis at Saïs (*KU*, 197 n.). Where in the tangle of nature does "surreption" begin or end? What about that face of nature that is as close to the human heart of hearts as anything can be—what about the human *body* in which the human *Gemüt* is entangled?

For all his emphasis on the noumenal human being (*KU*, 398), the soldierly spiritual human being who shows respect for and submission to the moral law, and for all his anxiety in the face of the sensuous and sensual human being (*KU*, 395), the human being caught up in enthusiasm, Kant, especially in his third *Critique*, remains relentlessly attached to the human body. Near the end of his "General Remark" on aesthetic reflective judgments, he writes:

> Nor can it be denied that all representations in us, whether in objective terms they are merely sensuous or altogether intellectual, can subjectively be bound up with enjoyment or pain, no matter how unnoticeable these two may be. (This is the case because enjoyment and pain collectively affect the feeling of life, and because neither of the two, inasmuch as they are modifications of the subject, can be indifferent.) Nor can it even be denied that, as Epicurus once put it, *enjoyment* and *pain* are ultimately corporeal, even if they are initiated by the imagination or by representations of the understanding. This is the case because life without the feeling of the corporeal organ is mere consciousness of its existence, but not the feeling of well-being or malaise, that is, the feeling of the furtherance or the inhibition *[Hemmung]* of the life forces, and because the heart of hearts for itself alone is all life (the principle of life itself), and obstacles or furtherances

must be sought outside of it but still within the human being, which is to say, in conjunction with its body. (*KU*, 129)

Schelling, to repeat, will soon be occupied by the question of *Hemmung*, although he will eschew the notion of a single life force. Novalis will be struck by the mysterious connection between our heart of hearts, our *Gemüt*, which is life whole and entire, and the bodily affects that nevertheless enhance or diminish life. He will find the ladder of soul and body to be a Heraclitean figure, inasmuch as the way up is the way down.

When we turn from the Analytic of the Sublime to that of Teleological Judgment, and also to the Doctrine of Method, matters related to the sublimely terrifying life of the body, the sentient, sensuous, surreptitious body that variously enables, enhances, and hinders life, rise to meet us. Let us emphasize here those that may have most troubled the generation after Kant.

1. *Contingency.* Nature, says Kant, is the realm of necessity, spirit the realm of moral freedom. Yet the Kant of the third *Critique* appears to say something quite different. He appears to say that the freedom that is most accessible to our reflection is the one we experience in the play of our faculties as they contemplate the beautiful. And he certainly does say that nature is the realm of *accident* or *contingency* even more than of necessity. The entire generation to follow will worry about such contingency in the realm of necessitous nature. For the more one tries to bracket out every vulgar sense of human intention *(Absicht)* in nature, and the more one matures and realizes that the Nile does not flood *so that* it deposits silt *so that* I can plant my wheat *so that* I will not starve *so that* I will fulfill my human destiny, the more powerfully present in nature is accident—and in me the realization that nature "could have shaped itself in myriad other ways" (*KU*, 269). The entire generation after Kant—indeed, all the generations of philosophers henceforth—will marvel over those "thousand other ways" of nature and will have to worry whether Kant himself successfully avoids vulgar anthropocentrism *(vestigium hominis video)* when he reverts willy-nilly to human reason, the regulative idea, the noumenon, and the moral law, or to intention, final purpose, and the suprasensuous substrate, in order to combat contingency (*KU*, 285; 387–90). They will have to worry whether the entire elaborate system of reason envisaged by Kant is a fortress in the air, a desperately contrived bulwark against the dire forces of nature. For

as Kant's system goes colossal, opting for magnitude and infinitude, the forces of nature go infinitesimal and microscopic. Secretly, and by secretion, they organize in the direction of infection by the forces of contagion.

2. *The organism as an organized, self-organizing, self-reproducing product.* Kant makes it perfectly clear that the search for purposiveness in nature has only one place to go: it must seek out the *organized* products of nature (*KU*, 282), that is, *organisms.* Organisms are those natural things whose composite parts are reciprocally related, that is, conjoined in such a way that they mutually influence one another, thus making the organic whole something greater than the mechanically calculated sum of its parts. Moreover, such a self-producing product, such a *growing* product, is also self-productive in another sense: it frustrates all the conceptions of mechanism and technicity by reproducing itself sexually (*KU*, 287). The very word *organ*, which means *tool*, will have to be taken with an extraordinary sense of irony and paradox, for the organ of the organism will be the tool that tools itself, and a tool that *brings itself forth* will ultimately not be a matter of production or τέχνη at all (*KU*, 291–92). In the Kantian and post-Kantian systems of reason, purposiveness will be ineluctably tied to growth, maturation, sexual opposition, and sexual reproduction—with all its foibles, *faibles*, and fabulations.

3. *"Communication," and the monstrous births of the primal mother.* In section 65 of the *Critique of Judgment*, which bears the heading "Things, as purposes of nature, are organized creatures," Kant pursues with a relentless eye the secret of organization. Organization is a self-organizing force *(Kraft)*, a force that shapes itself—and defines itself by tautology. Indeed, it is a force that *communicates* itself to the matter of which the living creature is composed. Kant has some trouble identifying what it is that gets communicated: in editions A and B, it is the *force* that communicates itself to matter: *die sie den Materien mitteilt;* in edition C, it is the *essence* or *creature (das Wesen)* in general that communicates *formative* force *(b i l d e n d e Kraft)* to matter. When and how such communication occurs is difficult to say, and Kant in fact says little about it. Perhaps he has in mind the spiritual anastomosis that Goethe at that moment is attributing to plant reproduction. At all events, it is clear that this sort of communication (but compare the *communicability* of a sensation, discussed in the Analytic of the Beautiful: *KU*, 151 n. and 153–56) has to do with the

reproductive function, *die Zeugung*, of organized creatures. Kant's full definition of the organized creature states that it is *eine sich fortpflanzende bildende Kraft*, "a force that reproduces [and] shapes itself" (*KU*, 293). Indeed, the generation after Kant might have expected the master to say more about sexual reproduction than about the moral law, inasmuch as the entire thrust of his *Critique of Judgment*, in each of its mutually influencing parts, takes him to the scene of creaturely communication. Yet that scene is also the place where nature's profusion, its excess of force, and even its sublimely dire forces, come to the fore: Kant refers in passing to one of the "most wondrous properties of organized creatures," namely, their proclivity to give birth to monsters and malformations (*Mißgeburten oder Mißgestalten im Wachstum*), a proclivity that will trouble Hegel repeatedly throughout his philosophy of nature. When in the Doctrine of Method Kant encourages philosophers to become "archaeologists of nature," tracing back the variegated forms of organized creatures to some common *Urmutter*, and even to "the womb of the Earth," he is doing so for the purposes of teleology—he wants to find the secret ends of nature's profusion of monstrous growths in her matricial beginnings. However, in terms of method, to combine ἀρχή and τέλος in this way seems adventurous and bold: Kant speaks of *ein gewagtes Abenteuer der Vernunft*, "a daring adventure of reason" (*KU*, 371 n.), and no doubt that adventure is what Novalis, Schelling, and Hegel thought they were engaged in. For even though like breeds like (*generatio homonyma*), many students of nature believe they can descry the development of sea creatures, via monstrous amphibians, into land creatures (*generatio heteronyma*). And perhaps even the homonymous generation that Kant avows opens itself to some fundamental ambiguity or double sense; indeed, it must do so, or else the archaeologist's search for the primal mother of all heteronymous forms is futile. Whatever the homonym within generation may suggest, however, the generation after Kant knows that mating (*Begattung*) is no mere formality on the way to the moral law (*KU*, 376). They also know that Kant, driven to the scene of sexual reproduction, seems in a hurry to leave it and all its "monstrations" behind, even though nothing else will bring him as close to the notion of intention (*Absicht*) and purposiveness (*Zweckmäßigkeit*) in nature. Thinkers and poets after Kant must have been struck by the *ambivalence* of the powerful, self-shaping, self-reproducing force in nature, which is both productive and dire, as Kant himself was struck by it—nowhere more so than on the scene of sex:

> There is but one single external purposiveness that is bound up with the inner purposiveness of organization, and, without posing the impossible question as to why creatures organized in this fashion had to exist, in the external relationship we see nonetheless a means serving an end. This is the organization of both sexes in relation to one another for the procreation of their kind. For here as well one can always pose the same question that one poses concerning the individual: Why did such a pair have to exist? The answer is: The pair first constitutes an *organizing* whole, albeit not one organized in a single body. (*KU*, 380–81)

The most famous of Kant's questions, *Was ist der Mensch?* here receives its most disquieting reply: the organized human being is, or rather *are*, essentially twofold, duplex and duplicitous. The individuals are at least two.

Was it this failure of nature to form an organizing whole in each individual—in each of the two—that discouraged Kant from tarrying on the scene of sexuality? Was it this unaccountable split in the life force of the ostensibly best-organized creatures in nature—best organized, yet oscillating somewhere between angel and beast—that sent him on to that final purpose he despaired of finding in nature, the final moral purpose that would rescue him from the indignation of seas, the anger of cliffs beetling o'er their base, the monstrosity of heteronymous births, the entire Chaos of nature?

Perhaps it would be instructive to read Novalis, Schelling, and Hegel—along with Goethe, Schiller, Schlegel, Tieck, Hamann, Klingemann, Brentano, Paul, Eichendorff, Hoffmann, and many others—with the following question in mind: Who among these thinkers and poets succumbs to Kant's despair concerning self-shaping, self-reproducing, duplicitous nature, and precisely when and where do they succumb? Who among them tarries on the scene of natural purposiveness, shunning naive anthropocentrism, to be sure, but unwilling to leap too quickly from nature's vital monsters into the lifeless arms of moral legislation? Who among them remains true to the Earth, even when its redoubled forces turn dire? And, finally, who will linger over these dire forces as they go microscopic, shrinking asymptotically to invisibility? For the generation after Kant, remembering Leibniz's *petites perceptions*, will experience the forces of nature not in the storm at sea or the blizzard on the mountain but in the *actio in distans* or touching-at-a-distance of the germ—both the miniscule seeds of fecundity and the impalpable source of fatal contagion.

This would certainly not be the only way to read Novalis, Schelling, and Hegel. Yet it is one way, and it is the way taken in the book at hand. I shall now introduce the three thinkers—among the many possible ones—who have come to dominate this text, and then present a brief analysis of each of the dozen chapters of the book's itinerary, merely by way of introduction. Finally, I shall add a word about the conclusions—tentative though they may be—that are drawn at the end of the book.

### NOVALIS, SCHELLING, HEGEL: A BIOGRAPHICAL INTRODUCTION

In this brief space and time, in a modest volume such as this one, nothing like justice can be done to these thinkers or to the theme of dire forces in nature, much less to German Romanticism and Idealism as a whole. Let us content ourselves for the moment—but remain wretched over the long haul—with brief glimpses into the work of Friedrich von Hardenberg, known to posterity as Novalis, Friedrich Wilhelm Joseph von Schelling, and Georg Wilhelm Friedrich Hegel. Because Hegel is surely the best known of the three, my introductory biographical remarks on Novalis and Schelling will be far more detailed than those on him; my hope is that one day their lives and work will be as well known to philosophers as Hegel's are.

In part one I examine Novalis's theoretical-scientific notebooks of 1798–1800.[4] The notebooks as a whole, which in book form represent approximately one thousand pages of material, virtually none of it translated into English and most of it ignored by philosophers both inside and outside Germany, contain in my view some of the most remarkable thoughts of that remarkable decade of the 1790s. In the present context, only those notes dealing with sexuality, illness, and death will draw our attention. I will then, in part two, turn to Schelling's *Erster Entwurf eines Systems der Naturphilosophie* (1799), another untranslated and relatively neglected text.[5] Yet it is the first and only text in Schelling's philosophy of nature in which the philosopher spells out in considerable detail his philosophy of *organism* and is therefore a text that merits careful study. Finally, in part three, I will take up some sections of Hegel's comparatively well-known course in *Realphilosophie*—focusing on his philosophy of nature there—taught at Jena in 1805/06.[6] Allow me to begin, however, with a few words concerning the lives of these three thinkers.

Novalis, toward the end of his life, was thinking more and more about illness, the illness that killed his fiancée Sofie two days after her fifteenth birthday and that was about to snuff out his own life as well. His meditation occasionally took on a personal note: "If I should now become ill . . . ," he wrote about a year before he died, proceeding to plan out the activities that might be propitious for a convalescence (2: 679). As he thought about how he might best use his remaining time, he mused, "Should not sleep gradually be abolished?" (ibid.). However, unending sleep overtook him early, as it did Keats and Shelley.

Novalis was born in Oberwiederstedt, Lower Saxony, on May 2, 1772, the second child and first son of impoverished aristocratic parents. Novalis's father, and later he himself, became a mining inspector for the state in an effort to keep body and soul, life and literature, together. In 1785 the Hardenberg family moved to Weissenfels, not far from the Naumburg that would become Nietzsche's home seventy years later. During his university career, which began in 1790 at Jena, Novalis met Schiller; from 1795 onward, he studied with Fichte. Novalis's *Fichte-Studien*, which consist of over two hundred book pages of intense, critical involvement with Fichte's system, are among the most fascinating of his notes. In January 1792, in Leipzig, Novalis first met Friedrich Schlegel, whose friendship and support were undeniably the crucial mainstays of his literary and intellectual life. In 1794 Novalis took a degree in law from the University of Wittenberg. Yet his own poetic, scientific, and philosophical preoccupations were by that time at the center of his existence.

In the summer of 1795, the summer when he first met Fichte, Novalis also met briefly with Hölderlin at the philosopher Immanuel Niethammer's house in Jena. Yet Novalis's name does not appear in the index of names devoted to Hölderlin's correspondence; likewise, there is no reference to Hölderlin in Novalis's journals and letters. During the autumn of 1794, young Hardenberg had met and fallen in love with Sofie von Kühn, who was thirteen years old at the time. They were unofficially engaged on March 15, 1795. In November of that year, Sofie became ill with tuberculosis; two years after their unofficial engagement—two years of fever, infection, agonizing illness, and horribly unsuccessful surgeries—on March 19, 1797, Sofie died. Novalis had spent the first ten days of the final month with her, but left some nine days prior to her death, unable to sustain the vigil. He was able to visit her grave for the first time on Easter Sunday, April 16; two days earlier, his younger brother Erasmus had died—also of tuberculosis; two days later, Novalis began to keep a journal that became, at least in part, a record of his peculiar devotion to the young woman he had called his *Schutzgeist*, his guardian angel: "22 May: The more the pain in my senses diminishes, the more my spiritual mourning grows; a kind of tranquil desperation is on the ascendant in me" (1: 466). Although he became engaged to Julie von Charpentier in December of 1798, no one replaced Sofie in his sensual, obsessive devotions. His engagement to Σωφία, to a "wisdom" of an intense and peculiar kind, never ended.

In the meantime, he had become involved in his father's work with the Saxon bureau of mines, eventually himself becoming inspector of mines. He studied in the famous mining academy at Freiberg under the leading geologist of his time, Abraham Gottlob Werner (1749–1817). He also studied chemistry and medicine, which became lifelong preoccupations. In December 1797 he met Schelling, whose work he vastly admired even as he sought critical distance from it; for his part, Schelling remained coolly reserved in the presence of this gregarious young man who perhaps threatened Schelling's otherwise unchallenged status as the *Wunderkind* of German Idealism.

In April 1798 Hardenberg's first major published text, *Blüthenstaub* (Pollen), appeared in the inaugural issue of Friedrich Schlegel's journal *Athenaeum*. It appeared under the pseudonym *Novalis*, a name that implied that the poet was the discoverer of new lands. At the same time, Novalis was working on a text that, although it remained a fragment, is one of the most inspired documents of German Romanticism, *Die Lehrlinge zu Saïs* (The apprentices at Saïs). I will say nothing here about the literary texts for which Novalis is best remembered, texts such as the series of poems entitled *Hymns to the Night* and *Spiritual Songs*, his famous *Monologue* on language, and the incomplete novel, *Heinrich von Ofterdingen*—except to urge my readers to give themselves the pleasure. Nor will I comment on Novalis's political texts, among the strangest of that entire genre *(Faith and Love; Christendom, or Europe)*. The principal groupings of the theoretical, scientific-philosophical texts are as follows: *Fichte-Studien*, written in 1795/96, divided into six groups of handwritten notes; studies on Hemsterhuis and Kant, beginning in March 1797; *Blüthenstaub*, published in spring 1798; *Vorarbeiten zu verschiedenen*

*Fragmentsammlungen* (Preliminary studies for various collections of fragments), written during Novalis's tenure at the Freiberg Academy in 1798 (see also the *Freiberger naturwissenschaftliche Studien* from this period); *Das allgemeine Brouillon* (The universal sketchbook), the single largest and most significant collection of theoretical, philosophical, and scientific fragments, begun in September of 1798 and designed as an encyclopedia, though never published; and finally, *Fragmente und Studien,* the last notes, divided into three groups, composed during the year 1800, increasingly focusing on matters of health and illness, religion and poetry.

Novalis participated in the famous "Meeting of the Romantics" in Jena, with the Schlegel brothers, Ludwig Tieck, Schelling, and Johann Ritter, from November 11–14, 1799. During the year 1800, he delved into the works of Jakob Böhme, whom Hegel was to call "the father of German philosophy," studying them as intensely as Schelling was to study them several years later. That summer he jotted down a series of notes on medicine, religion, and poetics. His health began to deteriorate, and by the fall of 1800 he was seriously ill. Friedrich von Hardenberg died of tuberculosis on March 25, 1801, almost exactly four years after Sofie's death.

If Novalis is undisputably the most "romantic" of the three authors I will be considering in the present volume, the one for whom nature is the source of all that is best and most beautiful in the world, it is also true that his thought reveals a core of skepticism—in the Greek sense of σκέψις—and realism that we find difficult to integrate into our notions of Romanticism. As exalted as nature undoubtedly is in Novalis's literary and scientific oeuvre, the enthusiastic poet and theoretician is keenly aware of the role that disease and death invariably play in the course of nature. A perpetual confrontation with mortality takes place in the reflections of this "physician of immortality," a strain of utterly unsentimental realism and empiricism that we are inclined to think is reserved for the twentieth century.[7]

Much the same could be said of Schelling, three years younger than Novalis and every bit as precocious. Even though Schelling is becoming much better known today in the English-speaking world, it may be advisable to offer a brief sketch of his life and work as well.

Friedrich Wilhelm Joseph von Schelling was born in Leonberg (in the southwestern German region of Swabian Württemberg) in 1775. At fifteen years of age he was thoroughly prepared for university:

he went to study in nearby Tübingen in the fall of 1790, where his roommates for the next four years in the *Stift* were Friedrich Hölderlin and Georg Wilhelm Friedrich Hegel. They studied philosophy and theology together, reading Rousseau and Kant—whose proscribed works they hid under the large stones that lined the Neckar River. In 1792 Schelling completed his master's thesis on the theme—for him the *lasting* theme—of the origins of evil. In 1793 he published his first work, again on a theme that would be a mainstay, *On Myths, Historical Legends, and Philosophical Themes of the Most Remote Antiquity*. During that same year, Schelling met Fichte and became a devoted though soon wayward disciple. In 1794 he published his first Fichtean work, *On the Possibility of a Form of Philosophy in General*, precisely at the time he was also engaged in studies of Plato—especially Plato's *Timaeus*—that would take him from Kantian-Fichtean subjectivity to the realm of nature.[8] There followed in 1795 *On the I as Principle of Philosophy; or, On the Unconditioned in Human Knowledge*, as well as a work in which his theory of tragedy played an important role, *Philosophical Letters on Dogmatism and Criticism*. Serving as a tutor in a private household, Schelling followed his employer to Leipzig, where he studied mathematics, the natural sciences, and medicine at the university. His study of Plato's *Timaeus* had doubtless already convinced him that the problem of *nature* loomed large even at the outset of Western philosophy. Although he devoted a part of the year 1796 to a *New Deduction of Natural Law*, the philosophy and the sciences of nature came to occupy the center of his thinking for the next several years.

It is perhaps merely of symbolic interest that Schelling's 1800 *System of Transcendental Idealism* appeared precisely at the time that the Jena circle was dissolving—largely because of Schelling's and Caroline Schlegel's love for one another and their decision to live together and eventually marry. Of Schelling's close work with Hegel during the years 1801 to 1803, and of the growing distance between themselves and Fichte, little need be said here. And perhaps nothing at all need be said of Hegel's famous polemic against Schelling in the 1807 preface to the *Phenomenology of Spirit* and elsewhere.

Schelling moved to Würzburg in the summer of 1803, then on to Munich in 1806. He became increasingly absorbed in the study of medicine, influenced by—and himself influencing—the noted physicians Andreas Röschlaub (1768–1835) and Adalbert Friedrich Marcus (1753–1816). The three of them were particularly intrigued by the theories of the Scots physician John Brown (1735–1788), theories that had also fascinated Novalis. Between the years 1806 and 1820, Schelling suspended all teaching activity. After publishing his 1809 treatise, *Philosophische Untersuchungen über das Wesen der menschlichen Freiheit und die damit zusammenhängenden Gegenstände* (Philosophical investigations into the essence of human freedom and related matters), he delivered a series of private lectures in Stuttgart; these *Stuttgarter Privatvorlesungen* proved to be the most important work on the threshold of his never-completed masterwork, *The Ages of the World*, on which he labored from 1810 to 1815. I will say nothing here about Schelling's late work, the 1821 *Philosophy of Mythology* and the 1827 *Philosophy of Revelation*, themes on which the aged Schelling continued to lecture in Berlin in 1841. If Novalis's flame was extinguished early on, Schelling's seems to have suffocated in the fumes rising from its own elongated wick. Nowhere was that flame brighter, however, than in those texts where it sputtered in the wind of the dire forces of nature—which Schelling confronted most stubbornly in his 1799 *First Projection of a System of Nature Philosophy*.

Only a word about Hegel's life and work. Born in 1770, the year also of Hölderlin's birth, two years older than Novalis and five years older than Schelling, Hegel ended his long philosophical apprenticeship under Schelling with his 1807 *Phenomenology of Spirit*. His next great work, the three-volume *Science of Logic*, published in 1812, revealed quite clearly the importance of nature, and within nature *life*, for his system: the final segments of the book, following upon a discussion of teleological judgment, focused on the life of the system of logic, whose very concept was nothing if not living. When the *Encyclopedia of Philosophical Sciences* appeared in 1817, with its three sections devoted to logic, philosophy of nature, and philosophy of spirit, respectively, it became clear that nature was the pivotal point for the concept. It had always been so, even for the early sketches of the system, which Hegel elaborated during his first year of teaching as an Adjunct Professor at Jena, during the winter semester of 1805/06.

It is the text of his *Realphilosophie*, more specifically, that of the philosophy of nature within his *Realphilosophie*, published today as *Jenaer Systementwürfe III*, to which the final chapters of the present book will turn. Even though Hegel himself preserved a great deal of this material for his lectures in Berlin on the philosophy of nature (from 1819 until his death in 1831), little of it appears in the handbook of the *Encyclopedia* as such. Only those editions that include the addenda, themselves problematic because they are lecture notes collated and edited by Hegel's students, reveal how much of the earlier Jena material on the philosophy of nature remains relevant to Hegel's final system. Here we will focus on the final pages of the Jena philosophy of nature, which treat of genitality, the mating process, disease, and death.

### SEXUALITY, DISEASE, AND DEATH: AN ITINERARY THROUGH THE DIRE FORCES OF NATURE

Part one of the present volume is entitled "Thaumaturgic Idealism," after Novalis's "magical idealism." It focuses on Novalis's relatively late and most encyclopedic collection of notes, entitled *The Universal Sketchbook (Das allgemeine Brouillon)*. Part one unfolds in four stages, constituting chapters 1–4.

1. The principal features of Novalis's magical idealism come to the fore in the motif of "the first kiss." For Novalis himself initiates his account of the human body with the lips and the entire system of the mouth—a complex system in which nourishment, elimination, sexuality, and speech are interrelated—indeed, by an "anastomosis of discursive individuals" (2: 350). The system of the mouth subtends a "theory of voluptuosity"; yet it is also subject to the dire forces of nature. Nature, characterized by the expansive force of eros, is nevertheless often described in the notebooks in the way a voice in *The Apprentices at Saïs* describes it, namely, as "a terrifying death-mill," "a frightful, rapacious power," "a realm of voracity and the wildest excess, an immensity pregnant with misery."[9] Novalis's theory of voluptuosity culminates in a "poetics of the baneful." The first kiss is always a kiss of death—and the first thing to die is the concept of "firstness," inasmuch as thaumaturgic idealism does not conjure up a theory of origins.

2. Novalis's poetics of the baneful is a principal part of his project of "romanticizing the world," that is, of developing a *lingua romana* for its descriptions. Such a project relies upon two opposed yet complementary methods. First, it requires a *logarithmic method*, that is, a method by which the most elevated spiritual matters receive an earthbound designation. Second, simultaneously with the search for logarithms for the supreme philosophemes, everything lowly is elevated in Novalis's *lingua romana* by the method of *exponentiation*,

or "raising to the powers." At the crossroads of such exponential elevation and logarithmic reduction lies the theme of illness. Novalis begins to speculate "on the attractive force of the dire" (2: 628).

3. Central to Novalis's reflections on illness is the theme of a touching without contact, traditionally defined as *actio in distans*. However, such contactless touching is every bit as much related to the reproduction of species, to the engendering of new life, as it is to illness. For Novalis's double method of logarithmic reduction and exponential raising to the powers, this intersection of the lines of demise and fecundity, the lines of illness and sexuality, becomes the principal point of focus. Likewise the "pharmaceutical principle," by which the ambiguity of poisons and healing powers is fully experienced, becomes an essential part of the Novalisian system. In a very real sense, all the forces of nature are (also) dire forces. Among these forces, the human soul stands out—precisely as "the most potent of poisons" (2: 706).

4. In Novalis's thaumaturgic idealism, the role of the physician is central. The physician must become an "artist of immortality." Yet, as in all things, Novalis's "immortality" is a strange beast, and death lies at the heart of it. Novalis does not dream of banishing human mortality and securing some angelic or divine status for the human; rather, the artist of immortality puts illness, old age, and death itself to work. The medicine of the future will integrate pathology with therapy, focusing on such matters as fermentation, oxidation, combustion, and inoculation—including inoculation with death. Novalis calls it "the pathological explanation of the human condition" (2: 716), and also, with reference to the logarithmic method, "infinitesimal medicine" (2: 549–50). In all this, Novalis seems to be the most important precursor of the postmetapsychological thinking that does not think life without death. His is a thinking of what Derrida calls *la vie la mort*, or *lifedeath*, a thinking that inevitably becomes a thinking of *contagion*.[10]

Part two, "Tormented Idealism," turns to Schelling's *Erster Entwurf eines Systems der Naturphilosophie* (1799). Three separate, large-scale works (there are several additional smaller works) are generally held to be the most significant for Schelling's philosophy of nature: first, the 1797 *Ideas toward a Philosophy of Nature*, which pledged but did not entirely fulfill the promise of a philosophy of organism;[11] second, the 1798 *On the World Soul: A Hypothesis of Higher Physics toward Explaining the Universal Organism*, which brought Schelling closer to his goal of a philosophy of organism, yet again left it strangely unfulfilled; third and last, and for our purposes the most important of the three, the 1799 *First Projection of a System of Nature Philosophy*. This strange work, no more than a rough draft of Schelling's inaugural lecture course at Jena during the winter semester of 1799, soon paled in the bright light of Schelling's first magnum opus, the 1800 *System of Transcendental Idealism*. Yet the deduction of organic nature in the latter work is so spare, the treatment of nature as a whole so scanty, that one would never be able to reconstruct from it the detailed reflection on nature that preceded it. Although matters here are controversial, one might go so far as to say that the 1800 *System* begins to obscure rather than illuminate the problems that Schelling's earlier texts had exhibited, problems for which the philosopher had sought radical solutions. In a second magnum opus, the 1809 *Philosophical Investigations on the Essence of Human Freedom and Other Related Matters*, Schelling complained that many so-called "solutions" merely push philosophical problems "one point farther down the line, without truly resolving them," and what he criticized in other authors he could hardly forgive in himself.[12] The 1799 *First Projection*—to repeat, a misnomer, inasmuch as it was at least the *third* projection of Schelling's system of nature philosophy—is significant precisely because it shows the torment of a system of reason that insists on responding to, rather than evading, what more innocent ages called "the mysteries of nature."

Once again, Schelling's analysis can be developed in four stages, here constituting chapters 5–8.

5. Schelling attaches to the script of his 1799 lecture course an "Outline of the Whole," which enables the reader to see at a glance the struggle between monism and dualism in his system. It also demonstrates the importance of theories of sexuality and illness for his theory of organism. In effect, sexuality and illness attach themselves to *every* site on the outline of the whole: they seem to infect the entire plan of the lecture course, from its account of the organic and anorganic realms to its postulation of a third, encompassing sphere, a sphere of "universal organism." As in Novalis's thaumaturgic idealism, Schelling's tormented idealism finds the imbrication of illness and eros at its otherwise unlocatable center—the center Schelling calls *duplicity*.

6. Sexual opposition, that is, the opposition of male and female, dominates Schelling's analysis of organism as the principal duplicity.

Similarly, at the level of universal organism, the opposition of infinite activity and infinite inhibition is the dominant opposition; at the level of the individual organism, the essential opposition is sensibility (receptivity) and irritability (efficacious activity). Yet all these oppositions are themselves menaced by the theme of contagion. *Contagium* is a word that arises in the discourses of sexual reproduction (for example, in William Harvey's *On Generation*) and pathology (that of the Scots physician John Brown). As these two spheres, the sexual and the pathological, begin to interpenetrate, however, every dualism and monism gives way to a theory of *duplicity*, which seems irreducible to any traditional dualism or any possible monism.

7. Sexual opposition and reproduction of the duplicity in nature come to be seen as "the ultimate source of life" *and* "the bridge to death" (*EE*, 89, 227, 236, 238). Thus, precisely for a theory of organism, which must be a theory of *universal* organism, life and nature are set at murderous odds: "Wherever life comes to stand, it comes to stand . . . against the will of external nature . . . , by means of a tearing away from her" (*EE*, 81). The forces that sustain life are the forces of death, and the factors of life are the factors of illness (*EE*, 222n. 1). For Schelling as for Novalis, all the forces of nature are dire forces. The Romantic concept of nature is anything but romantic.

8. Among the oppositions that become duplicities rather than dualisms is that of identity and difference. For A = A only if the A is iterable—and to that extent duplicitous—as such. In a sense that is at first difficult to comprehend, one may say that A is ill and is on its way to inevitable demise. Philosophers will continue to dream of singular identities, atoms, and monads, but, for a system that responds to organic life, such units, like all the constructs of logic and metaphysical discourse, will succumb to dire forces. Another way of expressing the impasse at which Schelling's tormented idealism arrives is to say that his attempted ontotheological monism dissolves into a dualism, his dualism into a trialism, his trialism into infinite regress and infinite regression. Near the conclusion of his lecture course, Schelling poses "the most universal problem, the one that encompasses all nature, and therefore the *supreme* problem, without whose solution all we have said explains nothing" (*EE*, 220). That problem is to identify the cause that "first tossed the seed of motion into the universal repose of nature, duplicity into universal identity, [and] the first sparks of heterogeneity into the universal homogeneity of nature" (ibid.). Schelling's tormented idealism never finds a satisfying reply to these questions. It remains thoughtful.

Finally, part three takes up some passages in Hegel's lecture course on *Realphilosophie*—specifically, his philosophy of nature—taught at Jena in 1805/06. The four stages of the discussion constitute chapters 9–12.

9. Hegel is principally concerned to exhibit nature's seductive impotence and spirit's ultimate dominion over nature. His "triumphant idealism" differs from Novalis's thaumaturgic variety and Schelling's tormented version in that it focuses on the rescue of spirit from the natural. Spirit and nature may be "reconciled" in the system, but the natural *(das Natürliche)* is destined for extrusion and oblivion. In Hegel's early system, however, the accounts of illness and sexuality show the selfsame imbrication or intertwining that they show in the systems of Novalis and Schelling. Perhaps it is this imbrication that the later philosophy of spirit struggles to escape?

10. Hegel brings home the lessons of Kant's Analytic of the Sublime: nature is incapable of sublimity and must submit to the human *Gemüt*. As nature swoons in powerlessness, spirit rises on the afflatus of the logic of the concept. Yet nature in a less demure guise appears to draw boundaries that even spirit cannot cross: "The impotence of nature sets limits to philosophy, and it would be utterly irrelevant to demand of the concept *[Begriff]* that it grasp *[begreifen]* such contingencies as these and, as people say, to construe or deduce them."[13]

11. However, the concept must perform one task alone: it must transform into yet another facet of interiority whatever at first is taken to be utterly extrinsic and exterior. The limits that nature sets to philosophy must therefore be overcome and nature herself secured in her subaltern position. As in the cases of Novalis and Schelling, Hegel's understanding of sexuality and illness in organic nature lies at the core of the philosophic project—in Hegel's case, the project of the concept's self-transformation and eventual encompassment of nature and history. Of the three thinkers, Hegel pays the closest attention to the structure of human *genitality* in the sexual relation. Whereas male genitality is directed "to the outside," thus taking up the position of an active spirit over against a fundamentally passive nature, female genitality remains interior and undeveloped, "undifferentiated." The sexual relation as such proves to be both permeating and debilitating; that is, sexual identity must permeate every level of reality, including the spiritual, even if the seed of reproduction is the seed of death in every living creature. Dialectic turned to the outside yields to dialectic turned to the inside: the death

of sexed individuals spawns consciousness. Whereas the organic is "weak" and is not "the ground," consciousness is the fulfillment of spirit's itinerary, consciousness is spirit's triumph. Individuality passes over to universality, not in the achievement of the animal genus but in the achievement of spiritual genius. Both sides of the sexual opposition fail to survive and establish the universal. Their failure is elaborated as illness. Both sexes, viewed as wholes, die as a result of the malady that arises from their internal doubling. They die because in each of them male and female elements try to mate: "The possibility of illness is that the individual is both of these—in the sexual relation it has surrendered its essential determinacy *to the outside*, inasmuch as it is in relation; now, in itself, as it were, it is mating with itself" (*JS*, 165). What seemed to be the τέλος of sexual opposition, namely, the unification of the two sexes in a perduring whole, is in fact the catastrophe of all nature: "Every individual is now itself the unity of the two sexes; but this is its death" (ibid.).

12. Whereas Hegel announces consciousness as the "result" of this natural process, nothing in the account of sexual opposition and illness clarifies the process as such. The *fever* of terminal illness is an expression of the Phoenix-fire of spirit; accordingly, the triumph of spirit itself is an expression of febrile *pathology*. Spirit-as-nature *suffers* consciousness, which is the duplicitous flurry of a racked body, the epiphenomenon of a redoubled and self-destructive organism. The entire phenomenology and philosophy of spirit, subjective and objective, that follows in the course of Hegel's career will be haunted by the epiphenomenal status of consciousness. Hegel will employ every means to censure, extrude, and obliterate the duplicitous genitality, genus, and generation of genius. He will ignite pyre after pyre. Yet he will also scour the ashes for traces of spirit's victories: spirit's will always be a triumph of ashes.

So much for a summary of the book's itinerary. What sorts of conclusions, starting with Hegel but remembering back to Schelling and Novalis, can one draw from it all?

For those who insist on at least the appearances of triumph, Hegel will always be preferred as more compelling and more satisfying than either Schelling or Novalis. For those who can experience the failure of a system, however, not as an objection to the system but as testimony to the honesty and fortitude of a thinking that guide us to the point of its inevitable demise, Novalis and Schelling will always be at least equally fascinating figures. The fact that Hegel has

overshadowed them says more about philosophy's desire for hege-
mony than it does about the requirements of thought. When thinking becomes the occupation of mortals and leaves triumph to the
gods—gods who, as Hölderlin knew, have always already flown—
Novalis and Schelling emerge from under Hegel's shadow as thinkers
of great stature. Yet is Hegel himself truly so triumphant?

Hegel's philosophy of nature, as we have it in part two of the
*Encyclopedia of Philosophical Sciences* (1817, 1827, and 1830), is always
touted as the weakest part of his system. Presumably, it is the weakest
part insofar as the necessity of its dialectical advances appears to be
less convincing there than it is in other parts of the system, and also
insofar as the distance between the logical structures that govern it
and the minute details that absorb it seems so vast. Should the polyp,
turned inside out, reveal the structures of positive rational speculative dialectics? Hegel himself speaks to the *necessity* of *contingency* in
philosophy of nature. And the details of the system of nature, details
to which Hegel remains true in spite of himself and his system, are far
more intriguing than any overarching aspect of the system itself. If
the system of nature often works by the simple declaration that a
prior conclusion now proves to be inadequate, so that the student
must agree to leap ahead or be dragged kicking and screaming on to
the next challenge, it is the fascination of the intricate details themselves—the phosphorescent slime of the sea, the compact metal of
the earth, and, yes, the reversible belly of the polyp and the interac-
tive innards of the beast—that most honors the Hegelian system.
The system goes to embrace recalcitrant materials, materials that
resist absorption into any logic, materials whose remnants perdure as
the trash of the system, monuments to its ultimate failure to encom-
pass without scraps and to distill without residue. And it is such
recalcitrance, resistance, and remnance (if one may coin a word in
recollection of Derrida's *Glas*) that grace Hegel's system more than
any of its triumphs.

The fact that the system of nature is called upon (by Hegel) to
contain more than it can is not a mark of its embarrassment in the face
of an *embarras de richesses;* it is rather a mark of Hegel's own greatness
as a thinker. In the end, it will not do to rescue Novalis and Schelling
by diminishing the stature of Hegel. Such diminution would insult all
three thinkers. And at all events, recalcitrant remnants are found
everywhere in Hegel's, Schelling's, and Novalis's "systems," whether
the region in question be that of aesthetics, religion, law, or history.

If Hegel's system seems more triumphant in these other regions, it is only because there the need for visible triumph inhibits the actual elaboration of the system. What is most intriguing about Hegel's philosophy of nature is that the overextension of the system is so pronounced, the ambition so palpable: spirit may be excused for all its false steps in history, may be forgiven for its Oriental infancy and its long and awkward adolescence in the West; yet its collapse into the stuff that has no history—the arid stuff of sidereal earth, the sticky stuff of the oversexed plant world, the repulsive stuff of the insatiable beast—is more difficult for metaphysicians to forgive. In the history of metaphysics, of course, it is this relation of spirit to dejected matter that cries out for explanation. Nature is the Achilles' heel, or the unheroic clay feet, of every system, not merely Hegel's. How does Milan Kundera put it? He notes somewhere in one of his novels that we can forgive God every moral evil He commits or allows, seeing in it some sort of necessity at work for the greater good; what we cannot comprehend, not ever, is his most innocent defecation.

By way of conclusion, we do have to concede that it is perverse of us to focus on an area of past philosophy that, as everybody knows, has been made obsolete by progress in the natural sciences themselves. Why not concentrate instead on questions of art and beauty, or law and justice, where science dependably falters and leaves us stranded? Why? Precisely because the primary metaphysical quandary—the relation of mind to matter, of spirit to the material world—demands that we go where science even today fears to tread. Whether or not our three thinkers—Novalis, Schelling, and Hegel—have something to teach today's scientist and philosopher has less to do with the limitations or even obsolescence of those thinkers than it does with the narrowness and the poverty of imagination in scientific and philosophic education today. The present volume is dedicated to those in whom a technologized science and an academic philosophy have not yet obliterated a sense of the mystery and power of nature—those possessed of a reverence for, and love of, even the dire forces of nature.[14]

PART ONE

# Thaumaturgic Idealism

*Novalis's Scientific-Philosophical*

*Notebooks of 1798–1800*

*We were but one blossom,*
*and our souls lived within one another.*
*When the blossom loves,*
*it conceals its tender joys in a closed calyx.*

—*HÖLDERLIN,* HYPERION

# CHAPTER ONE

# *The First Kiss*

When Novalis dreams that celestial bodies such as meteors and planets are actually petrified angels (2: 792), he is doing exactly what we expect of a Romantic. Even when there is talk of rock and petrifaction, the thought seems an idle, airy, and wingèd thing. Romantic thought must be romance, we think, and romance must spin out a sentimental and complacent view of the world—fluff washed in the wan light of setting suns. There are of course jarring moments, such as the moment in which the hero of Hölderlin's *Hyperion* confronts "the nothing":

> From time to time a force of spirit still stirred in me. But of course only a destructive one!
>
> "What is a human being?" was the way I might begin. How does it happen that there is such a thing in the world, a thing that ferments like a Chaos or rots like a dead tree and never reaches maturity? Why does nature deign to accept sour grapes alongside her sweet ones?
>
> To the plants the human being says, "I was once like you!" And to the pristine stars, "I want to be like you, I want to be in another world!" Meanwhile, he falls apart, working his old ploys on himself every now and again, as though he could put the pieces of the living back together again once they had disintegrated, as though he could mend walls. Yet he is not even chagrined when he sees that nothing is improved by all his labors, that everything he does is mere artifice.
>
> O you hapless creatures, who feel it, but who do not like to speak of what defines human beings; you who are transfixed by the nothing that governs us; you who thoroughly comprehend that we are born for nothing, that we love a nothing, believe in the nothing, toil away for nothing, in order gradually to pass over into the nothing: —what can I do to prevent your collapsing when you contemplate it in earnest? . . .

> Oh, I can fall on my knees, wring my hands, and plead (with whom I know not) that there be other thoughts. Yet I cannot suppress the crying truth. Have I not convinced myself twice over? When I gaze into life, what is the end of it all? Nothing. When my spirit ascends, what is the highest height of all? Nothing.[1]

Hölderlin's "Diotima," Susette Gontard, encounters the nothing in the very throes of romantic love: separated from her friend and lover for over a year, she begins to hallucinate, to see visions of him, but then hears the voice of reason: ". . . it was as though I went to embrace you and you had become a shadow, and this shadow, so dear to me, could have comforted me too, and, if my reason had demanded it, this very shadow would have vanished from me and left me—if such a thing can be thought—with a nothing."[2]

Other jarring moments, moments that complicate our romantic sense of Romanticism, punctuate the writings of "Novalis," Friedrich von Hardenberg. In *The Apprentices at Saïs* he writes that nature—the lactating mother of the Romantics, the figure, in *Heinrich von Ofterdingen,* he calls Ginnistan—herself sometimes seems, as we have already heard, "a terrifying death-mill," "a frightful, rapacious power," vast, turbulent, and merciless, "a realm of voracity and the wildest excess, an immensity pregnant with misery."[3] Indeed, the Derridian thought of holocaust and ashes, *der Aschenhaufen,* is never absent from the minds of the Romantics, or at least of those Romantics named Hölderlin, Novalis, Schelling, and Hegel, no matter how hard we try to turn them into harmless, bemused dreamers, no matter how hard we try to smother the smoldering fires of their meditations.[4]

In the present investigation it will be a matter of the forces of nature as dire forces, particularly the forces of illness and death, accompanying those of eros and sexuality, in the thought of Novalis, Schelling, and Hegel. All three thinkers respond to nature in subtly different ways, even if we gather them together under the rubrics of Romanticism and Idealism. Yet nothing gives us better leverage to separate one from the other than the theme of a baneful nature. Why? Schelling notes quite explicitly that nature is the realm of gestation and birth. That it should also be the mill of death and destruction is the lesson that seems so hard to learn—so hard that we could never expect any two apprentices at Saïs to learn it at the same moment or in the identical way. To speak or write of the dire forces of nature is to say the unsayable of our own mortality, inborn and inevitable, whatever the idols may be "to which we are wont to go cringing."[5] Such mortal saying does not come easy to any of the three, nor to any of those I am here ignoring—Hamann, Brentano, Bettina von Arnim, the Schlegels, Jean Paul, and so on. It is the struggle with nature's baneful aspect and dire forces—always a struggle that is obscurely but ineluctably bound up with love and sexuality—that perhaps best exposes each of these thinkers to our gaze.

Let us turn to Novalis's scientific and theoretical observations during the years 1798–1800. We will stress the following themes and theses there:

1. For Novalis, philosophy begins with embodied experience, indeed, with the experience of erotic love—the "first kiss." Further, the experience of the expansive force of love in the first kiss introduces us to other aspects of the system of the mouth—to speech, laughter, eating, digestion, and elimination.

2. The system of the mouth is a mortal system, bound up with the pharmaceutical principle—the principle that medicament and poison are synonymous—and thus with contagion, illness, and death. In a word, the first kiss and the system of the mouth are in essential communication with the *baneful* aspects of nature.

3. Such communication occurs as a touching that does not achieve contact. It is a touching that works its effects as an *actio in distans*, precisely through *contagion*.

4. The pharmaceutical principle extends to the most beloved oppositional pairs in philosophical cosmology, anthropology, and theology, so that meditation on that principle by any "artist of immortality" leads to the most radical results for philosophy in general.

For Novalis, philosophy, which is the love of learning and wisdom, is bound up with the human needs to eat, speak, and kiss. In his first published set of aphorisms, *Pollen*, he writes: "How can a human being have a sensibility for something if he does not have the germ of it in himself? What I am to understand must develop organically in me; and what I seem to learn is but nourishment—something to incite the organism" (2: 232–33). The drive to knowledge is thus equivalent (and not merely analogous) to the drive to survival. Yet Novalis prefers to call it the "drive to completion," or perhaps the "drive to supplementation," *Ergänzungstrieb*. In his early studies on the philosophy of Fichte, he writes: "If the sphere of a particular force expands in a particular way, the necessary result is a drive. Drive is the striving of a force to realize itself" (*Fichte-Studien III*; 2: 134). It will therefore always be a matter of force and forces, although it is still unclear whether or how such forces could ever be dire. The first hint concerning the baneful is the thought that the system of the mouth, as a system of nourishment, is based on hunger, and that a system based on hunger or lack must be bound to mortality. It is a lesson Timaeus of Locri had learned, for the first thing he tells us about the immortal, self-sufficient universe is that it needs no digestive organs since there is nothing outside it that it might ingest.[6] Novalis echoes Timaeus's thought: "If every organic part had the life-duration of eternity, it would need no nourishment in the stricter sense of the word, no renovation, no elimination" (2: 563). It is also a lesson learned by Novalis's friend Friedrich Schlegel, who in his insolent novel *Lucinde* observes the two-year-old infant Wilhelmine and writes:

> It lies deep within human nature that it should want to eat everything it loves and put every novel thing that appears to it directly into its mouth, in order, if possible, to reduce it to its constituent parts. The healthy craving for knowledge desires to seize its object entirely, to penetrate to its innermost core and chew it up. In contrast, touching merely remains isolated at the outside surface; likewise, every conceptualizing proffers incomplete and only mediate knowledge.[7]

However, to return to the first point, and to summarize it as forcefully as we can: even when a philosopher asks for reasons and searches for the grounds of a phenomenon, what his or her spirit yearns for is nourishment—the appropriation (*Zueignung*) and assimilation (*Essen*) of the object, the absorption of whatever has stimulated one in the first place, the transformation of what is *foreign* into something *the same as oneself*, flesh of and for one's own flesh (*Vorarbeiten 1798*; 2: 418–19). A later note adduces the rhetorical question, "Are the external senses *devourers?*" (*Das allgemeine Brouillon*; 2: 504).

In the preliminary studies of 1798, Novalis refers to one of Goethe's most important notions in *The Metamorphosis of Plants*, which we touched upon in the introduction. Goethe describes the development of the venous system in leaves—by which the process of nourishment spreads across the entire leaf, exposing the refined liquids within the leaf to the gases of the air and the action of the sun—as *anastomosis*. As we heard, *anastomosis* is the branching system of the mouth of a river, for example, in a delta near the sea. Yet the anastomosis in a leaf, and, still more strikingly, the "spiritual anastomosis" that occurs in pollination, are essentially truncated systems. For even the venous system of leaves does not rely on true contact. Rather, there is a kind of spiritual *contagion* operative even in the leaf, though Goethe does not call it that, by which nourishment is somehow *communicated to* the plant by sun and air. Novalis now describes human discourse, speech and writing, as such a network of synaptic gaps, as it were, as a truncated system of the mouth: "Everything must become a foodstuff. The art of drawing life from everything. The goal of life is to vivify everything. Pleasure is life. Unpleasure is the means to pleasure, as death is the means to life. . . . Anastomosis of discursive individuals" (2: 350). Another note from the *Universal Sketchbook* observes the similarity between learning and eating: "Thus learning is quite similar to eating—and *a priori* knowing is satiety—a nourishing without eating" (2: 685).

For Novalis, however, the expansive force, the drive to completion or supplementation, is as much palpation as it is ingestion—no matter what Schlegel's little Wilhelmine may have insisted. And the palpation is gentle—more touch than grapple, more kiss than bite, more caress than engulf. Such palpating expansiveness—what Goethe and Schelling called expansion, *Ausdehnen*, and what Whitman was to call *dilation*—is philosophizing: "In the most authentic sense philosophizing is—a caress—testimony of the most intense love of meditation, absolute pleasure in wisdom" (*Logologische Fragmente*; 2: 314). For Novalis, there can be no doubt that the kiss—not the analogy or the metaphor of a kiss, but the *first* kiss, unless, in the *first* of the first kiss, osculation, analogy, and metaphor cannot be separated—is the nascent act of philosophizing, the *incitement* of nourishment that leads to the embrace of the world. The kiss is therefore the act that mediates between the systems of nourishment and reproduction, an act whose implications extend much farther than the system of the mouth. In a long note preparatory to various collections of fragments (1798), Novalis anticipates matters that will soon engage Schelling, Hegel, and Hölderlin:

> We seek the *projection* that suits the world—we ourselves are this projection. What are we? personified *omnipotent points*. However, the execution, as an image of the projection, must also be equal to the projection in its free activity and self-relation, and vice versa. Life, or the essence of spirit, thus

consists in the engendering bearing and rearing of one's like. Thus, only to the extent that a human being engages in a happy marriage with itself, constituting a loving family, is it at all capable of marriage and family. Act of self-embrace.

One must never openly proclaim that one loves oneself. Maintaining the secret of this confession is the life principle of the sole true and eternal love. The first kiss in this accord is the principle of philosophy—the origin of a new world—the beginning of absolute time-reckoning—the completion of an infinitely waxing bond with the self.

Who would not be pleased with a philosophy whose germ is a first kiss?

Love popularizes the personality. It makes individualities *communicable* and *comprehensible*. (Amorous understanding.) (*Vorarbeiten 1798*; 2: 329–30)

The lips of self-embrace in Novalis's meditation, in that happy marriage of self to self, may therefore be two, four, or more. They await other lips, but their contact with one another—if *contact* is the right word—is in a sense always already given: the first kiss is never truly first, but always second, or always uncountable. The lips, whether we are alone or in company, serve as the portals of incoming nourishment and outgoing speech or song. Novalis has a particular song in mind, Mozart's *"Wenn die Liebe in Deinen hellen blauen Augen,"* or *"An Chloe,"* Köchel-Verzeichnis 524. Reflecting on the "musical accompaniment" that might suit various "meditations, conversations, and readings," Novalis writes: "I wish my readers were able to read my remark that the beginning of philosophy is a first kiss at the very moment when they happened to be listening to Mozart's composition, 'When Love Shines in Your Bright Blue Eyes,' being sung most passionately—if indeed they were unable to be in tremulous proximity to a first kiss" (*Vorarbeiten 1798*; 2: 331). Let it be noted that this most innocent of songs, Mozart's "To Chloe," nevertheless proceeds rather rapidly from first kiss to total exhaustion: *ermattet, ermattet* is the repeated word that resounds at the song's apotheosis.[8] Likewise, Novalis's first kiss, which can never be the first, is also never the last word. It is the overture to a growing warmth, the kindling of a flame, the leaping of that personified omnipotent point—the human personality—outside itself in ardor and ecstasy. The leap is one of fecundity, faith, and philosophy alike:

The act of leaping out beyond oneself is everywhere the supreme act—the primal point—the *genesis of life*. Thus the flame is nothing other than such an act. Philosophy arises whenever the one philosophizing philosophizes its self, that is, simultaneously consumes (determines, necessitates) and renews again (does not determine, but liberates). The history of this process is philosophy. In this way all living morality arises, in order that on the basis of virtue I act against virtue—thus begins the life of virtue, a life that perhaps augments itself into infinity, without ever confronting a limit. The latter is the condition of the possibility of losing its *life*. (*Vorarbeiten 1798*; 2: 345)

That the first kiss, and the life of virtue and vice that it initiates, stand in proximity to both the caress and nourishment, both loving and eating, is suggested by the following three notes from the 1798 *Vorarbeiten*. The first asks, "What is the human being?" and answers, "A perfect trope of the spirit." It concludes: "All genuine communication is therefore replete with sensuous imagery [*sinnbildsam*]; and are not caresses therefore genuine acts of communication?" (2: 354). The second relates such communicative caressing and kissing to "magical idealism," a term that Novalis sometimes selects as a rubric for his system as a whole:

> All spiritual touching is like touching with a magic wand. Everything can become the instrument of enchantment. Yet whoever takes the effects of such touching to be altogether fabulous, whoever takes the effects of magical incantation to be merely marvelous, should remember the first touch by the hand of his beloved, the first meaningful glance from her, wherein the magic wand was but a refracted beam of light, the first kiss, and the first loving word—and then he should ask himself whether the entrancement and the magic of these moments too are not fabulous and wondrous, indestructible and eternal? (2: 354)

These thoughts on the refracted gaze, the caress of light and love, marriage with oneself, and the inaugural kiss—which, as we said, may be a kiss of two lips, four, or more—these thoughts that are among the most sustained of the *Vorarbeiten*, culminate in a long third note on philosophic nourishment:

> The philosopher lives on problems, as human beings live on foodstuffs. An unsolvable problem is an undigestible foodstuff. . . . A digestible means of nourishment—that's the way everything should be. As for the condiments with regard to foodstuffs, they are the paradoxes in problems. A problem is truly resolved when it is annihilated as such. So it is with foodstuffs as well. The gain in both cases is the activity that is stimulated by both. Yet there are nourishing problems, just as there are nourishing foodstuffs—the elements of which constitute an augmentation of my intelligence. Through philosophizing, insofar as it is an absolute operation, my intelligence is constantly ameliorated—which is true of foodstuffs only up to a certain point. A rapid amelioration of our intelligence is as dubious as a sudden increase in our weight. The true step to health and improvement is a slow step—even if here too it is true that, as there are various constitutions, so there must be various

velocities in the sequence. Just as one does not eat in order to ingest an altogether novel and foreign matter, one does not philosophize in order to find entirely novel and foreign truths. One philosophizes about why one is alive. If one were ever to achieve a life without any *given* means of nourishment, one would also get to the point where one would not philosophize about any *given* problems. Perhaps a few are already that far along. (2: 354–55)

Philosophizing about problems that are not *given*, admittedly an activity for those few who are that far along, requires an especially inventive sort of dietetics: that is what Heidegger, for example, who studied Novalis's *Monologue*, calls *thinking*.[9]

In the philosophic sequence, as I have already indicated, Novalis does not stop with the first kiss. He is interested in the ascent of the body and simultaneous descent of the soul, leading to the erotic leap or embrace of coitus, *die Umarmung*. Once again, in this first act of coitus between body and soul, it is difficult to say whether the human being is alone or in company. In any case, Novalis calls this proto-coitus "the *dythiramb [sic]* among sensuous actions," a Dionysian hymn or dance that, if it is to be judged at all, must be judged "in accord with its own natural laws" (*Vorarbeiten 1798*; 2: 359). Indeed, the first kiss and the first intercourse imply an entire theory of language and speech, which the following note develops across a considerable range of activities, powers, and genres:

> Language to the second power, for example, the fable, is the expression of an entire thought, and it belongs to the hieroglyphism to the second power — in the *imagistic language*[2] [i.e., imagistic language *squared*] *of sounds and written characters*. It has poetic merit and is not *rhetorical*—subaltern if it is a complete expression, if it is *euphonic*[2] [i.e., again, euphonic *squared*]—correct and precise; if, so to speak, it is an expression *that accompanies*, and is for the sake of expression, if at least it does not appear as a medium, but is itself a complete production of the *higher faculty of speech*.
>
> Language in the genuine sense is *a function of an instrument as such*. *Every instrument expresses, coins*, the idea of its composer.
>
> If one organ serves another, then it is, as it were, its *tongue*—its throat, its mouth. The instrument that serves spirit most willingly and is most readily capable of manifold modifications, is above all its linguistic instrument—and thereby the language of mouth and fingers.

Among Novalis's jottings toward a system of the mouth, his *Teplitz Fragments* hold a special place. They contain notes on daily life—sleep, leisure, and (underlined by Novalis) *food* or *eating* [Essen], and *nourishment* (2: 385, 402). Novalis invariably associates such questions with woman. He devotes several of the *Teplitz Fragments* to that figure—all of them given the number 17, the original of which reads, "Sofie; or, concerning women" (2: 387). In our time, of course, such an identification means trouble: if woman is to be consumed, and if the male is to be the consumer, the power relations are in place and are seemingly immovable. It is fully in keeping with Novalis's sense, however, that one feel free—or, indeed, compelled—to alter the sexual identities and identifications in these notes, that one take one's nourishment not where it is traditionally given—or taken for granted—but where surprises and reversals are always in store. One cannot expect Novalis to have lived two centuries ahead of his time; one cannot demand that he do all the work of thinking that is yet to be done—in order to serve it up to us, as it were. In what follows, therefore, we should always pose the question of a possible *translation* or *modulation* of gender and even genital identifications and identities. Interspersed among the notes on woman are those related to number 8 of the *Teplitz Fragments,* on daily life and on *eating* in particular. One of the later notes, a note that most successfully interweaves numbers 8 and 17, encompassing the two themes of woman and nourishment by the ring of *religion,* is the following:

> Eating is but an accentuated living. Eating, drinking, and breathing correspond to the threefold division in the body into things firm, things fluid, and things gaseous. The entire body breathes—the lips alone eat and drink—they are precisely the organ that excretes in manifold tones what spirit has prepared, what it has received by means of the other senses. The lips are so important for sociality; how very much they deserve the kiss. Every soft and gentle elevation is symbolic of the wish to be touched. Thus nature invites us all, elegantly and modestly, to partake in enjoyment—and thus the whole of nature must be female, virgin and mother at once.[10]

"Every soft and gentle elevation. . . ." The upper lip, no doubt, but—given the projections and associations of Novalis's "magical idealism" as a whole—also any other part of the human body, male or female, fetish or flesh, that invites the lips' palpation. Novalis's "Moral Psychology" concerns itself with such sublime elevations: "The female breast is the chest *elevated to the status of a mystery*—the moralized chest" (*Das allgemeine Brouillon;* 2: 524). Such elevation to the status of a mystery expresses the very relationship of soul, spirit, and matter in the cosmos (2: 527). Another of the many "number 8" fragments of the Teplitz notes takes this thought in the direction of the eucharist, the meal of grateful remembrance or commemoration. Because memory is unstoppable, and the human fancy a Protean thing, the eucharist that commences with the body of Christ the bridegroom ends by imbibing the milk[11] of the (m)other:

> The shared meal is a deed symbolic of unification. All unifications outside of marriage involve actions that take a particular direction, actions determined by an object, actions that are mutually determinative of that object. All enjoyment, appropriation, and assimilation is an eating; or rather, eating is nothing other than appropriation. All spiritual enjoyment can therefore be expressed as eating. In friendship, one eats of one's friend, lives on one's friend. To substitute the body for the spirit is a genuine trope, and in the commemorative meal for a friend we enjoy with a keen suprasensuous imagination his flesh in every bite, his blood in every draft. To our effete age, this seems barbaric—but who says one has to think of raw, corruptible, flesh and blood? Corporeal appropriation is mysterious enough to be a lovely image of the way I make something *mine* in spirit. And then, are flesh and blood in fact so repulsive and base? Truly, there is more than gold and diamonds here, and the time is not far off when one will have a more elevated concept of the organic body.
>
> Who knows what a sublime symbol blood is? Precisely what is repulsive in its organic components is what allows us to conclude that there is something utterly sublime in them. We shiver before them, as though before ghosts, and with childish terror we sense in this bizarre mélange a mysterious world, which may turn out to be something like a woman we knew long ago.
>
> But to return to the commemorative meal: may we not think that our friend is now a creature whose flesh could be bread and whose blood could be wine?
>
> Thus we enjoy the genius of nature daily, and every meal is a Mass—an agency for the nourishment of soul and maintenance of body, a mysterious means of transfiguration and deification on earth, an animating intercourse with what is absolutely alive. We enjoy in slumber something that has no name. We wake as a child wakes on its mother's breast, and we know that all this replenishment and nourishment came to us as a free bestowal of love. We know that air, drink, and food are the constituents of an ineffably loving person. (*Teplitzer Fragmente*; 2: 409–10)

Novalis's thaumaturgic thought of osculation, better, of succulation (to coin a much-needed word), assimilation, and nourishment is an ardent thought, a thought of blood and flame. It is thus related to the combustive heat of fermentation, and thereby to the entire digestive system, including excretion. Among the *Freiberg Scientific Studies* of 1798/99, written while Novalis was studying at the mining academy, the following note develops an expanded notion of excrement as a fiery excrescence or product of spirit, inevitably bound up with those excrescences we call words:

> 4 kinds of flame—1. that whose excreta are the anorganic natures; 2. that whose excreta are plants; 3. that whose excreta are the animals; 4. that whose excreta are human beings. The higher the flame, the more full of *artifice*, the more complex the excrement that is formed.
>   All devouring is a process of assimilation, binding, generation—
>   The flame is *that which devours* in and for itself.
>   *Fermentations*—excreta too still possess the nature of a flame—they still devour—in the way, for example, that rust devours *metals*.
>   The metals that *decompose* water surely constitute such groups.[12]

As a thought of flame and of complex, manifold excretion, Novalis's is also a thought of spirit. Every system of the mouth leads eventually to the thought of soul and spirit, sometimes by the more traditional route of speech and thought, sometimes by the rarer way of the first kiss, and sometimes by the complementary thought of liquidity—of the liquids involved in salivation, ingestion, assimilation, excretion, and reproduction. A note from the third group of notes for the *Universal Sketchbook* takes the traditional route, referring to a "simultaneous, mutually related *speaking* and *thinking*" as productive of a miraculous substance—*flame*—which "harmoniously excites and shapes both speech and thought" (*Das allgemeine Brouillon*; 2: 685). Another note from the first group of those notes offers insight into the more foreign reaches of this fiery complex—an uncertain insight, to be sure, if one is trying to be certain about identities and identifications, uncertain inasmuch as the imbibing mouth or receptive orifice is difficult to locate or specify in Novalis's text with perfect assurance: "Semen is a means of nourishment and stimulation for the woman as a replacement for the *menstrua*. Thus in the most authentic sense the man *shares his life* with woman" (*Das allgemeine Brouillon*; 2: 554). Another note, within parentheses, also sheds light on this complex: "(*Life* in general is the genuine, absolute *Menstruum universale*—and the universal *coagulant*.) (There are infinitely many kinds of life. Every organ is *excrement* or *product* of *life*)" (2: 514–15). A later note, entitled *Physical Doctrine of Meaning*, traces, again in barest outline and thus cursorily, the itinerary that Novalis's *Encyclopedia* was to have pursued, developing a system of the mouth as knowledge, speech, ingestion, excretion, eucharist, and sexual embrace:

Speaking and hearing are fecundating and conceiving. / PSYCHOLOGY. *Shame*—shyness before an announcement— / ART. symbolic, religious mimicry—mimicry within the community—greetings, etc. What, for example, does it mean to bare one's head?

Synthesis of man and woman. / PHYSICS. Basis of the hospitality of the ancients—*The Last Supper*—communal eating and drinking is a kind of *unification*—a generative act.

No doubt *laughter* is also a topic essential to any system of the mouth, and if it were not for extrinsic constraints of time and space, it would behoove us to consider Novalis's reflections on it.[13] Yet let us be satisfied—although we are telescoping far too much material here into an all-too-narrow presentation—with the following two brief meditations on excretory thought and the nourishing sensibility: "Is thinking too an eliminating—? Then sensing is perhaps a devouring. Self-thinking thought is perhaps a vital process—a process of devouring and eliminating at once, thinking and sensing at the same time" (*Das allgemeine Brouillon*; 2: 522). Self-thinking thought, including all a priori thinking, is here no longer conceived of as satiation without eating; it is now subsumed under the process of ingestion and excretion. Perhaps the strangest of Novalis's thoughts on the system of the mouth, both humorous and profound, inviting both laughter and rumination, is the following note under the rubric "Poetic Physiology":

> Our lips often show great similarity to the two will-o'-the-wisps in [Goethe's] fairy tale. The eyes are the higher pair of siblings to the lips. They close and open a holier grotto than the mouth. The ears are the serpent that hungrily swallows whatever the will-o'-the-wisps let fall. Mouth and eyes have a similar form. The lashes are the lips. The eyeball is the tongue and the gums, the pupil is the gorge.
>
> The nose is the mouth's brow, and the brow is the nose of the eyes. Each eye has a cheekbone as its chin. (*Das allgemeine Brouillon*; 2: 557)

Tongue and lips—these essential elements of any system of the mouth, including that of Novalis's Mr. Potato Head—are the organs of speech. More than that, they are the prosthetic elements of vision and of language as such, reaching across space and time as a sort of primal *telegraph*. (Long before the electric telegraph, there were the telegraphs of semaphore and light; it is to these that Novalis refers when he calls tongue, lips, and the other features of the mouth "parts of a telegraph," that is to say, of "an artificial linguistic instrument.") He continues: "The eyes are telescopes—the telescopes eyes—the hand, as an instrument of language—acoustic stimulator and non-conductor—as paintbrush—as universal instrument of direction—*lever,* handle—as support, foundation" (*Das allgemeine Brouillon;* 2: 639). Yet the prosthetic, telegraphic, proleptic aspect of tongue, lips, eyes, and hands should not conceal the essentially *eucharistic* and *voluptuous* character of the body and its communications, as the following note—anticipating what Max Scheler came to call the *ordo amoris*—suggests:[14]

> Dancing—eating—speaking—communal sensing and working—being to-gether —hearing, seeing, feeling one another, etc.—all are conditions and occasions and even functions—of the efficacy of the *higher*—of human beings who have been brought together—of the genius, etc.
>
> Theory of Voluptuosity
>
> It is *Amor* that presses us together. The basis of all the functions mentioned above is voluptuosity *(sympathy).* The genuinely voluptuous function is the one that is most mystical—well-nigh absolute—or the one that compels us toward the *totality* of unification (mixture)—the *chemical.* (*Das allgemeine Brouillon;* 2: 666)

Voluptuosity is ubiquitous in Novalis's notes because it is everywhere in the universe. It constitutes the mysterious center of the system of the mouth (the microcosmic palate, as it were) and the mystic center of nature (the tasted macrocosm). It is the theory of voluptuosity that Novalis uncovers at the heart of the philosophical system of the somewhat more reticent Schelling: "*Observations* of voluptuosity in the whole of nature. . . . (The feeling *of the world soul,* etc. in voluptuosity . . .)" (2: 664). Such voluptuosity is no doubt related to philosophy as nostalgia or homesickness: "Philosophy is genuine homesickness—*the drive to be at home everywhere.*"[15] Yet these references to an apparently more attenuated, domesticated, sublimated, or universalized voluptuosity are undergirded by reminders of specifically sexual voluptuosities: "On the mystic members of human beings—it is voluptuous merely to think of them, to say nothing of setting them in motion" (2: 693). And: "In the act of procreation the soul *needs* the body, and vice-versa perhaps—the mysticism of this operation" (2: 700). Such thoughts inform the kind of science of which Novalis dreams, a precursor of Nietzsche's "gay science," which Novalis calls "*voluptuous* knowing" (ibid.). In these same pages he writes: "*Voluptuosity* of *generation* [Erzeugen]—all reproduction is thus a polemical *operation.* Voluptuosity of synthesis"

(2: 694). The πόλεμος of which he is thinking is no doubt that of Heraclitus and Empedocles. And, to be sure, Novalis's polemical voluptuosity is polymorphously perverse—otherwise it could not be religious, mystical, and magical.

Even though, in Novalis's thaumaturgic idealism, voluptuosity is properly associated with the flame and all that is ardent, it is, as we have already seen, essentially *liquid*, as it is in the much later thought of Gaston Bachelard and Luce Irigaray. In the "Fragments and Studies" of 1799/1800, Novalis writes, "Intense *well-being* of water. — The voluptuosity in the touch of water" (2: 771). In *The Apprentices at Saïs* we read: "Water, this firstborn child of pleasurable fusions, cannot deny its voluptuous origins; it shows itself to be the element of love and of the commingled omnipotence of heaven on earth" (1: 228). In the very late "Fragments and Studies III," from late 1800, we hear that "water is the fish among stones" (2: 822). One might compare Novalis's voluptuous account of water to the mature Goethe's account in *Faust* of homunculus at the Aegean Sea; or to the young Schelling's account in *Ideas toward a Philosophy of Nature* and *On the World Soul* of the first rainstorms of spring, in which electricity and water alike are wedded to the soil; or to the young Hegel's account of baptism in *The Spirit of Christianity*, an account that is considerably more voluptuous than any other account of baptism I know.[16] Finally, one might also compare this notion of voluptuous liquidity with Hegel's account of Mary Magdalene, also in *The Spirit of Christianity*, in which Mary's anointing the feet of Christ with chrism is recounted in terms of ejaculation and orgasm—again, a more voluptuous account than anything we might have associated with the name of Hegel.[17]

When and whether a theory of voluptuosity can fully satisfy its appetite for ardent, chemical unification remains to be pondered, inasmuch as Novalis's *Encyclopedia* never saw the light of day. Novalis approaches something like satiety—the elusive a priori, the a priori itself consumed in the process of ingestion and excretion—when his theory repeatedly brings the systems of assimilation and sexuality to converge on the aperture of the mouth: "On sexual pleasure—the longing for *fleshly* touching—the delight taken in the naked bodies of human beings. Might it be a camouflaged *appetite* for human flesh?" (*Fragmente und Studien 1799/1800*; 2: 771).

Such a system of the mouth and theory of voluptuosity, however, cannot be merely about pleasure, even the pleasures of cannibalism—the particular pleasures that ostensibly cause Hegel to expel Africa from universal history.[18] The forces that Novalis's theory goes to kiss are potent, and they are not always conciliatory, not always propitious. For there is a *second* first beginning of philosophy, so to speak, in Novalis's thought. A sheet of paper containing a number of fragments written soon after Sofie's death opens with the following:

> The genuine philosophical act is suicide; this is the real beginning of all philosophy; every need for philosophical disciples leads in that direction, and this act alone corresponds to all the conditions and characteristics of the transcendental attitude.
>
> Detailed elaboration of this supremely interesting thought.[19]

The first kiss opens upon what Novalis himself calls a "poetics of the baneful."

# CHAPTER TWO

# A Poetics of the Baneful

$\mathcal{N}$ovalis's notes on health and illness appear principally in the context of his projected *Enzyklopädistik* (1: 477), an ambitious attempt to synthesize—or, as he and Friedrich Schlegel are fond of writing, symphilosophize—the findings of all the sciences, whether natural or historical, with a transcendental philosophy and a universal poesy. His dream is to translate all lore, from the fairy tale to the findings of chemistry and physics, into a common code, which he calls the *lingua romana*. In the "Preliminary Studies" of 1798, Novalis writes:

> The world must be romanticized. In this way one will find its original meaning once again. Romanticizing is nothing other than a qualitative raising to the powers *[Potenzirung]*. The lower self is identified with a better self in this operation. Thus we ourselves are a kind of qualitative sequence of powers. This operation is still altogether unknown. Whenever I give the common a higher meaning, the usual a mysterious aspect, the familiar the dignity of the unknown, the finite an infinite appearance, in this way I romanticize it—Opposed to that is the operation for the higher, unknown, mystical, infinite—by connecting these matters we find their logarithms— They receive a customary expression. romantic philosophy. *Lingua romana*. Alternating elevation and degradation. (2: 334)

The fragmentary syntax and the "altogether unknown" symphilosophical content of the note we have just read—on the *lingua romana*—ought to give us pause. Indeed, anyone who has suffered through the first chapter of the present book and made it thus far has a right to ask whether and why such an ambitious and inchoate task as von Hardenberg's, which is both encyclopedic and aphoristic, is to be taken seriously. Or, less polemically, we still confront the question as to how these fragments and notes are to be read, especially by those of us who have been trained—and tested—to identify reading with reading comprehension ("Thou shalt immediately understand everything at all times both in itself and in its connection with everything else"). No doubt, Novalis frays the nerves. He seems content to scatter seed promiscuously in all directions, trusting in our powers to glean (the German *lesen*, "to read," "to gather") his drift. He seems content to be as wasteful as dehiscent nature herself. One is tempted to agree with Anni Carlsson when she says that fragmentary writing is fragmentary knowledge and when she wonders whether Novalis is Jean Paul's Quintus Fixlein—an irrepressible romantic dabbler who is an ancestor of the Sartrean autodidact and the Flaubertian *Bouvard et Pécuchet*—all of them reveling in "literary Saturnalia" instead of preparing sober festivals for the crystalline analytical intellect.[1]

If Novalis's *lingua romana* at first seems arcane and impenetrable, and if we are nostalgic for the *lingua franca* of analytical thought, it may help if we remember some of the more recent lessons we are supposed to have learned. At least if we are to believe Georges Bataille and Maurice Blanchot, an erotics that is more devoted to the *discontinuity* of being than to any dream of uninterrupted continuity may be conjoined to an infinite entertainment of interruption, multiple truth, plurality, and separation—the earmarks of what Blanchot calls "fragmentary writing," for which Novalis seems to be the perfect preparation.[2]

No doubt, the more mathematical traits of Novalis's *lingua romana*, his qualitative raising-to-the-powers, potentiation, or exponentiation, could also apply to Schelling's system of nature philosophy. Schelling's preoccupation with a "sequence of stages" or "potencies" in nature is perhaps also a romanticizing of the world, even though the young Schelling is apt to insist that the potencies are embedded in the world of nature and are almost independent of thought, rather than being in the first place exertions of a positing reason. Also significant—and in the long run, that is, in terms of the history of metaphysics, as of the *end* or *closure* of metaphysics, even more significant—is Novalis's logarithmic method. By means of it, the elevated, mystical, and infinite receive a lowly, profane, and finite name. Perhaps Schelling and Hegel ought to have learned more of this logarithmic method from Novalis—not in order to reduce or insult the spiritual but to make all its earthly and unearthly connections more tenable, all its potencies more subtle, all its logics more supple and persuasive.[3]

One might say that a test case or even a limit-situation for Novalis's romanticizing project, for its raising-to-the-powers of the humble and its taking the logarithm of the elevated, is the matter of health and illness. It is not merely that both health and illness can serve as the logarithm for a loftier, more "spiritual" significance, health for the sanctity of the soul, illness for the condition of malignancy; it is also that health and illness are themselves bound to a vertical axis, health being superior to illness, and illness comprising a "fall" from health, a state of decline or diminution. Yet how can the state of decline, the "wreck of body, / Slow decay of blood, / Testy delirium / Or dull decrepitude," which Yeats laments,[4] be given a "higher meaning," a "mysterious aspect," the "dignity of the unknown," and an "infinite appearance"? A note from *Das allgemeine Brouillon* of 1798/99, having to do with "The utility of illness—*the poesy of illness,*" begins skeptically enough (2: 475): "An illness cannot be a life, otherwise the *connection with illness* would have to *elevate* our existence. Continue this bizarre thought" (ibid.). The "bizarre thought" occurs to Novalis that the connection between life and illness might in fact be elevating rather than distressing and depressing. No doubt he is thinking of the imbricated structures of excitability—that is, sensibility and irritability—and reproduction, as developed in the physiological and diagnostic system of the Edinburgh physician John Brown. That system, based on the work of Albrecht von Haller, had become well known in Germany thanks to the proselytizing efforts of Karl Friedrich von Kielmeyer, Adalbert Friedrich Marcus, and Andreas Röschlaub, all associated with Schelling during the period of his influential work *Von der Weltseele* (1798).[5]

Brown's *Elementa medicinae*, which intends to provide a complete nosology, that is, a classification of diseases, offers in addition a general theory of physiology. Although quite convincing in its general outlines, at least for the German authors we are discussing, albeit admittedly less so back in Edinburgh, even Brown's German disciples note that the theory does not sufficiently distinguish between health and illness—Brown seemed to appeal to the identical factors and processes when describing both states.[6] Indeed, the principal purpose of Brown's theory is to blur the distinction between health and illness. For each of these states Brown introduces an "indirect" state that serves as a transition from one to the other. Novalis, following Brown, notes the following:

> Just as illness is a symptom of health, so must health manifest symptoms of illness.
>
> 1. *Direct health*— 2. indirect health. 3. Direct illness— 4. *indirect illness.* No. 1 elides with 4, as no. 3 elides with 2.
>
> Repeated *indirect illnesses* ultimately elide with direct illness, and vice versa—repeated indirect health elides with direct health. Indirect health follows direct illness as surely as indirect illness follows health. (2: 452)

An equally bizarre thought now occurs to Novalis. No matter how elevating illness in general might be in and for a romanticizing tendency, as though illness were the logarithm of well-being, the soul itself, the most elevated principle of life, may serve to aggravate the worst illnesses of the body. The soul thus partakes of the secret ambivalence of all φάρμακα. Novalis develops what one might call the *pharmaceutical principle*, which has to do with the discomfiting proximity of medicines and toxins. Novalis does not shrink from speculating that the soul itself might be the prime instance of the pharmaceutical principle. That is to say, the principle of life itself may be the most poisonous of entities:

> Among all *poisons*, the *soul* is the most potent. It is the most penetrating, the most diffuse stimulus. — All the effects of the soul are therefore supremely harmful when it is a question of local illness and infection.
>
> A local illness often cannot be cured except by means of a general illness, and vice-versa.
>
> Curing *one illness* by means of *another.* (2: 706)

Novalis begins to speculate that sheer *love* of illness can transform a malady into "supreme, positive pleasure," that illness may be a means toward a higher synthesis. Illness may be the secret symphilosopheme and the proper potentiation; it may open a path that will return us to a state of intimacy with nature. To such intimacy the poet gives the name of his dead fiancée, *Sofie*, the young woman he admitted "loving more almost on account of her illness."[7]

There is something *uncanny* about Novalis's thinking concerning health and illness, something beyond the bizarre. Its uncanniness is corroborated by the fact that the *fairy tale*, which Freud in his famous essay on "The Uncanny" cites as the proper genre of uncanniness, is Novalis's most beloved genre: "In the fairy tale the genuine anarchy of nature lies concealed."[8] Novalis's *lingua romana*, itself radically anarchic, would have to learn a new language with regard to illness, a language for which John Brown had provided the first runes: Novalis's project would have to involve a *Poetik des Übels*, a poetics of the baneful and malignant, of which the fairy tale provides the most fecund source. Novalis elaborates the way in which the action in fairy tales often depends on a double transformation, whereby one impossible occurrence induces another impossible occurrence: as soon as the princess overcomes her disgust in the face of the frog, as soon as she does the impossible and confesses her love of the beast, bestowing on it her first philosophical kiss, the frog is transformed into a prince. Yet the transformation of the ugly into the beautiful comes about if and only if the beautiful (inexplicably, monstrously) comes to love the ugly. If the Beauty believes that the ugliness of the Beast is but a facade concealing a beauty equal to her own, if she surmises that a prince hides behind the horror, the magic will not work. Yet once the kiss has been given, the Beauty loves the Beast—and not the handsome prince. Novalis now muses on the uncanny relation of illness to his theory of voluptuosity:

> Perhaps a similar metamorphosis would occur if human beings could come to love what is *baneful* in the world—the moment a human being began to love its illness or pain, the most stimulating voluptuosity would lie in its arms—the summit of positive pleasure would permeate it. Could not *illness* be a means to a higher synthesis—the more horrific the pain, the higher the pleasure concealed within it. *(Harmony.)* Every illness is perhaps the necessary *commencement* of the more intense conjunction of two creatures—the necessary beginning of love. Enthusiasm for illnesses and pains. Death—a closer conjunction of lovers.
>
> *Poetics of the baneful.*
>
> Does not the best everywhere begin with *illness?* Half an illness is baneful. A whole illness is pleasure—indeed, a higher form of pleasure.
>
> On the attractive force of the dire. (2: 628)

Novalis's poetics of the baneful, celebrating the attractive force of the dire, tends to identify the forces of good health with those of a "whole" illness, and to identify the embrace of lovers, culminating in their "little death," as the fulfillment of what began with illness and, paradoxically, with death itself. In one of the final notes, jotted down near the end of his life, he elaborates:

Illnesses are surely a *supremely important object for humanity,* for they are numberless, and each human being has to struggle with them so often. It is only that we know so little about the art of using them. They are probably the most interesting stimulus to our meditation and our activity. . . . What if I should become the prophet of this art? (2: 828)

Novalis—again like Schelling, who had written his master's thesis on the subject—uses the term *Übel,* the baneful, in both a nosological and moral sense. It is not as though illness were a metaphor for evil, or evil a metaphor for illness, or that the two stand in analogical relation; rather, both Novalis and Schelling take moral and physical evil to be in some very deep sense *one.* Deep if only because both the malignant and the malevolent are for these philosophers of unification principles of separation, *Trennung.* Ironically, to try to separate off good from evil, the healthy from the ill, or moral evil from physical malaise, is to be both evil and sick. (Yet had not all the institutions of Christendom tried to effect such a separation? Was not such a separation the point of all moral education and sacramental administration?) Only greater synthesis, achieved through symphilosophizing, only integration, concatenation, ramification, alternation, and reciprocity will avail. In contrast, isolation is wickedness and decrepitude. Nor can one say that for Novalis and Schelling there is no radical evil; rather, we encounter radical evil precisely in those who believe they can separate off evil from good. That would explain the reluctance that Jesus tried to inculcate, the reluctance to toss the first packet of gravel. One will find radical evil, Novalis and Schelling propose, precisely among those who believe that they can separate off soul from body, vice from virtue, or even, say, law from medicine. For all these things are bound up with one another in nature. In the very first group of his notes on Fichte, from the fall and early winter of 1795, Novalis lists the following topics, which presumably are in some as yet unknown sense contiguous: "Critical physics. Vices. Criminal law. History. Medicine" (2: 47). In the sixth group of his notes on Fichte, from summer–fall 1796, under the general heading "Conceptual Developments," we find the following expanded list: "Love—natural law—criminal law—sociality—*art* —the state—constitution—religion—marriage—illness—political economy" (2: 196). In short, for Novalis's critical physics and thaumaturgic idealism, matters of medicine and illness, along with questions of vice and law, are not remote from either politics, religion, or art. Precisely how such "conceptual developments" are to be joined systematically or encyclopedically is a question that plagues Novalis throughout the philosophical-scientific notes. In the sixth group of notes in the *Fichte Studies* we also find the following two observations on philosophy and systematicity:

> The properly philosophical system must be freedom and infinity—or, to express it in a poignant fashion, systemlessness—brought together in a system. Only that kind of system can avoid the mistakes of the system, in such a way that neither *injust*ice nor anarchy can be held against it. (2: 200)

And:

> The universal system of philosophy must, like time, be one thread along which one can run through infinite determinations — It must be a system of the most manifold unity, of infinite expansion, with the compass of freedom —neither a formal nor a material system—
> We must search out the dichotomy everywhere. (2: 201)

That could have become the legend on Schelling's escutcheon as well: "We must search out the dichotomy everywhere."

An important aspect of Novalis's thaumaturgic idealism—his poetics of the baneful is an essential part of his total project, and so we should be able to turn from the kiss to disease to idealism without feeling the least violence or physical discomfort—is his theory of association, anticipating the psychoanalytic sense of *free* association. Novalis is willing to push association as far as it can go, into injustice and anarchy, and it is often likely to go in the direction of erotics and sexuality: "If the usual associations do not strike home, then unusual associations will help—for example, in order to excite the genitals" (2: 796). Indeed, Novalis puts the entire human body to work in what are otherwise thought to be thought processes:

> In the formation of thoughts it seems to me that all the parts of the body play a role. These parts too seem to be results of actions and concatenations of events—and in this way we can explain the necessary impact of *altered trains of thought, alien claims*—striking aphorisms—sudden windfalls—on the state of the body. The soul strives after the novel even in states of anxiety and perturbation—often it strives after the old—in short, it strives after something *other*.
> A sudden terror can also work advantageous effects. (2: 796).

Among the requirements of thaumaturgic idealism, none is more important than the faculty of free association, and the exercise of that faculty—the exercise Novalis calls *Fantastik*, a word that he takes to be homologous with *Logik*: "If we only had a *fantastic* as well as a *logic*, the art of invention would have been—invented. To the *fantastic* belongs also an aesthethics *[sic: die Aestethik]*, so to speak, in the way that the doctrine of reason belongs to logic" (2: 697). No doubt, Novalis's *Fantastik*, along with its odd hybrid of ethics and aesthetics, will be put to work on the most recalcitrant of philosophical problems, that of a poetics of the baneful. The prospects for such a *Fantastik* are only improved by the fact that magical idealism, according at least to a number of late notes, is itself laced with illness, marbled with malady, marked by a sublime hypochondria.

From the time of Novalis's Kant and Hemsterhuis studies, during the year 1797, we find a series of notes on hypochondria. Novalis avers that hypochondria may be "petty" or "sublime," the latter variety being equivalent to introspection—the capacity to gaze into the soul. Such a capacity for what in effect amounts to intellectual intuition, according to Novalis, who here once again anticipates Freud, employs one emotional disorder *(Gemüthskranckheit)* in order to discover other such psychic illnesses: like jealousy, hypochondria awakens the soul to vigilance and self-knowledge (2: 344). When Freud says that the great system-builders in the world of thought are philosophers and paranoiacs, with philosophy and paranoia possibly elided in and as psychoanalysis, he is building on Novalisian insights that no doubt were unknown to him, though adrift in the general culture and intellectual climate of nineteenth-century Germany and Austria. Indeed, there might be some grounds for considering psychoanalysis *as a whole* in terms of a poetics of the baneful. Be that as it may, Novalis, somewhat later, in October–November 1798, notes that hypochondria is "pathologizing fancy, bound up with *belief* in the reality of its productions, its phantasms" (2: 595). Such belief does not vitiate the power and efficacy of hypochondria, at least in its sublime form, but institutes it. Pathology, then, is not in the first place that which causes suffering but that which grants knowledge: "The pathological explanation of the human condition—our world—our constitution—these are *attunement*—stimulability and sensibility" (2: 716).

However, Novalis's understanding of the intertwining of thaumaturgic idealism and illness does not stop with the thought of hypochondria. His poetics of the baneful takes him to more explicit forms of illness, including those that arise from *contagion*, to which we must now turn. For contagion will have begun prior to the essentially undecidable moment of the "first" contact, the "first" touching, the "first" kiss.

## CHAPTER THREE

# *Touching, Contact, Contagion*

*A*t first blush, Novalis's ideas about *touching* seem to hold little promise—even though we saw them playing a central role in his system of the mouth and theory of voluptuosity. At all events, there is something literal and lapidary, something well-nigh mechanical, about the following observation in *Blüthenstaub* (Pollen) from 1797/98: "In every touch a substance originates whose efficacy lasts as long as the touch does. This is the basis of all synthetic modifications of the individual. However, there are one-sided and mutual touchings, the former grounding the latter" (2: 269). It is as though Novalis were trying to elaborate a phlogiston theory of palpation, and, moreover, a theory that is solipsistic. Yet from the outset of his thought, Novalis privileges practical over theoretical philosophy, identifying the practical as "a longing," *ein Sehnen* (2: 57), a yearning that is, as we have seen, bound up with touch and contact, kiss and coitus. Anything but lapidary, anything but *solus ipse*.

Among the most interesting uses of touching *(berühren)* and self-touching *(sich berühren)* in Novalis's notes is one that invokes the mutual touching—equivalent to coupling, *sich paaren*—of fancy and judgment, or reason and the arbitrary, *Logik* and *Fantastik*: when fancy and judgment touch one another, he says, perhaps echoing his friend Friedrich Schlegel, *wit* comes to be; when reason and the arbitrary mate, the result is *humor*. In short, mutual touches are fructifying (2: 239–41). The touch that most fascinates Novalis is that between soul and body as such, or the touch of world soul and the organism. He calls such touching the "mysterious tie" and adds: "Life is perhaps nothing other than the result of this unification—the *action of this touching"* (2: 415). Novalis emphasizes that touching is nothing extrinsic or mechanical—he denies, for example, that the imagination depends on the "presence" and the "touching" of "external stimuli," after the manner of classical typography.[1] One of the most striking notes on touch does relate palpation to the Brownian theme of stimulation and also to the general theory of excitation; it therefore broaches the dire proximity of life to illness as such, inasmuch as illness is caused by either excessive stimulation (hypersthenia) or understimulation (asthenia). In the 1798 *Vorarbeiten* Novalis writes, once again in language that is close to that of Freudian metapsychology:

> Stimulus from without is indirect—stimulus from within is *direct* stimulus. External stimulus presupposes internal stimulus. Stimulability is *indeterminate life—oscillating action*—indirect stimulus—Cancellation of equilibrium—Heterogenization—determinate direction. Life, like illness, originates from a *faltering* [Stockung]—delimiting—*touching.* (2: 350)

Novalis appears to be following the insight of the ancient Atomists (2: 621) when he identifies all sensation—and not only palpation—with touching. Yet, oddly, it is a touching without contact: "To look upon something is an *elastic enjoyment* [Genuß] of it. . . . The mere *need of an object* results from a touching-at-a-distance *[Berührung in distans]*" (2: 509). Thus touching and ingesting, as we noted in chapter 1, are as much a part of "epistemology" as of "dietetics" (2: 511). An apprentice at Saïs never needs to lift the veil of Maya; he or she merely moves to touch it, "for the softest touch dissolves the veil into a magical fragrance, which becomes the nebular vehicle of the seer" (2: 650). Later we will see Hegel touch the veil. Indeed, he will grasp it vigorously, only to have it "melt" under the solar ray of his thought, leaving no residue, no trace of fragrance. Novalis's touch is considerably lighter, his *move* to touch considerably more tremulous.

The theory of palpation is for Novalis a theory of transition. *Übergang* is one of the essential words in Novalis's thaumaturgic idealism. In one note he calls the theory of touch "the mystery of transubstantiation" (2: 622). It is clear from other remarks of his that touching is the very essence of Galvanism, that is, the relation of electrical energy to organic tissue (2: 591). The privileged moment of touching between soul and body, as we have already heard, occurs in sexual embrace, itself related to other forms of palpation, including ingestion. "When organs touch one another, souls harmonize," reads one note (2: 527); Novalis adds the parenthetical remark: "(Without separation there is no conjunction. Touching is separation and conjunction alike.)" A moment ago, in the context of illness and evil, we said that for a syncretic-synthetic, thaumaturgic idealism, separation itself is radical evil. Novalis's theory of touching now appears to contradict this when it suggests that touching requires both conjunction and separation—that, as Merleau-Ponty will say, the reversible touched-touching is only incompletely reversible.[2] Yet the apparent contradiction merely points to the *problem* of touching, which is the problem of contactless contact, the problem of contagion. In magical idealism, touching and being touched, activity and passivity, the elevated and the base, health and illness, good and evil—all these will no doubt be among the opposites that contaminate one another.

One of the most far-ranging notes on touch in the *Universal Sketchbook* (found in the first group of notes, dated September–October 1798) reads as follows:

> Held over against the life of animals, the life of plants is a ceaseless conception and giving birth; held over against the life of plants, the life of animals is a ceaseless eating and fecundating.
>
> In the way that a *woman* is the *supremely visible* means of nourishment, constituting the *transition from body to soul*—just so the genitals are the supreme *external* organs that constitute the transition from the visible to the invisible organs.

I interrupt to note that this notion of the genitals as the external paragon—more than an analogon—of the internal or spiritual organs plays a powerful role in Hegel's dialectic of genitality as well. As we will see in chapter 10, below, Hegel calls the genital member of the male "the upswelling heart," and at least suggests that it is the "active brain" of the body, as though the tumescent penis were itself in transition to heart and brain, to feeling and intellectuality. A noteworthy difference between Novalis and Hegel, however, is that Novalis does not seem to specify the male genitalia as the supreme organs of the transition to spirit—indeed, the opposite is the case. Like Hegel, however, he does see the complex of nourishment and the transition from body to soul as preeminently a matter of "woman." At all events, Novalis's note now continues, adding to his system of the mouth and eyes a system of hands and touches:

> The *gaze*—(speech)—*holding hands—the kiss—touching the breasts—reaching down to the genitals*—the act of embrace: these are all rungs on the ladder

down which the soul clambers. Facing it is a ladder up which the body clambers—to the heights of the embrace. *Premonition—pursuing the scent—the act.* Preparing the soul and the body for the awakening of the sex drive.

Soul and body *touch one another* [berühren sich] in the act. Chemically or galvanically or electrically—or *ardently*—the soul eats the body (and digests it?) instantaneously; the body conceives the soul (and gives birth to it?) instantaneously. (*Das allgemeine Brouillon*; 2: 497; cf. 487)

The soul, as animal, that is, as voracious, devours the body; the body, as plant, that is, as rooted in the earth, conceives the soul. And the soul digests the body? And the body gives birth to the soul? And each excretes or exhales the other? It is difficult to know what is ascent, what descent, on the ladders of love, palpation, nourishment, elimination, and reproduction. However, it is clear that for Novalis the eminently spiritual ladder is the body of woman, with the eyes of her moralized chest promising the most visible means of nourishment, the folds of her sex embracing the not entirely invisible organs that are closest to the unseen soul of what in baby-talk used to be called *man*. And it is clear that whereas the first kiss—the kiss of two lips—can occur without company, the touching of soul and body requires a kind of fourfold, a fourfold or infinitesimal folding "in the act," and can never transpire in splendid solitude.

Further, the palpation between soul and body—or between souls and bodies—imitates divine creation itself, creation as generative, that is, as bound up with both the genitals and genius. While God, nature, and the person are the Kantian-Fichtean categories with which Novalis is working early in his career of thought, that is, in 1795, the categories or *Gattungsbegriffe* themselves are always bound up with begetting, the genuses and geniuses with generation, and the generated persons with men and women: "*Zeugung. Mann und Weib*" (2: 68; cf. 97). Much later, in the *Universal Sketchbook*, Novalis relates the genius of generation to the creation of the world—once again declining to privilege either male or female genitalia: "The organs of thought are the parts that procreate the world, nature's genitals *[Die Denkorgane sind die Weltzeugungs-, die Naturgeschlechtstheile]*" (2: 719). One of those parts does seem to entertain a certain privilege: like Hegel, Novalis finds a distinct similarity between testicle and brain (2: 686); unlike Hegel, however, Novalis will not privilege the up-swelling heart (that is, the penis) over the putatively inactive brain (the testicle), nor either of these over the variegated sex of woman.

In a very late note, one of the last, the connection between sexual reproduction and health and illness is made: "The healing power of nature is closely related to the reproductive power—that is why we cannot count on it among overly sensitive human beings. The nobler the human being, the more artificial his or her preservation. The study of medicine will become a duty and a necessity" ("Fragments and Studies III," from early summer to October 1800; 2: 822). The thought of *genius* alone is sufficient to make that connection: "Well-nigh everything ingenious heretofore was one-sided, the result of a sickly constitution" (2: 271).

Novalis expatiates on the concept of touch and its relation to *force*—including, presumably, *dire* forces—in the second group of notes toward a *Universal Sketchbook* (2: 577):

> Force *[die Kraft]* comports itself toward the soul as the soul does toward the spirit. All touching occasions an excitation of the unifying and systematizing force—i.e., of the world soul—or of the soul in general. The more animated the matter is, the more effective the touching will be—for here too force cannot be oversaturated with *soul*. Touches themselves have degrees and magnitudes—and *directions*, i.e., figures. Inefficacious touches are not touches in the stricter sense—they are merely *apparent* touches. Apparent and real touches are not always bound up with one another. Genuine touchings are mutual excitations.

Nevertheless, a less harmonious kind of touching than the mutual sort is also envisaged—briefly, rarely—in Novalis's notes. For touchings can be baneful: "Just as good spirits, genies, are formed out of coexistence and congruence, or appear in these latter, so also, by contrast, evil spirits such as *pain* and so on are formed from *discrepancy*, enmity, etc. Pain is at all events a *substance*—originating from inimical touches" (2: 677).

With that, we both return to our point of departure, namely, Novalis's "phlogistical" account of touch, and broach our subject proper, *contagium*, as a mutual touching to the detriment of at least one of the living substances involved. It is in these pages of the *Universal Sketchbook* (the third group of notes, from November to early December 1798, the period of Novalis's engagement to Julie von Charpentier and a year before the acute stage of his own tuberculosis) that Novalis invokes the possibility of his own illness. If all *accident* is wonderful *("Aller* Zufall *ist wunderbar"),* inasmuch as it is "the touch of a higher essence" (2: 682), and if all past philosophers have dwelt in that ethereal place where the invisible world touches us *("die*

*Berührungsstelle mit der unsichtbaren Welt")* (2: 711), Novalis still must wonder about the unseen contingencies of illness and death, contagion and infection, that have by now touched him. He is interested in contact, whether it be *"Contact* with the spirit of history" (2: 504) or the above-mentioned "touching at a distance *[Berührung in distans]"* that occurs when we perceive an object or feel a need for it (2: 509), or the *actio in distans* by which remote mountains, remote events, or remote people touch the Romantic poet (2: 537).

The theme of *touch* in fact plays a role in Novalis's critique of Schelling. In his last notes, Novalis asks concerning Schelling: "In Schelling's nature philosophy a limited concept of nature and of philosophy is presupposed. What is Schelling's nature philosophy, really?" (2: 828). In the *Universal Sketchbook* he had criticized Schelling's preference for what we today would call the efferent nervous system ("irritability") over the afferent, affective, or receptive system ("sensibility"):

> Schelling takes as his point of departure merely the *phenomenon of irritability*—his basis is *muscle.* — Where do we find in him the *nerve*—the arteries—the blood—and the *skin*—*cell tissue?* Why doesn't he, the chemist, take as his point of departure the *process*—the phenomenon of touch—the *concatenation?*[3]

In his last notes Novalis is himself touched more and more by the strangeness of his most bizarre, beloved thoughts, his most uncanny and untimely meditations. "It is certain that the *highest*, the universal, the most obscure is always in play, and that every investigation must therefore quickly collide against obscure thoughts" (2: 792). At the same time, a kind of Nietzschean nervousness in the face of hybris is also there: "A human being cannot climb any higher than insight into the kinds of knowing that are suitable for the stage he or she occupies. . . . One should not promote in a pathological way the drive to know—rather, one should bring it into harmony with the rest of one's forces and conditions" (2: 793). In spite of the worry about pathology, the tendency of Novalis's final thoughts is to locate illness ever more centrally and irremovably in the terrain of life. *"Illness in the genuine sense* is a wondrous product of life," he writes. And Novalis well-nigh thinks the reverse as well, namely, that life may be a wondrous product of contagion (2: 794). In any case, excitability *(Erregbarkeit)* is "wondrous and mysterious"; this is what he learns by stroking in experimental ways the limbs of Julie: "Should not one be able, through thoughts, beliefs, etc., to put the body in the position of wondrous efficacy—vis-à-vis another?" (2: 795).

Finally, in these last notes, Novalis becomes increasingly convinced that the realms of birth and death, health and illness, generation and corruption, pharmacology and nosology, are coterminous: "All the forces of nature are but one force" (2: 820). And that force, to repeat, is "the attractive force of the dire." Hence it is often difficult to identify the *tendency* of Novalis's notes on illness, notes such as the following: "Earmark of *illness*—the instinct of self-destruction. — So it is with everything incomplete—so it is with life itself—or, better, with organic matter. . . . Cancellation of the distinction between life and death. Annihilation of death" (2: 417).

The parataxis and apparent apposition of the phrases "cancellation of the distinction between life and death" and "annihilation of death" is troubling: annihilation of death sounds like the Pauline project ("Death, thou too shall die!"), and there would be little reason to remember Novalis if he were merely another freerider on the salvationist bandwagon. Perhaps the genitive is subjective, however, with death performing its inalienable nihilative task? Annihilation by death, or at the very least, cancellation of every facile distinction between life and death, introduces into Novalis's magical idealism something like *lifedeath*. Lifedeath would presumably mark out the domain of the physician, though not the naive physician who tinkers with symptoms. Novalis can accept only the physician who has learned from the prophet of the art of illness. Such a doctor would himself or herself become an artist of a new kind, an artist of immortality, whereby both *artist* and *immortality* would have to be pronounced in an as yet unheard-of way.[4]

# CHAPTER FOUR

# The Artist of Immortality

$\mathcal{N}$ovalis recognizes that the pharmaceutical art, the art of mixing and administering medicines, is "the art of *killing,*" and that there are at bottom no healthy medicines: "All remedies are such because they are *efficacious* in general, *harmful*" (2: 501). The name of Helen's maid, the one who teaches Helen the pharmaceutical art she has brought back with her from Egypt, is *Polydamna.* It is this multifariously murderous side of pharmaceuticals that reminds Novalis again and again of the soul, the principle of life. If the stimuli that diffuse quite readily are generally characterized by their "narcotic nature" (2: 590), then the immortal soul, which diffuses most readily throughout the body, appears to be the most potent narcotic, the fatal toxin.

The soul works as salves, balms, and unguents do *(wie Oele),* "and also like narcotic poisons—depressing and also exciting" (2: 711). Yet balms or salves are themselves spiritual entities, inasmuch as they contain highly volatile substances; it is as though only an essence, only a fragrance, only a spirit, could be narcotic. Yet it is not that *narcosis* is simply to be condemned, not in this complex world. Still on the trail of the oleaginous, Novalis writes, "Temporal natures are like wine—the older they are, the more delicious" (2: 504). When a wine has "legs," as we say in English, meaning that it is viscous, rich in fruit and full-bodied in texture, the Germans call it *oily,* and the confusion in the ear of the English-speaker—for whom *oily* is a matter of machines and soiling—is one that would have amused Novalis. His note continues: "Fermentation—settling—spiritualization—the wines become *more oily.* (Oil, symbol of spirit—its body)" (ibid.).

It is this pharmaceutical—or, now, oinological and oleaginous—principle, as we may call it, that relates the themes of soul and poison to the sexual process. In a tantalizing note, Novalis writes, "Poison and antidote—gradual intensification of the two-sided process—in the process of generation" (2: 502). Also related to the pharmaceutical principle is the practice of inoculation, which Novalis hales as "in every respect a supremely remarkable thing" (2: 545). Among the inoculations he envisages, as a physician and artist of immortality, are those with aging and death. He writes:

> Every illness is a musical problem—its healing a *musical solution*. The more succinct and yet complete the solution, the greater the musical talent of the physician.
> Illnesses admit of manifold solutions. The choice of the most appropriate solution is what defines the talent of the physician.
>
> Inoculation with age *[Inoculation des Alters]*. (ibid.)

Inoculation with senescence and death, as strange as it may sound, may well be the therapy of the future. Novalis grows increasingly occupied with what we heard him call "the pathological explanation of the human condition" (2: 716). The art of healing, he says, "like physics and philosophy, is as much a theory of *making* as of annihilating," and its future course may lead to the most radical measures: "In the general therapy of the future not even *inoculation with death* will be missing—in the way that many illnesses are counted among the best educational methods, our pedagogues demanding the appropriate remedies for them."[1]

Whatever the art of healing may be in the future, it will not be simple trial and error, which has characterized the history of medicine thus far—each advance being made, Novalis wryly notes, on the basis of "an overfilled cemetery" (2: 566). Novalis is not thinking of injecting death as in *Dead Man Walking*, or after the manner of Dr. Death. Rather, death is to become a major heuristic principle, a field of discovery, as opposed to the charnel house of ignorance and defeat. Novalis asks himself, "How many kinds of *killing* are there?" and he replies: "The kinds of killing, like the kinds of noxious infection, would have to shed great light on the kinds of life and animation there are, and on the ways we make beings healthy" (2: 604). Inoculation with death, understood in terms of the pharmaceutical principle, has more to do with the *saving* grace than with the *coup de grace*.

The art of healing becomes the principal concern of Novalis's "magical idealism" toward the end of his own life. Novalis strives to be "the artist of immortality," who is also precisely a mathematician of mortality, elaborating what he calls "infinitesimal medicine":

> Death is nothing other than the interruption of the *alternation* between inner and outer stimulus—between soul and world. The middle member— as it were, the product of these two infinitely variable magnitudes is the body, the excitable—better, the medium of excitation. The body is the product and at the same time the modifier of the excitation—a function of soul and world. — This function has a maximum and a minimum; once reached, the alternation ceases. Death is naturally twofold. The relation between *x* and *y* is alterable forwards and backwards—but the *function as a whole* is also *alterable*. The *mass of one's constitution* is capable of expansion and narrowing. The doctrine by which we regulate our lives in the stricter sense actually contains the art of shaping and improving one's constitution. The genuine art of healing merely contains the prescriptions for preserving and restoring the special relations and alternations of the stimuli or of other factors. The artist of immortality practices the more elevated form of medicine—infinitesimal medicine. — He constantly observes the two factors simultaneously as one, seeking to bring them into harmony—to unify them in accord with one principle. (Should not a king who is simultaneously a moral genius on his own terms be immortal?) The external stimulus, in its immeasurability, is always already there, so to speak, and for the most part is under the control of the artist. Yet how slight is the power of the inner stimulus against *the external! Gradual* increase of the inner stimulus is therefore the main concern of the artist of immortality. With what right, one cannot say, for here too the poet has *prophesied* in a remarkable way— claiming that the Muses alone grant immortality. The learned estate too now appears in a new light. My magical idealism. (2: 549–50)

Among the more concrete therapies to be prescribed by the artist of immortality, all of them based on a critical reception of John Brown's nosology and theory of excitability, as sensibility and irritability along with reproduction, Novalis recommends not only an increase in inner stimulations but also *"more rapid alternations"* in stimulus.[2] Such concrete therapies, however, always take Novalis to the most general principles of his thaumaturgic idealism. One of these general principles, or general confidences, has to do with the refusal to accept random events or haphazard stimulations in nature, the refusal to accept the "mere" of "mere contingency." Novalis writes, "Nor is even contingency *inexplicable*—it has *its own* regularity."[3] Occasionally these general principles sound like thoughts that might have inspired a Merleau-Ponty, who certainly knew of Schelling but who may not have done extensive work in Novalis's scientific notebooks:

> Stimulability and sensibility stand in a relation similar to that between soul and body—or spirit and human being or world. The world is the *macro-andropos*. It is a world spirit, just as there is a world soul. The soul is to become spirit—the body is to become world. The world is not yet finished—neither is the world spirit. — Out of one god, a universal god should come to be. Out of one world, a universe. Vulgar physics—higher physics. The human being is common prose—it should become higher prose—all-embracing prose. Formation of the spirit also forms the world spirit—and is thus *religion*. (2: 551–52; cf. 558–59)

Tempering Novalis's enthusiasm for the arts of immortality, however, is the recurrent sense of the "infinite difficulty" of the problem with which he is engaged. That problem can be resolved only "successively," step by step, along an "infinite gradation of solutions" (ibid.) At the end of a long note on infinite difficulty, the parenthetical remark appears, "(Now we clearly see the imperfection and the ideal of our corporeal and human system)" (2: 564). It is as though Novalis is tracing the epochs of the world back to the era of Chaos, searching for the point at which the human body and all other living organisms, whether under the reign of Zeus or Kronos, took their departure from anorganic matter (2: 565). Early on in the *Universal Sketchbook* he writes: "In the world *to come*, everything will be as it was in the *former* world—and *yet it will be altogether different*. The world *to come* is *rational* Chaos—the Chaos that has permeated itself—that is in itself and outside itself—Chaos² or ∞." Among his last notes we find the following: "*Stones* and *matter are* the highest—the human being is the genuine *Chaos*" (2: 795). Novalis therefore also fears Chaos, fears its primordial, dire forces, the forces that long ago unsettled stones, the forces that once upon a time disquieted matter. Even though he embraces magical idealism, there are moments when it too seems to him sick, and these are the moments when magical idealism wants the world to be complete and perfect:

> An absolute drive to perfection and completion is illness as soon as it betrays its destructive attitude, its disinclination with respect to the *imperfect*, the incomplete.
>
> If one wants to act in such a way as to achieve something in particular, one must stake out boundaries that are determinate, even if provisional. Whoever cannot bring himself to do this is the perfectionist, the one who refuses to swim until he knows precisely how to do so. —

He is a magical idealist, just as there are magical realists.[4] The former seek a miraculous motion, a miraculous subject; the latter seek a miraculous object, a miraculous configuration. Both are caught up in *logical illnesses*, forms of delusion, in which, to be sure, the ideal reveals or mirrors itself in a twofold way—[both are] holy—[both are] isolated creatures—that refract the higher light miraculously—true prophets. . . . (2: 623; cf. 481–82, 499, 624)

Logical illness is fantastic health, however, and fantastic health is contagious. Delusion and prophecy are perhaps inseparable, or, if separable, are in constant contact, or, if not in contact, are continuously caught in the contiguity of contagion. The only thing that prevents Novalis's thaumaturgic idealism from degenerating into a facile optimism and subsequent baneful disillusionment is his sense of the *complexity* of his subject. However universal illness may be, it is everywhere intricate:

Similarities of diseases. — Every organ can have just about all the illnesses of the others.

All diseases are composed of other diseases. The entire body becomes ill when *individual organs become ill*. Relations of diseases of particular organs to one another—their mixtures—and complications.

*All diseases* originate from diremptions *[Entzweyungen]* of organs. (Illness belongs among the positive traits of the human being, as does death.) (2: 686)

The complications of disease reduce the similarity only now invoked, but they also encourage and instruct us in the *art* of healing. They exhibit the imbrication of illness with all the positive traits of organic life as such—an imbrication that all three of our authors, Novalis, Schelling, and Hegel, are on the verge of discovering:

Most illnesses seem to be as individual as any given human being, or flower, or animal. *Scabies, pox*, etc. could not be imitated by any sort of art. Many diseases, however, do seem to me to be excitable through art. All true illnesses are inherited—or epidemic—or, in short, *organic*—they can originate only through generation and reproduction. Therefore the natural history of diseases, their affinities for one another (whence the *complications* arise), their comparison, are so interesting—and if one can kill them too in manifold ways, nothing would be more desirable than to get to know their mutual blood-relations and their mutual enmities, their seats, etc., in order to learn how to have them destroy one another. (2: 797)

The sheer variety of palliatives and cures for diseases is what fascinates Novalis. He compares this variety to the sundry ways a composer can resolve a dissonant chord (2: 818). For all that, illness is fundamentally one, and its origin is coeval with sentient, nervous nature, equiprimordial with spirit itself:

> From of old there has been only one illness and likewise only one universal pharmacy. With sensibility and its organs, the nerves, illness enters on the scene of nature. With that, freedom and the arbitrary are brought into nature, and thereby *sin*, infraction against the will of nature, the cause of all that is baneful. There are diseases of the musculature that arise solely from the despotism of nerves. The ethical human being must also have a free nature—a counterstriving, educable, peculiar nature. If animal life is a phlogistical process, all diseases are antiphlogistical processes—disturbances of combustion. Their manifold character testifies precisely to their personal origin. Illness is the conflict of organs. The universal must almost always become local, as the local necessarily passes over into the universal.
>
> Transiency, vulnerability *[Vergänglichkeit, Gebrechlichkeit]* is the character of a nature bound up with spirit. It testifies to the activity, the universality, and the sublime personality of spirit. (2: 818–19)

If Romanticism and German Idealism are the movements in which *spirit* comes to hold sway, and to hold sway *absolutely*, it is important to observe that for Novalis the sublimity of absolute spirit expresses itself first and foremost in the *transiency* and *vulnerability* of nature. If absolute spirit is nervous tissue, spirit's nerves are absolutely frayed from the outset. Personality is contagious.

Novalis's final notes, his "Fragments and Studies of 1799/1800," as the editors designate them, evince the poet-philosopher's growing conviction that illness is not a mere anomaly, that the dire forces of nature are not mere exceptions to the rule. "All the forces of nature," we heard him say, "are but one force" (2: 820). If that force be identified with oxidation—as it most often is in both Novalis and Schelling—the nature of oxidation is far from clear. If *phlogiston* can still be retained as a name for combustible substance (Novalis knows of Lavoisier and oxygen, yet he persists in naming the principle of inflammability *phlogiston*), that substance appears under contradictory guises: "All dead matter is *phlogiston*," and, in the next fiery breath, "*Phlogiston* = spirit," drawing perilously close to the conclusion that spirit is dead matter, stone (ibid.). In any case, "*Rest* is peculiar to spirit"; and "mass *[das Schwere]* stems from spirit" (ibid.). However shocking it may seem to a tradition constituted by the unbearable lightness of being, "God is of infinitely compact metal—the most corporeal and most massive of all essences"; and "annihilation of air produces the Kingdom of God" (ibid.). If, on the one hand, "in matter itself lies the ground of life—the play of the drive of oxidation and deoxidation," then, on the other hand, "oxidation comes from the devil."[5]

In a world where opposites meet, at the closure of the circle, we are required to speak of *contagion*. At the closure that is contagion, ease and disease are discomfitingly close; illness is a myopic word for the good health of a spiriting and spirited life. Illness now comes to be equated with sensibility as such, that is, with the very principle of organic life: "With sensibility, diseases win the upper hand"; and "life is an illness of spirit—a passionate activity *[ein leidenschaftliches Thun]*" (ibid.). *Passionate* here means *born to undergo* passio, *to suffer and die*. In one of his last notes, Novalis affirms that "human beings are born to suffer," namely, to suffer the *Leiden* of *Leidenschaft* (2: 828). Life, albeit *one* force, ultimately and invariably turns against itself. Novalis's earlier criticism of John Brown, which was that Brown's schema had "served for both *life* and *illness*," (2: 695), now goes up in smoke, and Brown is vindicated. The only cure for life seems to be an eternal mud bath, which feels very much like interment, along with subsequent liquefaction and decomposition:

> Life is an expression of force—but at the same time a product of opposing factors. . . .
> The most incoherent, most decomposable forces are those that last longest.
> Should not the long life that has been lived in water become a method of achieving cures—also continuous mud baths?
> What possible means of healing are there still? (2: 821)

In the end, human beings return to the muddy ferment of Chaos whence they rose. "In the end, human beings are but the final Gaic formation" (2: 822). For this final formation of Gaia or Mother Earth, the only possible means of healing—a healing that will always be temporary, and a health that will always be indirect—are related to sexual reproduction; as we have already heard, such therapeutic means are not for the weak of heart or pusillanimous of spirit:

> Nature's healing force is very much related to the reproductive force—one cannot therefore count on it when it comes to oversensitive human beings.
> The nobler the human being, the more artificial his survival. The study of medicine becomes a duty and a necessity. (ibid.)

The affinity of reproductive force and healing power is expressed as *secretion*, the excess or lack of which accounts for most of what happens to our organs—and Novalis now provides the list of secreting organs and organ systems:

> Lungs. Liver. Gallbladder. Stomach. Spleen. Kidneys. Bladder. Prostate gland. Testicles. Prepuce. Seminal ducts. Intestines. Mesentery. Heart. Vascular system, including arteries and veins. Nerves. Muscles. Bones. Tendons and ligaments. Skin. Cellular tissue. Brain. Throat. Windpipe. Mouth. Eyes. Ears. Nose. Tongue. Teeth. Nails. Hair. (2: 823)

While it may be difficult to think of secretion in terms of teeth, nails, and hair, difficult at least if one is ignorant of Plato's *Parmenides* or psychoanalysis, the final Gaic formation seems to be essentially secretory—secretive, as it were, secretly sexual, secretingly liquid, and constantly in search of healing. It is therefore regrettable that Novalis's list—after duly recording the prostate, testicles, prepuce, and seminal ducts—overlooks some of the most significant human organs of secretion, those perhaps closest to Gaia herself and all her arts of polydamnic healing. Perhaps it is the omission of those organs so faithful to the earth that prompts Novalis to think of secretion in terms of transcendence, and transcendence in terms of transgression. The labor of secretion is indeed thought of as a kind of drive to transcendence, a drive that may be both the meaning of life and the origin of illness and evil:

> The system of morality must become a system of nature. All illness is equatable with sin, in that both are kinds of transcendence. Our illnesses are all phenomena of enhanced sensibility, which wants to pass over into still higher forces. When human beings wanted to become God, they sinned.
>
> Diseases of plants are animalizations. Diseases of animals are ratiocinations. Diseases of stones are vegetation. . . .
>
> Plants are deceased stones.
>
> Animals—deceased plants, etc.
>
> Theory of metempsychosis. . . .
>
> Every illness can be called an illness of the soul. (2: 824)

The immortal, poisonous, and sick soul is, of course, originally a Christian concept. What would this imply concerning the relation of Christianity to illness? Novalis's reply seems to anticipate that of Nietzsche in *The Antichrist* and *On the Genealogy of Morals:* "Universal presentation of Christianity. Love is through-and-through *illness*—hence the wonderful significance of Christianity."[6] All of which, to be sure, alters the sense of health as a purely positive notion: "The ideal of perfect health is interesting merely from a scientific point of view.

Illness belongs to *individualization*" (2: 835). The following excerpts exhibit something of the program—the program for life—that is gradually forming at the end of Novalis's own life, at the terminus of his own brief individualization:

> The feeling of health, well-being, contentment is thoroughly personal, contingent, and depends only indirectly on external circumstances. All the searching in the world will therefore not bring it forth; perhaps the real ground of all mythological personifications lies here. . . .
>
> Illnesses are particularly recalcitrant; they are the learning years of the art of life and the formation of the heart *[Lehrjahre der Lebenskunst und der Gemüthsbildung]*. One must try to use them by means of daily notations. For is not the life of an educated human being a constant insistence on learning? The educated human being lives altogether for the future. Its life is struggle; its survival and its goal is science and art.
>
> The more one learns to live no longer in moments but in years, etc., the more noble one becomes. Restless haste, petty preoccupations of the spirit, pass over into grand, tranquil, simple and encompassing activity, and splendid patience enters on the scene. Religion and ethicality, these fundamental fortresses of our existence, become ever more triumphant.
>
> Every crowding close of nature is a remembrance of a higher home, of a higher nature, to which we have a greater affinity. (2: 841)

Religion and ethicality, ever more triumphant? Perhaps. Yet triumph is not Novalis's specialty. The higher home and higher nature had for him always been the proper objects of logarithms. While one of the functions of thaumaturgic idealism was to elevate the lowly, its other function was to bring back down to Earth the high and mighty names of religion and ethicality. Elevating the lowly, yes, but also climbing back down the ladder, learning how to embrace.

The artist of immortality would no longer consent to paint the ceiling of the pope's chapel. He had mixed on his palette all the colors of mortality, and the forces that invigorated the art of a thaumaturgic idealism proved to be dire forces.

# $\mathcal{T}$ORMENTED
# $\mathcal{T}$DEALISM

*Schelling's* First Projection of a System

of Nature Philosophy *(1799)*

*At festivals no one goes wanting, not even the neediest. Yet only one celebrates his festival among you. That one is death.*

—HÖLDERLIN, HYPERION

# CHAPTER FIVE

# First Projection

## AN OUTLINE OF THE WHOLE

$\mathcal{S}$chelling's *First Projection* is actually one of his most mature works in the philosophy of nature.[1] The philosophy of nature was an area in which he showed intense interest from at least the time of his commentary on Plato's *Timaeus* (1794). It became the principal area of his research while he was working as a private tutor in Leipzig (1796–1798), where he studied mathematics and the natural sciences.[2] Whereas his two earlier works, *Ideas toward a Philosophy of Nature* (1797) and *On the World Soul: An Hypothesis of Advanced Physics toward an Explanation of the Universal Organism* (1798), had already stated the thesis of universal organism, the *First Projection* of 1799 was the first work in which Schelling elaborated an account of the organic as such in some detail. Among those details concerning the organism, as we shall see in chapter 6, is the issue of *contagium*.

In its opening pages, the *First Projection* offers a *Grundriß des Ganzen*, an "Outline of the Whole," that is, a presentation of the book's principal arguments. In spite of its enormous concision and its often quite cryptic nature, the "Outline" does grant us a view, however provisional, "of the whole." It behooves us therefore to study the entire "Outline," interrupting it from time to time with brief comments, before proceeding to the theme of contamination or contagion.

## Outline of the Whole

### First Major Division

**Proof that nature is *organic* in its most original products.**

I. Because to philosophize about nature means as much as to create it, we must first of all find the point from which nature can be posited into *Becoming* (11–13 [i.e., pages 11–13 of the *Erster Entwurf*]).

One must interrupt already in order to record some astonishment over what seems to be Schelling's desire to arrogate to himself a forbidden *intuitus divinus,* a power that could posit nature into becoming *(Werden).* Yet we should not make the unwarranted assumption that Schelling rejects the sobering lessons of Kant's doctrine of receptivity; indeed, receptivity within the organism—a Kantian receptivity given flesh by Spinoza's concept of substance and John Brown's physiological theory of sensibility—will be a central concern of Schelling's text.[3] In the opposition of *Seyn* to *Werden,* Schelling is clearly on the side that is becoming. The opposition of being and becoming is mirrored in that of the absolutely active or unconditioned deed and the conditioned or compelled activity. Schelling's desire is to reveal "the concealed trace of freedom" in nature *(EE,* 13); for him, the "formative drive" is the drive to freedom *(EE,* 6n. 1). According to Schelling, "the essence of all organism is that it is not absolute activity. . . . For the subsistence of the organism is not a *being* [Seyn] but a perpetual *being reproduced* [*ein beständiges* Reproducirtwerden]" *(EE,* 222). Productivity and infinite activity doubtless have to do with *freedom,* or at least the trace of it, in nature. Yet how could such infinite activity ever submit to compulsion, or to a condition or determination of any kind? Let us continue with the outline:

> In order for a real activity to come to be out of an infinite (and to that extent ideal) productive activity, that activity must be inhibited, *retarded.* Yet because the activity is originally an infinite one, it cannot result in finite products, even when it is inhibited; and if it should result in finite products, these can only be merely *apparent products;* i.e., in every individual the tendency to infinite development must be contained once again; every product must be capable of being articulated into products (11–20).
>
> II. III. The analysis thus may not be permitted to stop at any one thing that is a *product;* it can cease only with the purely *productive.* Only this *absolutely* productive character (which no longer has a substrate but is rather

the cause of every substrate) is what absolutely inhibits all analysis; it is precisely for that reason the point at which our analysis (experience) can never arrive. It must be *straightforwardly posited* into nature, and it is the first *postulate* of all nature philosophy. — It must be that which is *insurmountable* in nature (mechanically and chemically); such a thing is thought to be nothing other than the cause of all *original* quality (19). Such an absolutely productive character is designated by the concept of *simple action*. — (Principle of a dynamic atomism) — (22ff.).

*If* the absolute analysis were to be thought as actual, then, inasmuch as an infinite product evolves in nature as object, there would have to be an infinite multiplicity of simple actions, thought as the elements of nature and of all construction of matter (20).

(Here we must immediately remember that it can never come to this absolute analysis in nature, that those simple actions are therefore only the ideal factors of matter.)

To begin with the last-mentioned issue, that is to say, with matter as a *"particular degree of action,"* rather than as the stuff of mechanics (discussed by Schelling in the *First Projection* at *EE*, 26–27), the question remains as to "how matter in general is originally generated [*erzeugt*]." Perhaps the generation of matter requires a twosome, a *duality*, *dualism*, or *duplicity* of some kind; in any case, matter cannot be produced mechanically but must be the initial result of inhibited infinite activity. As we shall see, however, the "Outline of the Whole" will also *end* by invoking once again the mystery of a "real *construction of matter*," so that we should not expect to be clear about it at the outset.[4]

The notion of *Hemmung* (inhibition) is crucial for Schelling's *dualism*, which inevitably oscillates in the direction of a divine *monism*, precisely because the dualism is thought to be primal and originary. In other words, the *first* dualism must, it seems, be number(ed) *One*. When Schelling appeals emphatically to *"an original dualism* in nature" (*EE*, 16), however, the die of his system is cast: absolute or infinite activity will have to be inhibited absolutely or infinitely in such a way that the distinction between activity and inhibition will become tenuous in the extreme. *"If nature is absolute activity, such activity must appear as inhibited into infinity. (The original ground of this inhibition must, however, be sought **in nature itself** alone, inasmuch as nature is active **without qualification**)."* Schelling is aware that he is confronting here "an insoluble difficulty" (*EE*, 17; cf. 151 n., 169, 219), inasmuch as "inhibition" in the present instance means the presence in nature of "infinite negations" (*EE*, 20). Yet he sees no alternative. His system of idealism will never cease being tormented by the necessity of inhibition.[5]

One might wish to interrupt Schelling's account of inhibition—on which, to repeat, Novalis also speculated and Hegel too will write—with the following question: Might not a history of *Hemmung*, structured as a history of being in the Heideggerian manner, advancing from Hesiodic χάος and the Socratic daimon to Freudian metapsychology, be called for? Major way stations along the path of such a history of inhibition—to mention only a few in the epoch of in modernity—would be Spinoza, Leibniz, Fichte, Schelling, Freud, Nietzsche, Scheler, and Heidegger, among countless others. Because inhibition is not an extrinsic or exterior obstacle, but an operation within absolute activity as such, it will of course torment the absolute to death—that is why something like a history of being, a history recorded at the end or closure of metaphysics, seems appropriate to it. Indeed, it could be that the notion of inhibition might contribute to an understanding of what Heidegger calls the "mystery," that is, the withdrawal and the oblivion of being. Schelling knows about this torment of the absolute, knows about it at the very beginning of his "Outline of the Whole," with which we now continue:

> Yet these simple actions cannot be distinguished from one another in any other way than by the original *figure* that they produce (a point we owe to the atomists[)]. Yet because absolute evolution does not eventuate, due to the universal compulsion to combination that holds nature together as *product* (34), these fundamental configurations cannot be thought as existent, *contra* the atomists).[6] They therefore have to be thought as self-canceling, as *interpenetrating* (cohesion, 29ff.). The most original product of this interpenetration is the *most original liquid*—the absolute noncomposite, and for that reason the absolute decomposite. (A glance at caloric, electrical, and luminous phenomena from this point of view (34–36)[)]. — Such a principle would entail the cancellation of all individuality—hence also of every *product*—in nature. This is impossible. Hence there must be a counterweight in *nature*, by means of which matter loses itself from the other side into the absolutely *indecomposable*. However, this in turn cannot exist except by being at the same time the absolutely *composable*. — Nature cannot lose itself in either extreme. Nature in its originality [is] therefore a mediator on the basis of both (39).

The words *Indecomponible* and *Componible* (indecomposable, composable) in this section of the outline are difficult. The *Oxford English Dictionary* cites *indecomponible* as a variant of *indecomposable*, quoting Coleridge: "The assumed indecomponible substances of the Laboratory"; it defines *indecomposable* as "incapable of being . . . resolved into constituent elements." The word is apparently used by linguists to designate irreducible word stems. Schelling's dualism will surely have to do with this conflation of indecomposable and composable elements: dynamic atomism will dissolve every atomic unit into a subatomic duplicity, every solid into a flux.[7] But flux is merely another word for *liquidity*. *Liquidity ("the most original liquid")* plays an important role in Schelling's reflections on atomism and on the (im)possibility of an original type of matter, a type that would be absolutely noncomposite yet cohesive. It is also crucial for his account of the organic, as it was for Goethe's *Metamorphosis of Plants* and Novalis's magical idealism. Schelling's remarks on *blood* in this context are therefore noteworthy, and contemporary writers such as Irigaray would find much of interest here (see especially *EE*, 57, 179, and 213–14). According to Schelling, the liquid is not the formless element of water, not the Platonic μὴ ὄν, but the ἄμορφον, *"that which receives every figure,"* (*EE*, 31); it is then precisely the *Timaean* χώρα.[8]

Now that *becoming, matter, inhibition,* and *liquidity* have been mentioned, and now that a fundamental *dualism* has been implied, if not explicitly postulated, Schelling's "Outline of the Whole" finds itself already at the first turn of contagion—the turn of sexuality:

> The state of *configuration* is therefore the most original in which nature is viewed. — Nature = a product that passes from figure to figure—to be sure, in a certain order—through which, however, it cannot result in determinate products without absolute *inhibition* of the *formation.* — I demonstrate that this is conceivable only if the formative drive splits in opposite directions, something that on a deeper level will appear as *differentiation of the sexes* (44).
>
> Proof that by this means the permanence of various stages of development in nature is assured (49ff.).
>
> Yet all these various products = *one product that is inhibited at sundry stages.* They are deviations from *one* original ideal. *Proof* on the basis of the continuity of the dynamic sequence of stages in nature (63ff.); on that basis we discern the fundamental task of all nature philosophy: *to derive the dynamic sequence of stages in nature.*

Perhaps the single most important observation concerning *Hemmung* or inhibition is that it is itself defined as activity—not as a result, not as an extrinsic obstacle (*EE*, 42). As activity, inhibition insinuates itself into the very nature of infinite activity or *freedom* as such. Further, and for the purposes of the present book most significantly, inhibition is associated with a sequential formation of stages in nature, a formation that itself relies on sexual opposition and *Entzweiung* (diremption or severing in twain) as such: in short, diremption, severing in twain, halving, setting into opposition, doubling, and, "on a deeper level," sexual differentiation and opposition, all pertain to the infinite activity (*EE*, 44ff.). Such setting into opposition, separation, and counterposed development mark the "summit of formation in general," at least in the life of individual creatures, inasmuch as growth and maturation culminate in the onset of oppositional sexual and generative activity. Yet this summit, in turn, is in immediate proximity to death (*EE*, 45–46, 82, 89, 193).

Gender and genital separation, "universal sexuality" as sexual opposition (*EE*, 191, 207), constitute "the ground of inhibition" (*EE*, 49). Whence the force of that sexualized ground in infinite activity? Whence the originary doubling and opposition? In later chapters we shall have to work through as carefully as we can Schelling's notes on the fate of the individual and the individual's subordination to the species (*EE*, 50–53; see also 220). Our initial question, in the context of the dire forces of nature, must be: Does the (merely apparent) cancellation of individuality and the (affirmed) preeminence of the species (*Gattung*; see *EE*, 54ff. and 191) already point to something baneful in nature? Why must infinite productivity be inhibited and set in opposition in order to produce products—living individuals—in the first place? Why the (re)production of productive products at all; why not, as Leibniz invites the metaphysician to ask, far rather nothing? Or is the nothing given precisely in these productive products, precisely in the duplex nature—the duplicity—of these products, in terms of their sexual opposition and their proximity to illness and death? How can the duplicity of *natura naturata* and *natura naturans*, evinced primordially in the opposition of the sexes but also bound up with the nothing of dying, be thought to stretch all the way back to the source of life? One thing is clear to Schelling: nature abhors the individual, unless that individual *be* a duplicity. Oppositional sexuality is *one* natural operation, creating *one* individual; its operation is held to be primordial and universal.[9] Schelling's outline continues:

> IV. Individual products have been posited in nature, but nature devolves upon a *universal* organism. — Nature's struggle against everything individual.

Deduction of the necessary *reciprocity of receptivity* and *activity in everything organic* (which will be presented below as excitability) (73), and the cancellation of this reciprocity in the opposed systems
 A. of chemical physiology, which posits mere receptivity (no subject) in the organism, and
 B. of the system that posits in the organism an absolute activity (mediated by no receptivity)—an absolute force of life (81). Unification of the two systems in a third (79ff.).

The system to which Schelling refers here under "A" is the mechanist system of LeSage, related to the systems of Helvétius and the Baron d'Holbach. The second system, listed under "B," is the system of *Lebenskraft* or lifeforce as employed by Kant in the third *Critique* but going back to the physiologist Albrecht von Haller. For Schelling, the appeal to a *Lebenskraft*, whatever its attractions, and whatever its advantages over blind mechanism, is a blind appeal. "Life force" is a "principle of lazy reason" (*EE*, 80 n.; cf. 103 n., and 145). Yet whether his own *First Projection* is able to advance decisively beyond life force to the secret source of all nature's forces, and whether it is able to draw out all the implications of that more profound *receptivity* of which Kant himself is putatively unaware, remains to be seen. Schelling is searching for a unified system that can define activity or motion in nature without appeal to either mechanism or a mysterious teleology and entelechy of life force. Activity, even infinite activity, is inhibited by *Rezeptivität*, which, as the ground of *Erregbarkeit* or excitability, constitutes the essence of organism. Excitability points to an "outside" of the organism; it gives evidence of an inorganic—better, anorganic—realm.

> If, however, receptivity is necessarily posited in the organism as the mediator of its activity, there lies within the organism itself the presupposition of a world that stands opposed to it—an *anorganic* world that has a determinate effect on the organism. — This world, however, precisely because it is a determinate (unalterable) world, itself has to be subject to an external effect (it must be, as it were, in a state of compulsion), in order that it may form, together with its organic world, once again through some kind of commonality, something *interior.*
> This would have to be derived from the conditions of an anorganic world in general.

Receptivity points to the opposition of an organism to an exterior *anorganic* world that compels it and threatens its life. No matter how exterior or how compulsive such a world may be, however, the mere fact that it impinges on the organic indicates that some more vast site, some larger system, some greater third, encompasses them both. Schelling therefore riddles on this third, the *triplicity* that conjoins the duplex of organism and the anorganic in some interior, intrinsic, and thus ultimately *organic* way. Such an interiority, brought to light by an intrinsic deduction, would be the condition of anorganic nature as such, which thus becomes as problematic as the organic itself. Schelling's outline now proceeds to its

Second Major Division

**Deduction of the conditions of an anorganic nature.**

Deduction of the possibility of sheer contiguity and exteriority (94). Because such a thing is conceivable only as a tendency toward penetration, a cause is postulated that entertains this tendency.

A. Deduction of universal gravity (94–95). Opposed systems, the mechanical system and the metaphysical system of attraction (98–104). A third system on the basis of the other two: a system of physical attraction derived from the theory of universal cosmic formation (104–26).

B. With universal gravitation, the *tendency* in nature to universal intussusception is founded. Accepted as a hypothesis, namely, that there is *real* intussusception, the action of gravity would be only the first impulse toward it; thus another, different action would have to be adduced to it in order to make it actual. — We are required to demonstrate such a thing in nature (128).

Intussusception, a key term in Goethe's account of plant assimilation, is discussed at several places in the *First Projection* (see, e.g., 128, 166, and 260). The *Oxford English Dictionary* tells us that the word derives from the Latin *intus*, within, and *susceptionem*, "a taking up": "1. A taking within, absorption into itself. 'Plants receive their Nourishment by intus-susception.' 'A particle of gelatine may be swelled up by the intusussception of water.' 2. *Physics* and *Biology*: the taking in of foreign matter by a living organism and its conversion into organic tissue. 'Increase in the unorganized world happens through *juxta-position*, in the organic through *intus-susception.*' 3. *Pathology*: the inversion of one portion of intestine and its reception within an adjacent portion; invagination, introversion." Kant uses the word in the "Architectonic of Pure Reason" of his *Critique of Pure Reason* to indicate what a rational system must be: its parts must be related to one another not as mere aggregates but as organic members. Only in this way can a system of reason "grow," that is to say, "only through internal action *(per intus susceptionem)*, not externally *(per appositionem)*, just as the body of an animal does not grow by adding limbs but rather by strengthening each of them and making it better suited to its purpose without any change of proportion."[10] Indeed, the more one examines Kant's "Architectonic of Pure Reason," which everywhere *resists* the force of the merely "technical," the more one realizes that for Kant the architecture of pure reason is a *living* architecture, an "archeticture" grounded not on τέχνη but on τίκτειν, which is to say, on living, organic, reproductive being.[11]

It is therefore noteworthy that Schelling's discussion of the "tendency toward" intussusception occurs here in his discussion of the supposedly *anorganic* world, with gravity as a "first impulse" toward it; he thereby confirms the *Oxford English Dictionary*'s complacent juxtaposition of physics and biology for the second meaning of the word and Kant's more passionate elevation of biology over physics in the Critical project. Intussusception is also discussed in the context of assimilation and nutrition in the *First Projection* (see *EE*, 70, 172, 214; note especially the remarks on poison, 73, including the footnote, to which I shall refer later.) But to continue with the outline of the second major division:

> *Proof* that the principle of all chemical process of a determinate sphere is not in turn a product of the same sphere, but of a higher sphere. (Deduction of oxygen) (129–31). — Conclusion that the positive action in every chemical process within the lower sphere must take its point of departure from the higher one.
>
> Proof that in the part of the universe that is known to us as *light* there occurs the phenomenon of such a dynamic action, exercised by celestial bodies of a higher order on subaltern bodies. (Combustion = a transition of opposed spheres of affinity into one another) (131–36).
>
> C. Deduction of a relation in all terrestrial substances that is opposed to that action—*electrical* relations of bodies.
>
> Distinction between the electrical and chemical processes. The principle that immediately intervenes in the one is the mediate determination of the other (140–42).
>
> D. Relation of the action of gravity to chemical action (143ff.).

Chemical processes, such as combustion, oxygenation, respiration, light and photosynthesis, electricity, and magnetism are all interrelated in Schelling's system (see *EE*, 128–31, 137–38, 247–49). Oxygenation, as Novalis too knew, is the key to both chemical and electrical combination and reduction, as well as to organic activity. Such unity is crucial for Schelling's monism, dualism, *and* trialism

(*EE*, 116–20). With regard to the hazards of a possible infinite regress when it comes to these "higher orders," Schelling's dismissal sometimes seems quite confident (*EE*, 93); yet occasionally his mood is more circumspect and not so convinced (*EE*, 125n. 1).

All that really needs to be said about the *second major division*, at least for our purposes here and now, is that it resembles more closely than the first and third divisions do the work that Schelling had already done in the *Ideas* and the *World Soul*. For his opponents, it was simply evidence of Schelling's submission to the chemistry of salts and bases and his capitulation to the physics of electricity and magnetism. For his adherents, the move toward physics and chemistry—albeit a higher physics and a nonmechanistic, dynamic chemistry—was the only hope toward a unified theory of natural and spiritual activity.

With that, we pass to the final division, in which the common ground of the organic and anorganic realms is sought. Kant's Analytic of Teleological Judgment had defined the organic as such in terms of the reciprocal influence of parts within a whole: when Schelling argues that the organic and anorganic are *reciprocally related* he is in effect already insisting on *the eminence of the organic*. The universe is, in a word, *organized*. The principal aim of Schelling's project is to deduce or derive a *Stufenfolge*, a sequence of stages, in organized nature—what he here as well as later calls *Potenzen*, the potencies of nature. As we indicated in the introduction, one ought to compare to the Schellingian *Stufenfolge* Kant's search in the *Methodenlehre* of the third *Critique* (§§80–81) for the "primal mother" of the seemingly infinite organic forms. That bipolar search, which according to Kant must go upward and downward, forward and backward at once, inevitably links teleology to an archeology—Kant himself explicitly refers us here to the work of the archaeologist. However, let us now proceed to the final synthesis of Schelling's outline.

### Third Major Division

#### Reciprocal determination of organic and anorganic nature.

I. The supreme concept by which the nexus of the organism with an anorganic world is expressed is the concept of *excitability*. — Duplicity is thereby posited into the organism, and the derivation of duplicity from the general organization of the universe (144–48).

Complete unification of the opposed systems wherein the organism is posited as either mere object or mere subject in a third system, which posits the organism as *excitable* (148ff.). — Derivation of a *cause* of excitability, the condition of which is duplicity, a cause which in its tendency is chemical, and which precisely for that reason cannot originally be chemical; thereupon a grounded and complete demonstration of the *possibility of a higher dynamic process* (the same as the life process), *which, although not itself chemical, nevertheless has the same cause and the same conditions as the chemical process* (154).

With regard to *Erregbarkeit*, excitability, note that its single most important corollary, itself based on receptivity, is the twofold structure or duplicity that it presupposes—and that it shares with sexual opposition. The gravest problem posed by excitability is the possible regress of the twofold beyond the encompassing third to some fourth or *n*th ground or ἀρχή, which, being more an Anaximandrian ἄπειρον than an ἀρχή, would nevertheless be called upon to explain the coherence and genesis of the whole. One will therefore also have to examine the related problem of borderline, boundary, or limit *(Grenze)*, the traditional problem of the πέρας, to which Schelling himself refers (see *EE*, 147 n., 160, 186, 208, 221, 231–35, 243–45, and 264–65). As it turns out, even the principle of identity (A = A) must, in the philosophy of nature, be read as a duplicity (*EE*, 159–60, 218), so that the hope for clear and distinct borderlines is infinitely frustrated.

II. *Derivation of individual organic functions from the concept of excitability.*
    A. Because excitability presupposes duplicity—the cause of the former cannot be the cause of the latter. Thus a cause is postulated that no longer *presupposes* duplicity—a cause we call *sensibility*, as the source of organic activity (160).
    B. Determination of the activity whose source is sensibility, and the conditions of this activity (in Galvanism)—*irritability* (171).
    C. The extinguishing of this activity in the product—*force of production*, with all its offshoots (nutrition, 172–74, secretion, 175–78, growth, 179, the poietic drive [animal instincts in general], 180–91. Metamorphosis, reproductive drive, 191–94).

"Poietic drive" here translates *Kunsttrieb*, the drive or instinct that enables certain animals, for example, ants and bees, to work together in intricate, creative ways in the natural world. Whereas Hegel will regard the poietic drive as a form of excretion, bound up with the final stage of the process of assimilation, Schelling sees it as an ersatz—at a certain potency of nature—for mature sexual activity. Poietic activity also pertains to the drones, whose entire existence, however, still revolves about the queen. Following the discussion of secretion as an aspect of irritability, Schelling will cite the second turn of *contagium* or *Ansteckungsgift* as the secretion of contamination. (This is the point at which my own chapter 6 will begin: see *EE*, 177; cf. 73n. 1; and recall 192, where *contagium* means the reproductive "touching" that Kant described as a *mitteilen*, "communication.") For the moment, and despite Novalis's criticism, Schelling's analysis comes to rest on *sensibility* as the cause of excitability, the origin of that receptivity which goes beyond all lazy conceptions of the life force. The outline continues:

> III. Consequences of the preceding.
> A. That the organic functions are subordinated, one to another, in such a way that they are *opposed* with regard to their *appearance* (their coming to the fore), both in the individual and in the whole of organic nature.
> B. That by this opposition (because the higher function is repressed by the surfeit of subordinate functions) a *dynamic* sequence of stages in nature is founded.

Schelling now reverts to the question of *Scheinprodukte*, with which the "Outline" itself began: the ontological distinction between *Seyn* and *Erscheinung*, being and appearance. The dynamic, natural-historical, genetic sequence of stages *(Stufenfolge)* in which Schelling is principally interested has its source in some inhibition of the higher sphere's activity. Schelling's new word for this inhibition is *Verdrängung*—later to be Freud's central conundrum: repression now becomes a key term in that alternative history of being, being as inhibition, that we proposed above. Inexplicably, in Schelling's view the subaltern sphere outweighs and therefore "represses" the higher, which is associated with reason. Reason itself "is *one* without qualification," and yet it seems bent on "the restoration of duplicity" (*EE*, 182). In turn, the restoration of duplicity and the rebellion of the subaltern spheres menace the very distinction between higher and lower spheres or inner and outer relations. The hazards of duplicity for a system of reason will show themselves most clearly in Schelling's *Treatise on the Essence of Human Freedom* (1809), *Stuttgart Private Lectures* (1810), and *Ages of the World* (1811–1815); thus they far exceed the scope of the present inquiry.[12]

> C. Demonstration of this dynamic sequence of stages (194–96) on the basis of:

a) a reciprocal determination of sensibility and irritability (196–203);

b) a reciprocal determination of sensibility and force of production (203–204);

c) a reciprocal determination of irritability and force of production (205), throughout organic nature.

*Conclusion: that it is one and the same product which, beginning from the highest stage of sensibility, ultimately loses itself in the reproductive force of plants.*

D. Demonstration that *the same dynamic sequence of stages prevails in universal and anorganic nature as in organic nature* (207–20).

With regard to the expression "loses itself" *(verliert sich)* in the "Conclusion," we should note that Schelling is engaging in a regressive analysis, proceeding downward from the "higher" life forms, indeed, from the "highest stage of sensibility," to the simplest of vegetable forms—specifically, to their "reproductive force." Demonstration of "the same dynamic sequence of stages," the schematism of which now follows in the outline, is the high point of the *Erster Entwurf*. It reveals that the third, all-encompassing, "universal" sphere in the center has the same sequence of stages as the subaltern anorganic and organic spheres. Yet the demonstration is truncated at the very point where Schelling's earlier works on nature philosophy also had ended—at the interrogation mark of the "cause of magnetism," specifically, the cause of the form of magnetism that is appropriate to organic tissue, or "sensibility."

### *General schematic of this sequence of stages.*

| Organic | Universal | Anorganic Nature |
|---|---|---|
| Formative drive | Light | Chemical process |
| Irritability | Electricity | Electrical process |
| Sensibility | Cause of magnetism? | Magnetism?[13] |

E. *Supreme task of nature philosophy: What cause brought forth the first duplicity* (of which all other opposites are the mere progeny) *out of the universal identity of nature?* (220).

(Appendix to III: Theory of illness, derived from the dynamic sequence of stages in nature, 220–39.)

The deduction of the "supreme task of nature philosophy" ends, not with a satisfactory explanation or confident positing, but with a repetition of the question, "What cause brought forth the first duplicity ... out of the universal identity of nature?" Perhaps we may be permitted a proleptic look at that concluding repetition of the question (*EE*, 220; cf. 240), for it is that repetition which truly constitutes the outline of the whole. (Note, however, that the "whole" needs an appendix, will always have needed an appendix, on the theory of illness—as though the cause that brought forth duplicity out of universal identity and sensibility out of universal apathy also brought forth universal malady.) The appendix contains the second major turn on the itinerary of contagion; if the first turn was sexual opposition, the second will be illness. Both turns have to do with an original, organic duplicity. Schelling writes—and boldly underlines:

> **Thus a common cause of universal and organic duplicity is postulated.** The most universal problem, the one that encompasses all nature, and therefore the *supreme* problem, without whose solution all we have said explains nothing, is this:
>
> **What is the universal source of activity in nature? What cause has brought about the first dynamic exteriority [*Außereinander*],** with respect to which mechanical exteriority is a mere consequence? **Or what cause first tossed the seed of motion into the universal repose of nature, duplicity into universal identity, the first sparks of heterogeneity into the universal homogeneity of nature?**[14]

Such, at the end as at the beginning of the *First Projection*, is the supreme task of nature philosophy. However, close to the end, an "Appendix to III," that is, to the third subdivision of the Third Major Division, appears. A note by Schelling's son and editor Karl (*EE*, 205n. 1) indicates that his father had actually presented his "theory of illness" earlier in the lecture course, *prior to* the "Conclusion" of his "Demonstration" that a single product, "beginning from the highest stage of sensibility, ultimately loses itself in the reproductive force of plants." Thus, at least in terms of the Jena lecture course of 1798/99, illness and sexual reproduction through opposition are brought into proximity, as they have been since Plato's *Timaeus*. Infinite activity, the freedom of the higher sphere in all its simple actions, is itself bound up with love—and thus, at one stroke, with the dire forces of nature expressed in illness. Illness will prove to be related to inhibition, negation, opposition, repression, and deviation (*Abweichung: EE*, 68, 205 n., 228n. 3), if only because of "*the continuity of organic functions*" (*EE*, 69; on *Krankheit*, see also 89–90, 162).

In the present volume, chapter 6 will take up the *sexual* aspect of contagion; chapter 7 will turn to contagion as illness; and chapter 8 will try to understand the imbrication of sexuality and illness in

Schellingian duplicity, the tormenting duplicity of contagion as such. But now, moving more rapidly, let us continue with the "Outline of the Whole":

IV. Not only the subordinate functions of the organism but also the general forces corresponding to them (electricity, chemical process) presuppose an original heterogeneity—the solution of that task (What is the cause of the original heterogeneity?) is thus at the same time a theory of chemical process, and vice versa.

Universal theory of the chemical process (240–61).

A. Concept of the chemical process (240–42).

B. Material conditions of the chemical process. — Demonstration that in the chemical as well as in the electrical process only one opposition prevails (242–49).

C. Inasmuch as all chemical (and electrical) process is mediated by a first heterogeneity, the latter has for universal nature the same function that sensibility has for organic nature. Complete demonstration that it is magnetism that is for universal nature what sensibility is for organic nature, that all dynamic forces of the universe, such as sensibility, are subordinate to it, — that magnetism, like sensibility in organic nature, is universal in anorganic nature (and canceled, wherever it is canceled, only for appearance). — Conclusion: the identity of the ultimate cause of sensibility and of magnetism (257).

D. Complete construction of the chemical process and of all dynamic process (257–61).

a) Inasmuch as an intussusception between heterogeneous bodies is possible only insofar as the homogeneous is itself split in itself, no homogeneous state can be absolute; rather, it can only be a state of indifference. In order to explain this, we must suppose that there is in the universe a universal effect that replicates itself from product to product by means of (magnetic) distribution, which would be the universal determinant of all quality (and of all magnetism as universal) (260).

b) Further, in order to bring heterogeneity into the particular dynamic sphere, and thereby the possibility of canceling the dynamic state of indifference, there is a communication between the higher and lower spheres of affinity (through the medium of light, 261). By means of the lower sphere, the external condition of the dynamic process (heterogeneity) is given; by means of the higher sphere, the inner condition (the split in the homogeneous itself) is given.

The chemical twofold forms the neutralized or indifferent salt, as Kant had defined it in his Anthropologie.[15] However, in the organic realm, such chemical neutralization is nothing other than death. Whether the moves to sensibility and to universal magnetism advance a solution to the problem of a necessary duplicity in nature, or are merely different ways to pose it, must have given Schelling cause for concern. Because "only *one* opposition" (see IV. B.) prevails throughout the organic and anorganic spheres, that is, throughout the spheres of sensibility-receptivity and electricity-magnetism, and because "the homogeneous is itself split *in itself*," in order to make intussusception possible (*EE*, 127–28, 166, 240ff.), homogeneity cannot be absolute in any sphere. What Schelling discovers is that *the absolute is heterogeneous even before anything is "thrown" at it.* He writes: "But to *bring* heterogeneity *forth* [hervorbringen] means to create duplicity in identity. . . . Thus identity must in turn proceed *[hervorgehen]* from duplicity" (*EE*, 250). Here, as earlier in his *World Soul* and even in his *Ideas*, Schelling hopes that universal magnetism will unify all the spheres. Yet both earlier and later in his *First Projection* (*EE*, 89–90n. 2, and 258–60), he traces heterogeneity back to a homogeneity that is a "state of indifference," *Indifferenzzustand*. And such indifference spells the *death* of the organism (see especially *EE*, 90n. 2.) God himself will repair to such a state of *Indifferenz* in the 1809 treatise *On Human Freedom*. Whether he will be able to rouse himself from his indifference—literally, his lack of differentiation, the default of *différance*—by the effects of *light* or of some other *communication* between the higher and lower spheres, or whether the "split in the homogeneous itself" will always have been irreparable, will always have defeated every effort to define a borderline *(Grenze)* between inner and outer, remains a question for the future—the future that is ours.

For the moment, Schelling concludes by conjuring "an original duplicity in nature," which operates by the forces of expansion and contraction (as Goethe had described them in *Metamorphose der Pflanzen)*, along with gravity. The result is a triplicity, if not a reproductive quadruplicity (*EE*, 193n. 2), if not an infinite regress in infinite activity, which haunts all monism.

V. The *dynamic organization* that we have now derived presupposes the universe for its *scaffolding*.

 *Deduction of the forces by which* (presupposing an original duplicity in nature) *the evolution of the universe is conditioned—*

  of the expansive force,

  of the retarding force,

  and of the force of gravity,

which (in their independence from one another) alone make nature possible as a determinate product for every moment of time and space, and which alone make possible a real *construction of matter* (261–68).

Thus far the "Outline of the Whole." Now that our heads are brimming with all the details it takes to construct a material universe, let us proceed to the parts—doubtless the dire parts—of sexuality (chapter 6) and illness (chapters 7–8).

# CHAPTER SIX

# Sexual Opposition, Inhibition, Contagion

$\mathcal{T}$he word *contagium* appears twice in Schelling's *First Projection*. It first arises in a discussion of *secretion*, which for Schelling, as for Novalis, is perhaps the universal mark of life in its more highly organized, more irritable forms (*EE*, 177). Secretion is identified with the organism's capacity for self-reproduction, the power of (re)generation *(Zeugungskraft)*, both within the tissues of any given organism and for its species as a whole. Schelling defines the relation of the gallbladder to the liver, for example, in terms of such secretion—the release of an irritant that causes the liver to reproduce or regenerate itself. Such a specific irritant, in turn, is also described as toxic: it irritates precisely because it is a specific kind of sepsis, a potential source of infection, a toxin *(Ansteckungsgift)*, which Schelling also calls "a kind of *Contagium*."

The second use of the word occurs in a discussion of general or universal sexuality, that is, the general or universal formation of two distinct sexes for the purpose of reproduction within a given species. Just as sensibility and irritability are the poles that energize every living, excitable entity in nature, so the sexes occupy "the outermost limit of universal organic opposition" (*EE*, 191). What is the product of such opposition? "Its product is a *new duplicity*," replies Schelling, adding, "sexuality reproduces into infinity its *condition*" (*EE*, 192). Schelling seeks the ultimate source of this passing on of sensibility and irritability from generation to generation, which is also the passing on of the condition of sexuality. The answer cannot lie in "fructification" as such, which merely passes on the received "spark" of sensibility. Whence this "spark" in the first place? Schelling denies that it can be located solely in semen, which he calls the mere "excitant cause" of fecundity, the secreted irritant of reproduction. Indeed, fecundation transpires by means of a rarefied contact that is a kind of touching (Berührung), a word, as we learned in the foregoing part, that is also central to Novalis's thaumaturgic idealism.

Yet the word touching is inadequate. Like Novalis, Schelling appeals to a kind of touching at a distance, an actio in distans that is a Berührung in distans. Schelling may be thinking of the way Kant in the Critique of Judgment speaks of sexual reproduction as a process of mitteilen, a sharing or communicating that is not quite a touching. Sensibility is "awakened" in a new creature by this proto-touching that is not a touching, a contact that is both more and less than contiguity: Schelling calls it, to repeat, "a kind of Contagium," citing now William Harvey's "famous work" on the generation of animals. Most important to this concept of "awakening," the arousal of sensibility in a new creature through contagium, is the fact that the duplicity of the sexes is required for the production of each unit of inherently duplicitous sensibility/irritability. Only through sexual duplicity can the twofold "process of excitation" be "ignited" (EE, 192n. 2). It always takes two sticks to ignite the "spark," even if the tree and the forest from which they have fallen remain mysteries.

When we look to William Harvey's "famous work" on generation for insight into the mysteries of contagium, we find there a detailed account of sexual reproduction, an account that is based on, of all things, the famous conundrum concerning the chicken and the egg. Or, to complete the picture, the chicken, the egg, and the rooster—although, as we shall see, for Harvey the cock is considerably less important than one might have thought. In any case, the relationship between these three is fundamentally one of contagion rather than of a typically conceived typographic, mechanical, or physical contact. William Harvey writes:

> Nor should we so much wonder what it is in the cock that preserves and governs so perfect and beautiful an animal, and is the first cause of that entity which we call the soul; but much more, what it is in the egg, aye, in the germ of the egg, of so great virtue as to produce such an animal, and raise him to the very summit of excellence. Nor are we only to admire the greatness of the artificer that aids in the production of so noble a work, but chiefly the "contagion" of intercourse, an act which is so momentary! What is it, for

instance, that passes from the male into the female, from the female into the egg, from the egg into the chick? What is this transitory thing, which is neither to be found remaining, nor touching, nor contained, as far as the senses inform us, and yet works with the highest intelligence and foresight, beyond all art; and which, even after it has vanished, renders the egg prolific, not because it now touches, but because it formerly did so, and that not merely in the case of the perfect and completed egg, but of the imperfect and commencing one when it was yet but a speck; aye, and makes the hen herself fruitful before she has yet produced any germs of eggs, and this too so suddenly, as if it were said by the Almighty, "Let there be progeny," and straight it is so?[1]

Later in the same treatise Harvey confirms the fecund sense of that "contagion, by which, as by a kind of infection, she [the hen] conceives" (*AE*, 372). One must of course note that the eighteenth- and nineteenth-century uses of *infection* are broader than our own; we will see Hegel appealing to the notion of *infection*, for example, in his account of vegetable assimilation, where it means as much as the intussusception or intake of liquids. For Harvey and his followers, *infection* means infusion or adsorption by osmosis or porosity, or perhaps even an *affection* by means of an *actio in distans*. Nevertheless, the proximity to pathology in the word *infection* remains a significant overtone or undercurrent throughout the vocabulary of reproduction through *contagium*. Infection is simultaneously assimilatory, sexual, pathological, and, one must say, if only in memory of Novalis's pharmaceutical view of the soul and Goethe's *geistige Anastomose*, eminently "spiritual."

In an independent essay, "On Conception," Harvey writes of "a fecundating power by a kind of contagious property (not . . . in actual contact . . . but . . . previously [in contact])" (*AE*, 575). It is clear that *contagium* is a touching that does not touch, or at least *no longer* touches—the touch as *actio in distans*, the original, sudden, past yet perdurant creative miracle. *Contagium* unites not only cock and hen but also man and cock, and also cock and God, the artificer and the Almighty. *Contagium* names the *current*, activated state of the *formerly* touched, now rendered prolific through time. For the cock himself rises from the germ of the egg of the hen, rises from that very *contagium* of which it seems to be the most noble embodiment and agent. Or is it but a vestige? We are not so much to wonder at the cock as at the germ, Harvey insists, and at the ongoing "intelligence" of what ages hence will be called deoxyribonucleic acid. From Harvey through Hegel, the spark of that ongoing intelligence remains an unnamed cause that is as wonderful as the first cause of the soul—which is God—and more beautiful than the splendid Shanghai celebrated by Herman Melville in an inspiring, scurrilous tale entitled "Cock-a-doodle-doo."[2]

Schelling's two uses of *contagium*, however, relate the life-sustaining matters of secretion, fructification, and sexual reproduction to a more general structure of infection and toxification *(Ansteckung)*. It is therefore important that we expand our focus somewhat. There are three instances of such *Ansteckung* in Schelling's *First Projection* that demand comment. In the world of nature, assimilation—and the consequent bipolar or duplicitous structure of assimilator and assimilated—is universal. In the world of assimilation, in turn, a special place is occupied by the phenomenon of *failed* assimilation, that is, an ingestion that remains incomplete and potentially lethal. Schelling is speaking, of course, of poisoning. His interest in it is dialectical, to the extent—obvious yet crucial—that no poison does an organism harm unless that organism makes a move to ingest it. A poisonous mushroom does not attack us until we attack it at the table. There is no poison "in itself," Schelling notes, but only in and for us, as it were. He continues:

> The concept of poison, like so many other concepts—such as contamination *[Ansteckung]*—illness—medicine, etc.—only has sense for the organic product. — Every substance can become a poison. For only through the activity of an organism does a substance become poisonous. — Boundary between medicament and poison. Kant: that which simply cannot be assimilated. Every form of excretion is as such poison. Meanwhile, so much is true: poison is poison only insofar as the organism directs its activity toward it, strives to assimilate it.[3]

If one agrees with Novalis that speech is essentially a form of excretion, the identification of excretion with the septic and the absolutely unassimilable is disturbing. To be sure, sexual fecundation, for its part, is not an assimilation, at least not in any straightforward sense. Nor, for that matter, can the action of the gallbladder on the liver be called an assimilation. Yet Schelling himself, in his first reference to *contagium*, places immediately after it, in brackets, the word *Ansteckungsgift*—that word's second appearance *(EE, 177)*.

Whether fecundation too is not only a *contagium* but also a *contamination* by poison or excretion, is therefore a question we shall have to raise.

The third notable use of *Ansteckung* or contamination occurs near the end of the treatise (*EE*, 237n. 1) in the context of illness. Schelling observes that virtually all three categories of John Brown's system—sensibility, irritability, reproduction—can in one way or another be regarded as the "seat" of illness. Indeed, illness "is possible only through the (indirect) affection of the ultimate source of life itself *[der letzten Quelle des Lebens selbst]*" (*EE*, 236). Only the parenthetical word *indirect* can rescue—if rescue is at all possible here—the identification of the ultimate source of life with the ultimate source of disease and death. Schelling observes the following concerning contamination: "Even with every contamination (a concept that makes sense only for organic products of nature) something more elevated occurs than common humoral pathology can sense. The product is a homogeneous one; the affection of the formative drive is thus the same as in the case of more elevated operations" (*EE*, 237n. 1). Sexuality doubtless pertains to those more elevated operations; indeed, it is the summit of all that nature elevates. Yet if every contamination is elevated in the direction of sexuality, then sexual communication, by logarithm, is tethered to contagion. Schelling, like his contemporary Novalis, here envisages a monism of drives—but it is a potentially lethal monism. The homology of higher and lower operations makes the ultimate source of life the germ of death, the secret of thaumaturgy the seed of torment.[4]

For the remainder of part two of the present book, we will be occupied by two supplements, the first to the third section of the first major division, and the second to the third major division of Schelling's *First Projection*. For it is in a "Remark" and an "Appendix" that we find the most detailed accounts of sexual opposition and illness, respectively. What rises to disturb Schelling's account of inhibition is that if sexual opposition is the universal mechanism of inhibition, then illness too tends toward the universal, as though infinite activity itself were malignant. It becomes difficult, if not impossible, to locate the ultimate source of life without colliding against the ultimate source of illness and demise. For the moment, we will read those pages (*EE*, 44–53) of Schelling's "Remark," the *Anmerkung* to section three of the first major division, on sexuality and sexual duplicity.

"Absolute sexlessness is nowhere demonstrable in the entirety of nature," Schelling begins, taking as his point of departure a "regulative a priori principle" that sexual difference *(Geschlechtsverschiedenheit)* is the point of departure for organic nature as a whole—even for those primitive stages where the difference is cryptogamic. The productive or formative drive of nature requires—for reasons that resist simple deduction—that every life form be severed or cut in twain, dirempted *(entzweit)* in such a way that the two halves can develop to their full capacity and at that point reunite for reproductive purposes. Virtually every "organization" of life possesses a stage in its formation for which separation of the sexes is necessary *(EE,* 45). Whether the two sexes are conjoined in one individual or separated into two, that is to say, whether in the plant or the animal worlds, growth and maturation inevitably culminate in sexual activity and sexual reproduction. "The development of the sexes itself is but the highest peak of formation in general" (ibid.). The metamorphoses of plants, but most remarkably of insects, those untiring avatars of contingency, invariably culminate in maturation of the sexes and sexual activity. Schelling is able to identify sexual opposition and maturation as the summit of the formative principle if only because, once that summit is reached, it is all downhill for plant and animal alike: the petals of the rose wither and fall once pistil and stamen have done their work, and after copulation the insect soon dies.

Separation of the sexes follows a rule, the rule of duplicity, which falls back upon an ultimate homogeneity: each sex develops independently to its full capacity, only then rejoining the other sex and thus preserving the species. Sexual opposition is *one* formation, *one* operation of nature, as Kant himself had intimated: sexual duplicity reverts to a developmental monism.[5] Indeed, Schelling will soon insist that nature is careless of the individual, insofar as the individual is but one half of a sexual pair; the individual *as such* is consigned to death, precisely because nature loves the *one*—that is to say, the one *pair.* Yet if *monism* consigns the individual μόνος to death, there is something sick about its one and only *one,* something morbid about all its individuals; we may be certain that Schelling will have to return to— or, in effect, will never be able to abandon—the problem of this moribund monism.

Schelling now undertakes to demonstrate that sexual differentiation and separation constitute "the ground of inhibition," the basis of that retardation in infinite activity that results in a product of any kind, whether organic or anorganic. What must be shown, Schelling emphasizes, is that *"nature is actually inhibited by this separation, without thereby ceasing to be active"* (*EE*, 49). The condition of infinite activity in nature (again the insoluble problem of a conditioned unconditioned, a finitely infinite) is dualism (*EE*, 49n. 1). The product of any such activity is essentially incomplete, limited as it is to a particular stage of development *(Entwicklungsstufe)*. Yet Schelling does not mean by this the "wicked infinity" of Hegel—the fact that each newborn creature is repeatedly but one-half of the species. Rather, for Schelling, limitation to one-half of the sexual pair is the secret of nature's infinite activity, its successful continuation and continued development. However, though not wicked, nature is ironic: for the very "moment of culmination" in the development of the individual is the moment of its "annihilation" *(Vernichtung)*. "Nature strives constantly to cancel *[aufzuheben]* the duality and to revert to its original identity" (*EE*, 49–50n. 2). Yet that original identity is precisely the ineradicable tendency to dualism. "Such striving, however, is precisely the ground of all *activity* in nature" (ibid.). Nature without activity, without infinite activity, would be not divine but dead. Such an irony, such a paradox, forces Schelling into a double caesura: "—The duality that imposes on nature the compulsion of a constant activity is, wherever it is, *against the will* of nature, so to speak— —and thus it is here" (ibid.). Infinite activity, in which there ought to be at least a trace of freedom, is subjected to compulsion, an inhibition exacted of it against its will, as it were *(gleichsam)*, though infinite activity itself exacts this inhibition of itself. Schelling continues, "Nature did not intend the separation [of the sexes]. — Nature leads the product in both directions to the highest peak only to let it founder or sink back into indifference once that peak is reached" (ibid.). Nature's product, inhibited and limited within the graduated, developmental series of stages, "is subordinated to the *universal* striving of nature toward indifference" (ibid.)

Thus nature is monistic, even as it kills the monad. For each individual, each half of the sexual pair, when developed to its acme, both achieves and disturbs the balance *(Gleichgewicht)* of nature. Restoration of that balance, restitution to the community *(Gemeinschaftliches)* of its rights, return to the cycle *(Kreislauf)* of productive activity—these are the fruits of sexual reproduction. From this point of view, each individual product of nature must be seen as "a botched attempt to depict the absolute" (*EE*, 51n. 1). The individual is but the means, the species the end. However, each species and each stage of development, in turn, is yet another such botching. To what end, this moribund, morbid monism?

At this point in his analysis, Schelling interrupts with a question concerning these "botched attempts," namely, the individuals: "But is this really the case?" (ibid.). If it is, then one must be consistent and note that even among human beings, the so-called higher forms of life, the individual is but the misbegotten means to a dubious end. Even though human beings take longer to mature, and even though nature kills them off more slowly after they reach maturity, granting them a longer grace period for their dotage, human beings too would have to be regarded as nature's botchings. The most perdurant organizations of the sexes—and among these the human must be counted as eminent—are those in which the separation of the two is greatest; the more ephemeral the creature, the closer the two sexes are to each other. If nature wants to preserve the individuals of a certain complex species, she "explodes" the two sexes, separates them from one another radically, causes them to flee in the face of one another (EE, 51–52n. 2). If they are gathered like pistil and stamen in a single calyx, enjoying a single "conjugal bed," as it were, they soon wilt. What Schelling is not so much unable to decide as unable to ask is whether the delay in wilting where human beings are concerned, a delay that is due in part to the vast distance that these exploded sexes must cross in order to piece themselves together again in the labors of species preservation, truly constitutes a higher organization, or whether the botching consists in postponing the inevitable. As male and female human beings flee in the face of one another, their cultures posing ever greater inhibitions to the inhibitions already implanted by nature, are they enhancing organization or cluttering the stage? Schelling does not pose this question, to which his analysis nonetheless leads him—against his own will, as it were. He does concede an important point: even though he has shown that the diremption into two sexes, with the full development of each "in opposite directions" culminating in the reestablishment of the species, is necessary if production in nature is to be inhibited, he has not accounted for that Aristophanic severing in twain, that *Entzweiung*, as such (EE, 52n. 1). It is a necessary assumption, but it has not been demonstrated, neither by fairy tale nor science. "If our science is to be complete," Schelling concludes, diremption and duality themselves have to be explained. And they will be explained, as he later notes, only if we can locate that "one point of inhibition" *(Ein Hemmungspunkt)* that is original with nature herself.[6]

Schelling's note is puzzling. For sexual differentiation was introduced as the only possible explanation for the inhibition of infinite activity. What other kind of demonstration could Schelling be dreaming of? One recalls the abyss of reason into which Kant feared we might plummet when posing such a question, the question of the duality of the sexes.[7] What Schelling is searching for is one opposition, one pair, one relation of the twofold into which all other dualities will be absorbed, as though by infection. What he is missing are those links that would show how every oppositional pair can be subordinated to some original pair. In the *First Projection,* the two oppositional pairs that vie for originality are sexual opposition and the excitability (sensibility-irritability) paradigm. Schelling will be tempted—and Hegel will fully succumb to the temptation—to identify the female with (passive, affective) sensibility, the male with (active, effective) irritability. Yet even such an identification would not solve the problem of the original duality, the dualistic monism or monistic dualism that should constitute a rational system of nature philosophy. Thus there are places in the treatise where Schelling dreams of an "absolute organization," one that would dispense with duality while also accounting for its eventual emergence on the scene. One such place is the following, in which he conjures up an *Urbild* or proto-image of nature:

> This proto-image would be absolute, *sexless,* and would no longer be either individual or species; rather, it would be *both at the same time;* in it, therefore, individual and species are conflated. For that reason, the absolute organization could not be depicted by an individual product, but only through an infinity of particular products, which taken *individually* deviate into infinity from the ideal, but taken together as a *whole* are congruent with it. Thus the fact that nature expresses such an absolute original by means of all its organizations taken together is something that could be demonstrated simply by showing that all variation in the organizations is only a variation in the approximation of each to an absolute. We would then experience this absolute as though these organizations were nothing other than different developments of one and the same organization. *(EE,* 64)

Schelling's dream of a sexless absolute, while a *necessary* dream, turns into the nightmare in which the absolute is an undeveloped simpleton, the monotonous simplex that has not yet developed fully in those "opposite" or "counterposed" directions, *entgegengesetzte Richtungen*, that Schelling himself constantly invokes. The one-and-the-same organization of all organizations in the graduated sequence of stages in nature would have to be as complex as its most complex stage, and if its complex stages are always and everywhere *duplex* states, a simplex god looks a little silly. No, not merely silly. For what is the unexpected force of Schelling's suggestion that the various organizations of infinite organization "deviate into infinity from the ideal"? As we shall see, the word *deviation* is the key word for Schelling's account of *illness*. Furthermore, deviation *of* infinity *into* infinity sounds a little bit like an infinite regress, or an infinite regression, or a regression *of* the infinite *(genitivus sub. et ob.)*. The god of infinite organization should not be simpler than a sponge or polyp but ought to be at least as complex and duplex as, let us say, naming one set of living creatures among others, women and men. However necessary the dream of a sexless absolute may be, the dream of a common origin of all the deviations and gradations to come, the very necessity of those deviations, variations, and organic exfoliations rouses the deviant dreamer. Demonstration of a *dynamic sequence of stages* in the organization of nature cannot dream peacefully of an indifferent source. Schelling says at one point, invoking what one might call the χώρα-principle, "Nothing in the organization is a mere *container*" (*EE*, 67). For no mere container could explain the mysteries of *inhibition, deviation,* and *duality*.[8]

Schelling will return to the matter of separate sexes and universal sexuality in nature, indeed at the very place he invokes *contagium* for the second time (*EE*, 190–92). This is the place where that reciprocal determination of the organic and the anorganic is being sought in some "universal nature" (*EE*, 193). Here Schelling espies a kind of "duplicity of the second potency" (*EE*, 193n. 1), which Novalis would write as a *duplicity*,[2] a duplicity that prevents sexual duality from being a mere wicked infinity. For the productive power of nature is preserved precisely in the duplicity of sensibility-irritability. Each individual, unless stillborn, is marked by such a duplicity, which is the very mark of life. If that is the case, however, what are we to make of the cessation of duplicity? What are we to make of disease and death? What are we to make of contagion? What does contagion make of us?

# CHAPTER SEVEN

# The Bridge to Death

$\mathcal{W}$e have already noted the odd placement, or rather the displacement, of the "Appendix" on illness. The discussion of illness is appended to the third section of the first major division of the treatise (*EE*, 220–38), although, as the editor notes, something compelled Schelling to discuss illness earlier than he had planned (*EE*, 205n. 1). Indeed, it is surprising that Schelling was not compelled to discuss illness considerably earlier in his text, for example, at the moment when he discusses the effects of *poison* (*EE*, 73). Or perhaps even earlier, at the moment when he acknowledges the "theater of strife" as the site of the various actions of nature, the "egoism" of each action striving against all the others (*EE*, 40). Or perhaps from the very moment—the first page—when *drive* and *inhibition* are introduced as complications of the divine "infinite activity." Certainly by the time diremption (*Entzweiung*) becomes a theme, as it does with the assertion of universal sexual opposition (*EE*, 44ff.), something like illness seems already to have been made inevitable. For if sexuality is the summit, morbidity is the plummet, and unless one sex contrives to murder the other, or the inimical world conspires to kill them both, death seems to advene preeminently through illness. Among the accidents and contingencies—or brute necessities—of nature (*EE*, 55ff.), disease surely deserves a high place.

Yet no matter how detailed Schelling's account of Brownian nosology—and his objections to it—may be, much of the discussion in the *Erster Entwurf* devolves upon a point that is not difficult to grasp but impossible to accept, especially for a philosophy that insists that the third nature, the universal nature that embraces both the anorganic and organic realms, must itself in some sense be organic, alive. However much Schelling believes in and insists upon the world soul and the *life* of the cosmos, he also (at times) understands life as engaged in a life-and-death struggle with an intrinsically inimical nature. Incipient life, nascent life, neophyte life is dragged from a nature which, were she alive, would be kicking and screaming. In the context of life as fundamentally receptive, that is, exposed to external stimulus or excitation, Schelling writes:

> Wherever life comes to stand, it comes to stand, so to speak, against the will of external nature (*invita natura externa* [under external nature's objection]), by means of a tearing away from her *[Losreißen von ihr]*. External nature will therefore struggle against life *[gegen das Leben ankämpfen]*; most external influences that one takes to be in furtherance of life are actually destructive of it, for example, the influence of air, which is actually a process of consumption *[Verzehrungsprocess]*—a constant attempt to subject living matter to chemical forces. (*EE*, 81)

Oxidation, said Novalis, "comes from the devil." A century later, Freud will depict the scene of life's emergence in nature in terms of an emergency, or even a calamity: in the 1895 *Project*, which is Freud's *Erster Entwurf*, one might almost say, inasmuch as his *Project* is the *First Projection* of his metapsychology, he writes of *die Not des Lebens*, the exigency of life.[1] On the scene of exigent life, Quantity (of excitation or stimulus) inherently menaces Quality (consciousness). Were the dour neurologist and future psychoanalyst to go to meet the *Wunderkind* of German Idealists, there would not be a hint of disagreement, nothing that Freud would have to "correct." Yet Freud's puzzlement too is not different from Novalis's and Schelling's: given the enmity of nature toward life—which even Aristotle noticed when he said that touch is the proto-sense inasmuch as when we are touched too hard we die[2]—whence in all the world this fragile, tenuous, tremulous, precarious thing called *life? Natura externa* invites life but does so *invita*, unwillingly; nature is, with respect to life, uninviting, *invidiosa, inimica*. In the still life of nature, then, whence the life of all that moves? And in a world where life cannot be stillborn, what can the destiny of *illness* mean? Illness—to what end?

Schelling initially defines nature as the collective product of infinite productivity. His emphasis is always on the activity of production, the produc*tivity*, not the product. Why? Because the product is merely a botched attempt, a way station, a temporary interruption of production. "It sounds paradoxical," writes Schelling, understating the matter somewhat, "but it is no less true that precisely through the influences that are contrary to life, life is sustained" (*EE*, 82n. 1). Aristotle noted the paradox as well, and Freud was to build his entire metapsychology around it: the very sensibility and receptivity that enable us to move (in) the world and alter the conditions of our life are the portals of our death. Excess of light, excess of sound, perhaps even excess of taste or smell—from these we can at least try to flee, though we do so precisely in the directions opened up to us by our eyes, ears, and nose. By contrast, excess of touch, the overwhelming of the haptic sense by some bludgeon—say, Maxwell's Silver Hammer—means the end of us. To what end? The flesh that Aristotle in *On the Soul* calls the proto-sense, σάρξ, will inevitably be swallowed by the sarcophagus of the world. Schelling concludes, "Life is nothing other than a productivity that is restrained from passing over into the product. Absolute transition into the product is death. Thus what interrupts productivity sustains life" (ibid.). Sustains *and* destroys it, one feels compelled to interject, inasmuch as death proffers the leisure of permanent interruption to each of its individuals, products, and stages. We might then wish to put the question: If the interruption of productivity is what rescues life, there must be something in the very itinerary of productivity that enjoins death; but why does infinite activity culminate in death, even the "relative death" of which Goethe writes so hopefully?

Schelling feels the full weight of a question that Kazantzakis's *Alexis Zorba* puts to the Englishman after the murder of the widow. He asks the Englishman, "Why do the young die? Why does anybody die?" The Englishman answers, "I don't know." Zorba retorts, "What do you read about, then, in all your damned books? If they don't tell you that, what the hell do they tell you?" The Englishman replies, "They tell me about the agony of men who can't answer questions like yours." Whereupon Zorba says something like, "I spit on their agony."

Yet even if widows and widowers are not murdered, they will drift insensibly toward agony and demise. As fully developed in the direction of womanhood or manhood as they may be, they will deteriorate and die. As we heard earlier, William Butler Yeats lamented the wreck of body, testy delirium, slow decay of blood, and dull decrepitude of old age—indeed, was doing so continuously by the time he was thirty. What, then, about disease and death? To what end? Or will *contagium* make it impossible to ask for determinate ends? Will it be the ruin of teleology?

Schelling continues to approach the theory of disease, without taking it up explicitly, as he recounts the basic principles of John Brown's theory of excitability (through sensibility and irritability) and reproduction. Schelling accepts Brown's theory of disease as little as Novalis does, and his criticisms of it are quite similar; at the same time, Schelling concedes that no one has portrayed the ultimate paradox of organic life as convincingly as Brown has.[3] Schelling's criticisms of Brown's nosology are therefore criticisms that strike at the heart of Schelling's own philosophy of nature. According to Schelling, Brown is able to demonstrate in a convincing way that life is excitability, *Erregbarkeit*, arising from the reciprocal influence of sensibility and irritability, or receptivity and efficacious activity. What Brown is unable to explain is what excitability as such is. Nor do we know, says Schelling, precisely how excitability is effected or put into play in the organism. Thanks to Brown, we possess an empiricism of excitability, but we remain ignorant of its laws—which must be found in the relation of the organism to a higher physics, that is, preeminently, in the relation of flesh to electricity and magnetism. Schelling is convinced that he is in a better position than Brown to investigate the physical sources of excitability—to leave the Brownian system behind by pushing on to the covert electrochemical and magnetic sources of its efficacy. The harder Schelling pushes, however, the more paradoxical life itself, the entire realm of the organic, becomes to him.

Excitability and stimulation, the very sparks of life, invariably culminate in "absolute exhaustion," extinguishing the flame that drives combustion as such (*EE*, 89). Nature reaches its goal in every organization, but does so by means that are entirely opposed to her attempts. As a result, "life activity is the cause of its own extinction" (ibid.). Life gradually immures itself from external stimulation, but the ultimate walls are those of a vault or tomb. As the organism succeeds in surviving the throng of external stimulations—all those silver hammers that pummel its senses and threaten its very life—it shuts itself off from the only world in which it can live. "Life activity is extinguished as soon as it begins to become insensate with regard to external stimuli; life itself is therefore but the bridge to death" (ibid.).

Schelling now introduces a long footnote in order to get closer to this paradoxical life: to reach the verdant shore of life, he will cross the bridge to death. The details of his analysis are astonishingly close to Freud's theory of neural barriers and the successive filterings of quantitative energy flow—even though this is not the place to trace these parallels. Let us follow Schelling now over the bridge of a life and a death so joined that one might have to speak of them as *lifedeath*:

> Nature seeks to transform the receptivity of the organism vis-à-vis the outer world, which is always a determinate receptivity, into an *absolute* one. Yet precisely in this process receptivity is constantly diminished, and in the same ratio in which activity is increased. The organism thereby achieves ever-greater independence from the influences of external nature—although the more independent it becomes, the less that external nature excites it. Now, this excitability through external influences and receptivity with respect to them is itself the condition of life and of organic activity: when organic receptivity is extinguished, so too is organic activity. Thus nature reaches its goal, but by means of an altogether wrongheaded path [*auf einem ganz verkehrten Wege*]—and indirectly through organic activity itself. (*EE*, 89–90n. 2)

The wrongheaded path of nature—so reminiscent of what Hegel in the *Phenomenology of Spirit* will call the "inverted world"—now diverges. It deviates from itself, diverts and detours itself. It seems as though nature's ill will toward life, in some strange way and altogether by indirection, *rescues* life from itself—as though life were not really a part of nature, or were a truant needing the firm hand of the Instructress. The footnote continues:

> Life comes on the scene through a contradiction of nature, but it would be extinguished by its own hand if nature did not struggle against it. To be sure, life ultimately succumbs to nature. However, it does not succumb to the external throng; rather, it succumbs to the lack of receptivity for the external. If external influence, which runs counter to life, precisely serves to entertain life, then, in turn, what seems to be *most conducive* to life, namely, absolute insensibility to this influence, must become the ground of its decline. That is how paradoxical life is, right up to the point of its cessation. (Ibid.)

Schelling now expands his already oversized footnote—indeed, all the "action" of the lecture course, the entire oscillation between the desire for monism and the compulsion toward dualism, occurs within the footnotes of the text, so that one must wonder what they represent, what they *were* precisely in the oral presentation of the course—in order to apply to this situation the most general structures of his *First Projection*. In so doing, he appeals to the principle of *Indifferenz*, which will play the crucial role in his account (in the treatise *On Human Freedom*, ten years later) of the ground of God's existence. What will be invoked to save the life of God a decade hence, however, is now introduced in order to explain the death of the organism.[4] Yet that death, in a curious turn of dialectic, appears under the guise of immortality:

> The product, as long as it is organic, can never founder in indifference. If it is to succumb to the universal striving after indifference, it must first descend to a product of a lower potency. *As* an organic product, it cannot decline; and if it has already perished, it is no longer genuinely organic. Death is return to universal indifference *[Tod ist Rückkehr in die allgemeine Indifferenz]*. Precisely for that reason, the organic product is absolute, immortal. For it is an *organic* product for the very reason that in it there can never be a question of indifference. Only after it has ceased to be organic does the product dissolve in universal indifference. The constituent parts that were withdrawn from the universal organism now revert to it, and because life is nothing other than an enhanced state of common natural forces, the product, as soon as that state has passed, falls under the dominion of *these* forces. The same forces that preserved life for a while also destroy it in the end; thus life is not some thing; rather, it is merely the phenomenon of a transition of certain forces, out of that enhanced state, into the usual state of the universal. (Ibid.)

All that needs to be explained now is the secret of enhancement, *Steigerung*, along with the downside of enhancement, that is, the transition from inborn organic immortality to indifference, that is, death. For, if I read the footnote aright, the "curious turn of dialectic" is a *salto mortale* for the system of reason, inasmuch as *both life and death* are defined in terms of enhancement of forces: 1) "because life is nothing other than an enhanced state of common natural forces"; 2) "life is . . . merely the phenomenon of a transition of certain forces, out of that enhanced state, into the usual state of the universal." One may feel certain that the word *Leben* in the second phrase is merely a *lapsus calami*, a slip of the pen, a parapraxis, and that the sense of Schelling's entire endeavor demands that we read it as *Tod*. Yet the slip of the pen from death to life, life to death, would be more eloquent than any other phrase in Schelling's *First Projection*.

Both the enhancement and the fatal transition out of enhancement have to do with the introduction of excitability into an erstwhile inert nature. What did nature have to get excited about? Why did nature have to get excited about it? Why does that excitement ever have to end? To what end? And what about those forces that are nature's "usual" forces, the forces of nature's *gewöhnlichen Zustands*, the forces that rise to reclaim the constituents of organic life that were only borrowed from the anorganic—although, to be sure, the anorganic only borrowed them from universal organic life? Are they not—can they be anything else but—dire forces of nature, at least as far as life is concerned? Yet is not universal nature, embracing the organic and the anorganic, concerned precisely with life?

These are the questions that loom at the end of the first section of Schelling's tripartite *Projection*. We skip over the second part, on anorganic nature, at our own peril. Yet life is short, and the forces of life suffice only up to a certain point.[5]

Schelling's task throughout the lecture course and the treatise is to account for the reciprocal action of organic and anorganic realms in nature. He does not know whether nature can be explained "at *one* stroke," employing a phrase (*mit* Einem *Schlag*) that he will use in 1809 to describe the "magic" stroke by which good is sundered from evil and nature comes into existence. In the present case, that single stroke will have to do with a *doubling* of both the organic and anorganic realms of nature, in the hope that such a doubling will enable Schelling to unite the two realms in an intrinsic way (*EE*, 146–47). It can come as no surprise that the *boundary* between these two now doubled realms, the problem of the *Grenzen*, begins to loom as a central mystery of the *First Projection* (*EE*, 147n. 1, 160, 186, 208, 231–33, and 245).

The tendency of Schelling's analysis in the third and final section is to seek in the doubling of organism and external world a possible basis for unity, allowing perhaps for a kind of crossing, or perhaps an algebraic crossing out. The more precarious the method of doubling becomes, however, the more emphatic Schelling's text will be—that is, the more italic, bold, and spaced type we begin to see: "*The organism would have to be broken down into its appearance in two counterposed systems,* a higher and a lower system" (*EE*, 148). "In short: *every organization is an organization only insofar as it is turned simultaneously toward two worlds.* Every organization a *Dyas*" (ibid.). According to Karl Schelling, this last phrase is stricken from Schelling's own copy of the *First Projection*. The forces of monism, for which A = A, never cease to exercise their editorializing impact on Schelling. And yet it is the rational system itself, monism as such, that calls for a twofold, a *Dyas*, in this world of the quick and the dead. Duplicity is the one thing we can count on in a philosophy of nature. For A = A only insofar as the A reduplicates itself and is itself in some way duplicitous.[6] Such is the magnetism of identity, which can only be bipolar. If God himself is not *Dyas*, it is only because God is not discussed in the *Erster Entwurf*. In contrast, the reader of the later writings gets the sense that *Dyas* is indeed God. And even here in the *First Projection*, Schelling writes, "Thus, just as the organism is *duplicity in identity*, so is it also *nature*; the One, equal to itself and yet also counterposed to itself. The cause of organic duplicity must therefore be *One* with the cause of duplicity in nature in general, that is, with the cause of *nature itself*" (*EE*, 160).

It is at this apparent summit of the analysis, the exhibited duplicity of all identity, that the word *Krankheit* falls (*EE*, 162). "In the organism itself lies no ground *[kein Grund]* for its being disturbed," Schelling insists (ibid.), even though in the first section of his work we have seen that the organism could not be alive without such disturbance. Even if the *First Projection of a System of Nature Philosophy* cannot appeal to an experience that would take us back to the *first cause* of duplicity in nature (*EE*, 169), illness is an experience that a system sensitive to duplicity must respect. Soon the word *contagium* falls (*EE*, 177), and soon the discussion of illness forces its way forward in the presentation of the whole. That discussion interrupts the "meaningful dream" of Schelling's dualism, a dream Schelling describes in the following uncanny passage:

> It was surely a meaningful dream that dead matter be a *sleep* of the forces of representation, that animal life be a *dream* of the monads, that the life of reason finally be a state of universal vigilance. For what else is matter than *extinguished spirit?* In matter, all duplicity is canceled, its state is a state of absolute identity and calm. In the transition from homogeneity to duplicity, one world slips into twilight; with the restitution of duplicity, the world itself rises. (*EE*, 182)

If we read the passage backwards, we move from the waking state of reason, the reason that constructs systems, to a dream dreamed by the monads, a dream that causes the monads always and everywhere to be sundered into two—in animal life. Finally, from the dream of the monads we regress to a dreamless sleep of presentative or representative forces, the stony sleep of the presumably as yet unmagnetized anorganic. Whether we move forward or backward, it becomes impossible to account for waking and sleeping, and one wonders, with Keats, "Do I wake or sleep?" Soon the word *contagium* falls once again, whether in wakefulness or in the dream state, in a discussion of sexual opposition and reproduction (*EE*, 192). And so it is high time we wake up and turn to the "Appendix to the Foregoing Section" (*EE*, 220–38), the appendix on illness, following it quite closely.

# CHAPTER EIGHT

# The Ultimate Source of Life

$\mathscr{A}$n appendix is needed now, says Schelling, inasmuch as the attention he has paid to the totality of organic nature has slighted one very important aspect of that totality. We recall hearing earlier that even though systems of reason are monistic, the system of nature seems to abhor the individual: only through the demise of the individual do species establish and maintain their identity. Yet what about the individuals that are sacrificed to the species unity? Individual organisms, perhaps especially those frightened, bemused, but vigilant creatures that devise rational systems, deserve at least a supplement in the system. That supplement or appendix will turn out to be about disease or illness—the process of the decline and death of the individual.

Like nature as a whole, with its sequence of stages, the individual organism is *"a visible expression of a particular proportion of organic forces"* (*EE*, 220). Every organism, every organization, consists of such a ratio of forces, which implies both a norm and the possibility of deviation from the norm: "That the proportion in general is a *determinate* one, makes *deviation* from it possible; that the entire *existence* of the organization is *limited* by this proportion, makes deviation from it incompatible with the existence of the product as a whole—in a word, *both together* constitute the organization's capacity for **illness**" (*EE*, 221). Illness is therefore a "relative concept," in the sense in which Goethe speaks of "relative death" rather than "absolute death."[1] The degree of irritability that would make *you* feel ill, writes Schelling, employing the second person singular *familiar* form for only the second time in his treatise (*EE*, 158, 221), as though illness made us intimate with nature's individuals, would not disturb an organism at a lower level of organization.

Schelling takes considerable space and time to work out a theory of illness, one that builds upon the theory of John Brown. There is no need here to follow the ins and outs of Schelling's argumentation, which refine Brown's thesis that illness arises from a disproportion between stimulus and excitability in an organism.[2] Suffice it to say that Schelling argues two points convincingly: first, the proportion in question must be between the two factors that constitute excitability as such, namely, between sensibility and irritability; second, these two factors must be inversely related and yet tend to balance one another above a certain threshold or "boundary" *(Grenze)*. Below that threshold or boundary, however, sensibility and irritability are not in inverse relation; below that threshold, both decline until they reach the zero point, which is death.[3]

The initial assertion of Schelling's account of illness, which is not nearly as technical as the second avowal and not at all difficult to establish convincingly, is the assertion on which I wish to concentrate. That assertion arises from an argument we heard expressed only now, to the effect that the causes of illness (disproportion of natural forces, deviation from the norm) are identical to the causes of the sequence of stages in organic nature as a whole. The origin of illness and the scale of nature's potencies are therefore linked. Schelling develops two "principles" from his "concept of illness" (*EE*, 222), once again inserting a footnote. The footnote assures the reader that the theory of illness is now being elaborated "in order to prove that the sequence of stages that comes to pass in the entire organic chain is also expressed in each organic individual" (*EE*, 222n. 1), an assurance that might cause the reader to wonder why (and how, and to what end) an ostensibly permanent sequence of stages in nature was possible or necessary at all. Schelling now states his two principles:

> 1. That illness is produced by the same *causes* through which the phenomenon of life itself is produced.
> 2. That illness must have the same factors as life.

Another footnote appears (*EE*, 222n. 2) at this juncture—a juncture at which the entire first projection of a system of nature philosophy threatens to become unglued—and it is this footnote on which I wish to focus. The issue, to repeat, is the dire matter of the identity of the factors that cause illness and those that spark life in general. Schelling notes:

> It is therefore altogether nonsensical, for example, to call illness an anti-natural state, since it is every bit as natural as life. If illness is an antinatural state, then so too is life—and indeed to that extent life truly *is* antinatural, because life is actually a state that nature has been forced to yield, not one that it favors, but one that persists only against the will of nature, a state that she preserves only by struggling against it. In this sense one can say: life is a chronic illness, and death but convalescence from it.

What would happen to Schelling's account, to his entire *First Projection*, if one were to emphasize not the identity of the causes of illness with those of life but the identity of the organic realm with illness as such? If the entire sequence of stages in organization, the organism as such, with its drive to perfection, maturation, and procreation, were an expression of illness? If Hegel were right when he scandalized the citizens of Berlin by pointing out that Kant's great symbol of morality, to wit, the night sky of stars over their heads, was actually a kind of skin rash? If the starry sky of night is leprous, it is only because the general or universal nature that putatively embraces the organic and anorganic realms is itself contaminated. With what? With life, or with death—the answers come to the same. Contaminated with the original contagion. Infected with lifedeath.

As we have seen, Schelling argues that it is the essence of the organism to have to reproduce itself constantly. The organism is not a being *(Seyn)* but "a perpetual *being* [or: *becoming*] *reproduced [ein beständiges* Reproducirtwerden*]" (EE,* 222). The activity or movement of the organism is not an absolute activity but one that is mediated—and even inhibited—by *receptivity*, which is expressed most notably in the *sensibility* of the organism. If excitability, that is, sensibility and irritability in determinate proportion, is the formula for life, it presupposes "an original duplicity in the organism," more specifi-cally, "a constant restoration of the original duplicity in it" *(EE,* 223). Only such restoration or restitution of the twofold can prevent the organism from "sinking back into absolute homogeneity, which is death" (ibid.).

As Schelling goes in search of that duplicity, or of the secret of its perpetual restoration, he begins to repeat a particular phrase that eventually serves as a kind of refrain in the *First Projection.* He announces his search for "the ultimate source of life *[die letzte Quelle des Lebens]" (EE,* 227, 236, 238). He seeks this ultimate source precisely by investigating "the seat of illness" (*EE*, 224). He finds that seat first of all in *irritability*, in which the symptoms of a disease first express themselves. Yet the symptoms can emerge only after the disease has sufficiently *reproduced* itself. Finally, or ultimately, the symptoms developed through reproduction and expressed in irritability are seen as having their sovereign "seat" in originary *sensibility*.

Schelling is aware of the fact that the mere rising and falling of sensibility and irritability, in inverse ratio to one another, do not adequately explain how illness comes to pass: "We still confront the question as to how these two—become *illness*" (*EE*, 235). All he can ascertain is that if "illness is possible only through (indirect) affection of the ultimate source of life," then it must somehow have always already subverted the very seat of sensibility (*EE*, 236–37). The healing arts will have to devote their best energies to the vagaries of sensibility, not knowing whether the ultimate source of illness lies outside or inside the organism, uncertain whether the ultimate source of illness *is* the ultimate source of life. The healing arts will have to struggle against the very nature that struggles viciously against life, the life that struggles mercilessly against itself, so much so that only an unwilling nature can save it—all this struggle and enmity expressing the antipathy at the heart of all pharmaceutical homeopathy.[4]

Schelling now enters into the final pages of his *First Projection*, seeking in the principles of chemistry and physics, which are principles that always have a *duplicity* or *twofold* at their center, answers to all the questions he has posed in the course of his treatise. We cannot follow him through all the intricate turnings of his path. We must be satisfied to note that in these final pages as well it is always "the question of the ultimate origin of all duplicity," that is, of that duplicity which is *"in general* the source of all activity in nature" (*EE*, 249, 249n. 1), that drives him. His hope is that a monism will successfully embrace all the duplicities, that "there is therefore **one** universal dualism that runs through all nature" (*EE*, 250). Yet he cannot hope that such a dualistic monism will hide behind the traditional principle of identity. For to *produce* heterogeneity is to *allow* duplicity to insinuate itself into all avowed identity—as an unstoppable contagion. Schelling knows that the state of indifference back to which he will always be tempted can only be *magnetic* indifference, that is to say, an indifference that may seem utterly inert but is always already polarized (*EE*, 259). "Without this diremption in the homogeneous itself, there can be no solution" (ibid.). The *possibility* of magnetism does not quell the question that continues to disrupt these final pages: even if all the opposites we find in nature can be traced back to *one* proto-opposition, we still have to ask: "What invoked that primal opposition itself, calling it forth out of the universal identity of nature? For if nature is to be thought as the absolute totality, then nothing can be counterposed to it. For everything falls within its sphere, and nothing is outside it" (*EE*, 250).

In the following passage, where almost everything is set in spaced type (presented here as italic) and thus stated emphatically, there are nevertheless one or two important words *without* emphasis, words that we therefore ought to observe quite closely:

> *There is therefore **one** cause that brought the most original opposition into nature. This cause we can designate by means of the* (unknown) *cause of original magnetism.*
>
> *By means of this cause, there came to pass in the universe, into infinity, an efficacity conditioned by **distribution**, the latter being conditioned by a state of indifference for every individual product, this state of indifference in turn being conditioned by the possibility of a difference in the homogeneous, and through that the **possibility** of a dynamic process* (which is where the life process too belongs), *and especially the chemical process as a dissolution of the heterogeneous in the heterogeneous.*
>
> *The **actuality** of the dynamic process for every individual product is conditioned by **communication**, which occurs in the universe into infinity; its universal medium, for the part of the universe that is known to us, is **light**.* (*EE*, 260–61)

Is there not a need for yet another supplement, another remark or appendix, to remind us of the (unknown) circumstance that pits life (the life process) against nature, that turns nature against the very life that is wrested from it, "against its will, as it were"? Will there not always be a need for yet another supplement to account for the lack or the contagious negativity that can never have been in the universal but which must have been there from the start, or from before the start, having always already sundered the universal?

If the original lack expresses itself as illness in the organic individual, a similar series of questions arises. Why is the fate of the individual reduced to such a supplementary position in the sequence of stages that constitute organized life? What light, what magnetism, what communication, what distribution—and, above all, what tormented soul, spirit, idea, or ideal—forced a concession from nature that left us with the paradox of lifedeath? If the seat of disease is to be found at the ultimate source of life, is not life itself the disease of nature? To what end? Unless, to repeat, such questions of ends have gone to their ruin in ultimate sources of contagion.

Finally, if nature is itself universal activity, universal self-inhibiting activity, can we not descry something in it like absolute illness? What can life be for a system of reason other than an exercise in imprecision, a deviant ratio, a disproportion played out across inscrutable floating boundaries, an infinite boondoggle? What sort of life is it that perpetuates itself by the very mechanisms of death? What is this adventure in which we find ourselves caught? What is this ruinous lifedeath?

Such questions can be at home only in an idealism, such as Schelling's, that is tormented. No, not at home; such questions are never at home. They can only be visited—without end.[5]

PART THREE

# Triumphant Idealism

*Hegel's Early Philosophy of Nature in the Jena* Realphilosophie *of 1805/06*

*We are like the fire that sleeps in sapless limbs or flint; we spend every moment struggling, seeking an end to our narrow confinement. But they are coming, those moments of liberation, and we will have restitution for the eons of struggle when divinity destroys the prison, when the flame is released from the wood, leaping victorious from the ashes, and oh! when it seems to us that the unfettered spirit has returned in triumph to the halls of the sun, his sufferings and servitude forgotten at last.*

—*HÖLDERLIN*, HYPERION

# CHAPTER NINE

## Nature's Seductive Impotence

$\mathcal{I}$f the forces of nature are dire forces, that is, forces that threaten the very life that is wrested from nature, would not the idealism that goes to meet those forces have to be either thaumaturgic or tormented? What could it mean for idealism to be *triumphant*, except that its militancy and triumphalism perpetually miss the point—or understand the point well enough, but obfuscate it precisely in order to feign victory and walk off with the laurels? The Hegelian system certainly triumphs over the Schellingian, if the objective spirit of institutional academic philosophy is any measure, and the magical idealism of a Novalis was never even in Hegel's league. Yet, to repeat, if life defeats the systems of reason that go to meet it, what does triumphant posturing betray but its own redoubled failure and yet another scandal in the history of academe?

The materials that Hegel presents in his 1805/06 course at Jena, his inaugural course as Adjunct Professor of Philosophy, do not survive in presentations of his mature system. True, the *Zusätze* or addenda of the *Encyclopedia of Philosophical Sciences*—first published in 1817, reissued with substantial changes in 1827, then revised and released a third time in 1830—offer versions of some of this material, prepared and polished by Hegel's editors. Yet the rougher versions of 1805/06, with their elliptical phrases and half-meanings, with their marginal emendations and never-completed thoughts, have considerably more value than those later versions from the hands of Hegel's students and disciples. The fact that these materials are for the most part excluded from the mature system as we have it from Hegel's own hand does not diminish their importance but enhances it.[1] True, when these early materials are added to the mix, Hegel's system is less triumphant in its gestures; yet the system is also more doggedly faithful to the questions that drive it, questions of limits and accidents. For these materials, in the hands of lesser philosophers, are simply repugnant to reason. They are, as Hegel himself calls them, the *trash* of the system—*Abfall*, which is a special kind of contingency, *Zufall*, or even mishap, *Unfall*.[2] What sorts of materials are we talking about here? In what follows I will take up Hegel's dialectic of genitality, elaborated in considerable detail in the 1805/06 *Realphilosophie*, and his account there as well of sexuality as the onset of illness and death.[3]

Before we begin, however, we might look for several *points de repère* in Hegel's mature philosophy of nature as elaborated in the second part of the *Encyclopedia*. It would already be a help if we could identify the places where the Jena materials *might* have fit in, the places from which, in retrospect, they appear to have been removed. More than that, however, identifying these sites might help us to decide what is at stake in these two related questions of genitality and illness. To that end, let us discuss the following two points: first, Hegel's polemic against the Romantics, especially Schelling, which attacks accidental or merely contingent parallels in nature philosophy—nature's *Zufälligkeit* being, in effect, the source of its impotence, *Ohnmacht*; second, Hegel's proximity, in spite of that polemic, to something like a thaumaturgic idealism (Novalis) or a tormented idealism of parallels and potencies (Schelling). After discussing these issues in Hegel's mature system, we will then turn to the earlier Jena materials—still against the backdrop of the *Encyclopedia*, however—in order to elaborate our third and fourth points. The third point, discussed in chapter 10, is the dialectic of genitality and the nature and destiny of sexual reproduction in Hegel's early and mature systems. Finally, the fourth matter for discussion, undertaken in chapter 11, will be the dire forces of illness and death as depicted in the early and mature systems.

In the lecture courses on philosophy of nature that Hegel taught at Berlin between 1818 and 1828, he never missed an opportunity to slight the Schellingian system. Schelling has brought nature philosophy into "discredit" because of his lack of method, his lack of scientificity; what Schelling has produced is a kind of vertigo, reminiscent of the dizziness produced by pusillanimous skepticism, according to the account of historical skepticism in the *Phenomenology of Spirit*.[4] Yet "vertigo" in this case is also a swindle, or series of swindles, *Schwindeleien* (9: 9). What Schelling is possessed of is fancy. He is fully capable of developing Novalis's *Fantastik*, but what he cannot do is prevent his fancy from turning to fantasies, phantoms, and phantasms of *analogy* (9: 15). Schelling is like a medieval philosopher who has outlived his epoch, always ready to draw lessons from the open book of nature, which he apparently gleans with secret lights. Hegel's criticism could as easily apply to Novalis, if Hegel condescended to discuss Novalis's philosophy of nature, which he does not.[5] Both Novalis and Schelling are "Sunday's children," all sweetness and light, unable to work up a sweat in order to produce hard and fast results (9: 17). Instead, what we get from the Sunday's Children is *parallelizing*, that is, the employment of names from spheres other than the sphere of thought, other than the sphere of logic, to describe nature's infinite—and infinitely seductive—metamorphoses (9: 472). Hegel's objection to Schelling (and, tacitly, also to Novalis) is of course precisely the objection that virtually every twentieth-century critic of Hegel's texts raises against him.

These ostensibly innocent parallels and analogies in Schelling and Novalis betray, at least from Hegel's point of view, a fundamental weakness of will. The underlying problem with Schelling and Novalis is that they are reluctant to lay a hand on nature. For only if one exercises violence on this Proteus—and one recalls from Goethe's *Faust* how slippery a rascal this Proteus can be—can one force him (or her, inasmuch as Proteus is actually Eve, or Nature) to stand still long enough to exhibit his (or her) logical structures. Only the use of such violence or force *(Gewalt antun)* will enable the philosopher to wrest the truth from nature: only if the philosopher refuses to gaze on nature with the sensuous eyes, only if he diverts her mesmerizing influence with the mirror of philosophical speculation and strikes with the sword of logic, will philosophy prevail. Only such violence will counteract the Medusa effect—with Hegel cast in the role of Perseus. Perseus over Proteus. Hegel therefore alters the image of Novalis's *Apprentices at Saïs*, which recounts the adventures of those young enthusiasts who dare to lift the veil. Hegel's focus is not on the parergonal veil, nor on the naked goddess beneath, but on the *thought* expressed by the inscription on the pedestal of her statue—or, as Hegel would have it, the inscription embroidered onto the hem of her veil: "The inscription on the veil of Isis: 'I am what was, is, and will be, and no mortal has lifted my veil,' melts in the face of the thought" (9: 19).

Spirit recognizes nature as a blood relative, Hegel assures us, in the way that Adam, upon waking, recognizes Eve as the flesh of his flesh (9: 23). True, nature is a pagan; she is not of Paradise. "Nature is spirit estranged from itself, spirit merely *unrestrained* [ausgelassen], a Bacchantic god who does not rein himself in, who does not get a grip on himself; in nature the unity of the concept conceals itself" (9: 25). Nature therefore does not seem to be up to the measure of spirit; it seems inappropriate *(unangemessen)* to spirit; the wisdom of the tradition (apart from Novalis and Schelling) identifies matter as μὴ ὄν, *non-ens*, the *nihil* proper; nature appears as the purely *exterior* and *extrinsic* into which spirit has unaccountably *fallen;* nature is the *downfall* or *dejection* of spirit, the *trash* of the idea—in a word, the word we only now heard, *Abfall.*[6]

Nature (or spirit *in* nature?) appears to have abandoned herself (or himself? itself?) to an orgy of unrestrained contingency or accident. This lack of discipline can be seen in the superfetation of forms, *die zügellose Zufälligkeit*, that characterizes her; life itself, the very summit of nature, appears to have capitulated to the irrationality of the extrinsic *(der Unvernunft der Äußerlichkeit hingegeben)*. Nature is the fallen or mad woman whom spirit can love only insofar as he remembers her in her days of clean and sober glory. It is this troubled love that Hegel's idealism of nature represents. Because of its insatiable need for triumph, however, Hegel's troubled idealism suffers from the rancor and self-hatred that begin to fester when what one loves has fallen in defeat and ignominy.

Nature is essentially impotent. Hegel brings home the surreptitious lesson of Kant's Analytic of the Sublime: whereas nature with her blizzards, her beetling brows of cliff, and her churning seas at first appears as the power that will dash us, she submits in the end to the rational and moral superiority of the human being who—admittedly, from his safe refuge, hanging on for dear life—confronts her with *Gelassenheit* (though not *Ausgelassenheit)* and *Gemüt*, opposes her with that untranslatable releasement and interiority, that "heart of hearts" whose tranquillity runs deeper than the mind. *Gemüt* over *Gewalt*. Or, better, since *Gemüt* disciplines itself in all the masterful moves of logic, a *Gemüt* that exercises *Gewalt*. Hegel's triumphant idealism builds on Kant's sublime: nature, however seductive, proves to be impotent; not *Macht*, but *Ohnmacht*, is her earmark. "It is the *impotence* of nature that causes it to receive the conceptual determinations merely abstractly, and to expose the elaboration of the particular to extrinsic determinability" (9: 34). Yet if old Adam recognizes this flesh of nature, the flesh of Eve, as flesh of his own flesh, can we suppose that nature's impotence casts no light back on the omnipotence that once deigned to mingle with her? In an extraordinary "Remark," the *Anmerkung* to section 250, on the impotence of nature, Hegel concedes that nature's debility cannot reflect spirit's strength. Indeed, philosophy itself cannot lord it over a labile and docile nature, a slavish nature, without the most terrible of reversals ensuing. "The impotence of nature sets limits to philosophy," Hegel confesses, in one of his least triumphant moments, "and it would be utterly irrelevant to demand of the concept *[Begriff]* that it grasp *[begreifen]* such contingencies as these and, as people say, to construe or deduce them."[7]

Limits or boundaries to philosophy? Borderlines already drawn up or laid out for spirit precisely by the *impotence* of nature? Such imputed impotence would in fact be that of the daunting goddess whose nautical chariot carves islands out of the sea. Be that as it may, her impotence *and* power result in superfetation—that profusion of bad births, malformed creatures, and abominations *(Mißgeburten)* on which Kant had already commented in his *Critique of Judgment* (§§64, 81). Kant sees them sometimes as signs of nature's bounty, sometimes as marks of her monstrosity. Hegel's view is more consistent and dependably less trusting. What from one point of view is her profusion of forms is from another the staggering trash pile of botched types. Spirit's exposure to the exterior and extrinsic is its conceptual flaw; or, to put it less triumphantly, such exposure is the flaw of the concept as such. In its immediacy and exteriority, nature produces *life*, but exposes it invariably to *death*. That, at least, is what our intellect or understanding makes of her:

> The concept wants to explode the husk of exteriority and become for-itself. Life is the concept that has come to its manifestation; it has become the meaningful and interpreted concept. Yet at the same time it is most difficult for the intellect to grasp, because for the intellect the abstract and the dead, as simplest, is what is easiest to grasp. (9: 37)

Limits, therefore, to the intellect. It remains to be seen whether reason and philosophy can overcome such limits when nature shows itself to be not only unintelligible but also *unvernünftig*, recalcitrant to reason, and therefore beyond the pale of philosophy. In the end, Hegel will tell the philosopher that he or she is not to take so seriously the profusion of forms in nature, particularly in animality: that very copiousness of form marks the victory of contingency over necessity (9: 502–503). And so Hegel draws the final conclusion or ties the double knot of the Copernican Revolution in philosophy: if certain monsters of nature do not conform to the categories that our logic has been able to establish, that is *their* fault, the monsters' fault *(so ist es* ihr *Mangel)*; if there are botched works in human culture, there are infinitely more botchings in nature *(schlechte Werke)*; the forms of nature "cannot be brought into an absolute system," and that is *their* problem, not the system's. Which leaves only the question as to how spirit could at any point in his or her or its career have gotten mixed up in any of this. Nature's seductive impotence? Twist and turn any way you like: nature's lability is spirit's liability.[8]

Hegel is not always equal to such desperate triumph, such Pyrrhic victory, for spirit. In his account of sidereal Earth, of geology as the prelude to life, Hegel both consigns mineral Earth to contingency and death and reclaims her seas and soils for future life. At first, pure exteriority seems to have the upper hand, and Hegel sees what Leopold Bloom first descries in outer space, before the heaventree of stars discloses to him its humid nightblue fruit:

> Never know anything about it. Waste of time. Gasballs spinning about, crossing each other, passing. Same old dingdong always. Gas, then solid, then world, then cold, then dead shell drifting around, frozen rock like that pineapple rock. The moon.[9]

Hegel writes: "One cannot grasp *[begreifen]* everything in this corpse, for contingency has played its role here" (9: 349). Philosophy turns its back on stony Chaos and does not look for the sources of order in this veritable desert of disorder. Suddenly, however, the system takes courage, and even poor *intellect* is rescued for nature:

> Nature essentially has *intellect.* The configurations of nature are determinate, limited; they come onto the scene as such. *If* therefore the Earth too was once in a state in which nothing was alive, existing only in chemical process etc., nevertheless a determinate, complete configuration is suddenly there as soon as the lightning of the vital strikes into matter, like Minerva springing from the head of Jupiter. (Ibid.)

What was earlier defined as the impotence of nature, an impotence that drew boundaries around what philosophy itself might hope for, now becomes a merely temporary inconvenience; contingency now becomes a prelude to compelling necessity. The profusion of forms in the living world, Hegel now claims, "at first appears as accidental; but the activity of the concept is to grasp as necessarily determinate what to sensuous consciousness appears to be contingent" (9: 350). The triumph of idealism is to be found, then, in this nurturing and consoling *zunächst,* "at first." At first, ostensible contingency; in the end, reassuring necessity. Such reassuring necessity will enable Hegel to scorn Schelling's sensuous obsession with chemistry and electromagnetism: for a triumphant idealism, the binding power of life in the system will always be a *spiritual* cincture, *ein geistiges Band* (9: 394), careless of chemistry, empowered by logic. Yet as the polemic against the Sunday's Children subsides, and Hegel's confidence in his own system grows, that system surreptitiously takes on characteristics that one can only call Schellingian, or even, as monstrous as it sounds, Novalisian.[10]

For example, and it is only one of many possible examples, when Hegel is under Schelling's wing—during the period of his (junior) partnership with Schelling on the *Critical Journal,* the period following his own *Differenzschrift*—he is doubtless caught up in Schelling's fascination with the physiological and nosological system of John Brown. Even in the mature system there are signs of Hegel's own preoccupation with the system of sensibility, irritability, and reproduction.[11] And while Hegel would never define philosophy as the first kiss, his mouth does not altogether abjure all the receptivities of the mouth, including "laughter, and then too, kissing" (9: 456). Indeed, Hegel sees the mouth as part of that system which can as readily be called *excremental* as *oral,* that is, the system of assimilation. The ultimate process of animality is a *real* process (so that a *Realphilosophie* has to scrutinize it), and Hegel defines its three forms as follows: 1) the form of abstract, formal repulsion or excretion *(Abstoßen);* 2) the drive to construction, cultivation, education, and culture *(Bildungstrieb);* 3) the reproduction of the species. Hegel comments:

> These three processes, apparently heterogeneous, are in essential interconnection with one another in nature. The organs of excretion and the genitals, the highest and the lowest aspects of animal organization, cohere in the most intimate way in many animals, as do speaking and kissing on the one hand, and on the other eating, drinking, and spitting, all being bound up with the mouth. (9: 492)

The way in which the mouth here comes to represent (or parallel or analogize) the extension of the system as a whole is certainly reminiscent of Novalis; so too is this earlier passage from the Jena period, in which the mere planting of a seed—by a kind of magic—branches out into many different spheres, including the religious. Hegel writes, in 1805/06, in the context of the "vegetable organism" planted as a seed in the ground:

> This safeguarding *[Bergen]* in the earth is therefore a *mystical, magical* deed—just as the child is not only this helpless configuration of a human being that does not yet announce its capacity for reason but also the force of reason *in itself*, something altogether different from this little one who cannot speak and can do nothing rational; and baptism is precisely the solemn acknowl-edgment of this comrade in the kingdom of spirits—just so is the germ of seed laid in the earth, [allowed to] fall; this [is a] mystical deed, [in] that secret forces are in the seed which still slumber, that in truth the seed is something other than this thing that is *just existing there;* the magician gives this seed an altogether different meaning: the seed that I can squash with my hand, a seed which, like a rusty old lamp, contains a powerful spirit, is the *concept* of nature. The seed is the power that conjures the Earth so that her force can serve it. (*JS*, 122; cf. 9: 396)

Spirit is at once the squeezing and rubbing hand, the Aladdin's lamp, the seed, and—whether Hegel likes it or not—the soil. The farmer sees revalidated each spring the life in the stock of magical idealism, the stock onto which Hegel's more stern, sober, and logical varietal is spliced.

Or, if one is looking for ways to overcome Hegel's polemic against his predecessors' philosophies of nature, consider this second pas-sage, now not from the 1805/06 system, where one is presumably more likely to find Hegel's "romantic" passages, but from the lecture courses of 1818–1828. Once again it is the geology of the system, but this time its streams and seas, its fresh water and brine, that are at least reminiscent of a thaumaturgic idealism. For, after giving an account of the chemistry and physics of the water table, and of the geological relation of water and land, Hegel suddenly writes as though he were not only Novalis but also Hölderlin, the poet of the great river hymns:

> Thus I do not see the mountains as beakers that collect the rainwater that penetrates them. Rather, the genuine sources *[die echten Quellen]* that pro-duce such streams as the Ganges, the Rhône, and the Rhine, possess an inner life, a striving, a pulsing; they are like Naiads; the Earth expels its abstract sweet water, which in these outpourings of its concrete vitality hurries to the sea. (9: 363)

There is something dire about the sea, however, whose sublime power Kant went to meet with moral humanity on his mind and a life jacket firmly in hand. We shall therefore have to return to the sea. Indeed, if Ferenczi is right about the thalassic regressive tug, we shall always have been returning to it.[12]

For the moment, let us proceed to a discussion of Hegel's early account of human genitality, where one might have thought that contingency and superfetation had run rampant. Yet the necessity that Hegel sometimes despairs of finding in the forms and functions of nature expresses itself forcefully in the genitals of male and female and also in their genital contact. Whether Hegel's dialectic of genitality brings him into closer proximity to Novalis and Schelling, or removes him farther from them, is a question we can postpone, if not forget.

# CHAPTER TEN

## *Turned to the Outside*

### THE DIALECTIC OF GENITALITY

*T*he story of genitality starts in fact with the sea and the stars, with the mind-boggling effusions, outpourings, and ejaculations that are the night sky and the phosphorescent oceans. Yet sea and sky are not the obvious places to begin. The obvious place to begin, the *logical* place to begin, is with *the universal type*. For, in Hegel's early account of the genitals, it will be their isomorphism and their functional equivalence that guide his analysis—an equivalence or near equivalence, inasmuch as, until the end, there will always be one difference between male and female genitalia. At all events, a fundamental *type* will be seen to underlie genital difference, like the *one* opposition that Schelling hopes will guarantee monism in the face of duplicity. That underlying coinage will guarantee for Hegel, as it does for Schelling, the establishment and maintenance of the species.

Hegel refers to a "universal type" elsewhere in his analyses of nature in the *Enzyklopädie*—for example, at the end of the addendum to section 352 on animal organization. The universal type of animality, the very paradigm upon which animals are to be measured, though only to be found wanting, is the human animal:

> In the perfect animal, the human organism, these processes are most completely and most clearly elaborated. In this supreme organism, therefore, a *universal type* in general lies at hand, in which, and on the basis of which, the meaning of the undeveloped organism first becomes recognizable and can be developed. (9: 436)

The perfection or entelechy of the universal type will be read archaeologically, from human beings back to everything that is

behind and beneath them; it will not "lose itself in plant reproduction," as it did in Schelling's *Erster Entwurf*, but in archaic seas and
asteroids. Whether or not the teleoarchaeological perfection of the
universal type in this supreme organism (the human) extends to its
genitalia is the question Hegel will soon be posing. Whether or not
the retrospect provided by human genitality will justify sexual opposition throughout nature is the question that remains to be posed.

In the first subsection of "The Reproductive Process," namely,
"Species and Kinds," Hegel once again appeals to the *type* that is
determined by the concept in a species (9: 500). Yet a certain tension
subsists within that type, a tension between inside and outside. It is
similar to the tension that one sees or feels in the hills and valleys of
a block of type, which will strike the matrix of whatever surface is to
be printed, and so reproduce the content of the text. In the present
context, whose difficulty should not be underestimated, it seems to
be a tension between an organ that has a specialized function *within*
an organism, as a part of its innards *(Eingeweide)*, and a member
*(Glied)* that is turned to the outside *(nach außen gekehrt)* as a tool or
implement of spirit. The innards of an animal organism are not to be
spurned; they exhibit the more intricate development of the animal;
plants, by contrast, have no guts. Animals display those winding coils
of intestine to which Timaeus refers—indeed, precisely at the moment (*Timaeus* 73a 3) when for the second time he invokes the notion
of the ὑποδοχή, the "receptacle" that is eventually given the name
χώρα. The coils of the intestine retain food and drink, so that the
animal—in this case, the human animal—can finally break from the
feeding trough and turn its head to the stars and beyond the stars to
the idea. For Hegel, innards are a sign of *system* (9: 373). As opposed
to that, plants are mere agglomerates of independent parts. The
independence of the vegetable parts betrays "the *impotence* of plants"
viewed as a whole. Plants thus come to represent nature, swooning
nature, as such, whereas the animal, and especially the human animal,
with its coiling complexity of innards, its "nonindependent members," somehow gestures beyond nature toward another realm (9:
385, 395).

The promise of animals—with members added to their innards—
is that they move themselves out beyond themselves and are in some
sense and at least for some time *turned to the outside*. They therefore
come to represent a system or an organization that is no longer
complacent, no longer content to remain in self-absorbed, undiffer-

entiated unity. In the final moments of ingestion, with the production of chyle from the food taken in from the outside and the adsorption of nourishment in the capillaries of the coiling intestines, the animal reproduces its own self; the internal systems of blood and lymph too are therefore in some sense *nach außen gekehrt*, turned to the outside (9: 449). As odd as it may seem, mother's milk is precisely such a turning to the outside of ingestion: it is as though the mother or nursemaid is a kind of robin, feeding its young with food that has already been ingested and predigested by the adult. Hegel, like Novalis, and also in (critical) relation to John Brown, discusses milk in the context of poison, the ultimately unassimilable matter, which in so many cases can be counteracted by the ingestion of the already digested material of mother's milk (9: 529–30). The source of mother's milk, the breast, may itself be viewed morphologically and also functionally as "turned to the outside," very like a member, so that we can expect it to play a role in Hegel's dialectic of genitality.[1]

For the moment, it will do to conclude this brief overview of Hegel's account of the universal type in the mature system of the *Encyclopedia* with a reference to configuration *(Gestaltung)*, which is discussed prior to both assimilation and sexual reproduction. For here (§355) Hegel argues that the configuration of animals must develop in two counterposed directions at once, namely, to the inside and the outside. The development to the outside has of course the advantage that it embodies differentiation as such: turning to the outside is always what differing achieves: Hegel writes it as *"die* differente," that is, he writes the *differente* as a noun but (because of the lowercase "d") preserves its force as a present participle. The achievement of development in such self-differentiating, "differen-ting," or counterposed directions, as Schelling doubtless taught Hegel, is precisely the aspect of configuration that points ahead to sexual reproduction. Development to the inside, related to the superior integration of animal innards or guts, prefigures the female, at least when viewed not in terms of the elevated mammary gland but with a view to the genitals; development to the outside, related to the process of differentiation as such, and not merely in animal develop-ment, prefigures the male. With sexual reproduction, in other words, there is a redoubled move to the outside, a potentiated assimilation of the outside, insofar as each sex is outside the other. Hegel writes, in sentences that are certainly not easy to unravel:

The whole, taken as a configuration that has been completed as an autonomous individual, is, in this self-relating universality, at the same time
*specialized* in the *sexual* relation, turned to the outside in a relation with
another individual. The configuration in itself, while closed in on itself,
points toward its two directions on the outside *[die Gestalt weist an ihr, indem
sie beschlossen in sich ist, auf ihre beiden Richtungen nach außen hin]*. (9: 455)

However, in the same section in which Hegel prefigures the
inward-tending genitality of the female and the outward-turning
genitality of the male (about which more in a moment), he uses the
word *permeation* or *penetration—Durchdringung.* Configuration must
permeate or penetrate all the parts, not only the genitals, and it must
permeate the parts not only morphologically but also functionally.
Indeed, at the culmination of the addendum to this section (§355)
Hegel emphasizes the extent to which sexuality as such has to
permeate or penetrate the entire individual, even in the case of
human beings. Earlier in the *Encyclopedia* he has faulted plants—
which, as we noted, have no guts—for their luxuriant but almost
entirely superfluous sexuality. Plants are not "fully dipped in the
*principle* of their [sexual] opposition, because that opposition does not
saturate them" (9: 421). This becomes clear to us when we see a new
plant taking root at the spot where any given node of a pendant,
drooping stem happens to touch the ground—no need to wait for the
development and scattering of seed. The language of flowers is not
too sexy, in Hegel's view, but insufficiently sexual. Thus, for example,
even though Friedrich Schlegel understands the importance of the
thought of the genus, in which male and female finally achieve an
identity, his understanding expresses itself in the language of flowers
and thus loses itself in sentimentality. In *Lucinde*, Schlegel writes:
"One day the two of us will be one in spirit; we will see that we are
blossoms on one plant, or petals on one flower. . . ."[2] Looking ahead,
Hegel describes the genuine sexual opposition as one that is "spread
over the whole" of the individual; sexual identity is, or ought to be, a
determination "completely reflected into itself" (ibid.). "The entire
*habitus* of the individual must be bound up with its sexuality" (ibid.;
on *habitus*, see also 9: 501). Because plants often combine male and
female parts in the same individual—as Novalis said, pollen dust
gathers in the same calyx; as Schelling said, stamen and pistil share
the same conjugal bed—and because, as we have only now noted, a
plant can often reproduce by contingent contact with the earth,

sexuality in plants is "a game, a luxury, somewhat superfluous for reproduction" (9: 423). A besotted suitor says it with flowers, but flowers, all droopy with sex, are merely for show. The superfluous production of seed means that plants confuse the highest with the lowest: their sexuality, as a superficial organization, is in reality identical with the process of excretion (9: 482). Plants, deprived of innards, piddle away precious seed. That is perhaps why pollen works as a *"lethal poison"* on an otherwise flourishing plant: pollination stunts the growth of plants, and instead of being a mere love-bite, a *medico morsu*, in fact consumes the individual plant and kills it (9: 426–27). Plants may have no guts, but they can be poisoned. And they are poisoned by what is most superfluous in them—their genitality. One hopes that things will go better for people.[3]

Sexuality must permeate the individuals in the way that warm blood permeates the flesh of an animal. Only in this way will the parts become "essential members"; only in this way will "subjectivity exist as the permeating *one* of the whole" (9: 429). Sexuality does permeate the human individual, Hegel assures us, even though his lack of detail on this point makes it difficult to take him at his word. "By means of the male and the female there results a determination of the entire configuration, a differentiated *habitus*, which among humans also extends into the spiritual realm *[der bei Menschen sich auch aufs Geistige erstreckt]*, and results in a differentiated set of characteristics *[Naturell]*" (9: 459). The differentiated set of characteristics, the variegated temperaments and behaviors of male and female, are here called a *Naturell*. One must wonder whether the *Naturell* belongs to either nature or the natural. *Die Natur, die Natürlichkeit, das Naturell*—the difference between them makes all the difference. For whenever Hegel employs the words *natürlich, Natürlichkeit* in his system— whether in the philosophy of nature or elsewhere—he means that in nature or humanity which must be eradicated from a system of reason. Not canceled and preserved, not *aufgehoben*, but eradicated. Whereas *Natur* is the Eve of Adam, *Natürlichkeit* is the Eve—or Lilith—of Satan; if nature is the trash of the idea, the natural is the biohazardous waste in that trash, calling for special handling and careful evacuation.[4]

As for those traits of male and female that seem to stretch into the realm of the intellectual or spiritual, the male and female *Naturelle* at their most elevated moments, one might ask whether they extend into the realm of the concept. If they do not, logic is not alive. If they do, logic is not logic. Hegel maintains a discreet silence. Discretion is important where there is to be triumph. But let us return to the analysis.

Permeation by sexuality is of the essence. Permeation, however, describes what a poison does, and, at least in Novalis's account, what the soul does. Sexuality perhaps permeates in both ways at once. It dare not be for humans what it is for flowers, a game and a luxury item. Perhaps that is what sexuality is for the sensual human being— who does appear, briefly, in Hegel's text. The production of *members* idealizes the body, the body becomes subject: "The life of the animal is thus, as this summit of nature, absolute idealism" (9: 430). Yet the process of idealization and of subjectivity is hardly complete in the animal, which "only touches itself, intuits itself, but does not think," just as the sensual human being "can wallow in all his desires, but cannot get shut of them, in order thoughtfully to grasp himself as universal" (9: 431). Presumably, the universal lies far from the wallow and is not accessible by way of the *Naturell*. One can grasp oneself as universal only if one stops grasping oneself (or letting oneself be grasped) as particular. Presumably, sexuality does not and cannot permeate humanity to the core of the universality to which it has access; presumably, sexuality does not and cannot saturate the logic of the concept. And yet permeation *(Durchdringung)* is of the essence.

It is finally time to turn to the dialectic of genitality as such. In Hegel's mature system, as presented in the *Encyclopedia*, it appears as an addendum to section 369, which takes up "The Sexual Relation" as such. Hegel's focus here is not the permeation of the sexual, however, but its lack of measure, its inappropriateness *(Unangemessenheit)* in each of the two sides of the sexual relation. Yet the feeling of not measuring up, of being unequal to the species or genus of which one is a member, is perhaps not distributed equally across the two *Naturelle*. Let us take up the 1805/06 account, which serves as the source of the later addendum, interrupting occasionally for purposes of commentary.[5]

My presentation of the text—in the German original, with a tentative translation alongside—will begin at the point where Hegel takes up the themes of *craving, satiated desire,* and *the sexual relation* in animal life as ways the animal—or animal species—produces itself. Hegel is already relating these ways to the theme of *illness,* which I will discuss in chapter 11. In the first few paragraphs, he is running through the entire development of sexuality, illness, and demise, presenting it in outline form, so to speak. Thus the opening paragraphs are all but incomprehensible, and we will have to be patient:

Die gesättigte Begierde hat hier nicht die Bedeutung des sich als dieses einzelne hervorbringenden Individuums; sondern als allgemeines, {*Am Rande:* Die unorganische Natur ist durch sein Ganzes hindurchgegangen—*Verdauung* ist hier des *Ganzen*, das sich selbst verdaut; *Schlaf,* seine allgemeine Nacht; seine Tätigkeit nach außen, ebenso gegen sich; —denn das Andere ist es selbst, Vergewisserung seiner selbst an *ihm*, durch die innere Aufzehrung seiner} als Grund derselben, an dem die Individualität nur Form ist; der innere Organismus, das Fürsichsein, das zur Äußerlichkeit geworden. (*JS*, 159)

Satiated desire does not here mean that the individual produces itself as this singular individual; rather, [it produces itself] as universal, {*In the margin:* Inorganic nature is permeated through its entirety. — *Digestion* is here of the *whole*, which digests itself; *sleep*, its universal night; its activity toward the outside *[nach außen]* likewise goes against itself; —for the other is it itself, corroboration of itself in *it*, through the inner devouring of it} as ground of the same, in which individuality is merely the form; the inner organism, being-for-itself, has become externality.

Hegel's point appears to be that whereas inorganic nature is permeated by a kind of lapidary, impassive identity with itself, the animal achieves a more elevated, more reflexive, relation to the universal as such—both by ingesting elements of the outside world and by finding its partner out there in that same world. Yet when the organic individual, driven by cravings, achieves satiety, it enters into the long night of the anorganic, becoming the universal shell of its former self. Hegel continues with his proleptic outline of the whole:

Die befriedigte Begierde ist daher das *zu sich zurückgekehrte Allgemeine*—das unmittelbar *die Individualität* an ihm hat; —die theoretische Rückkehr—des Sinnes in sich bringt nur den *Mangel* im *Allgemeinen* hervor; die der Individualität aber dasselbe, als positives. Dieses {*Am Rande:* inneres Organ. Gefäß, Blut, System—*Herz*, Gehirn und Verdauung—Ganzer Organismus nachgebildet} Mangelnde ist mit sich selbst erfüllt—es ist ein gedoppeltes Individuum. Geschlecht—(a) Idealität, beide dasselbe—Allgemeine, Gattung, (Gehör)—(b) und beide selbständig— (Mangel des reinen Selbst erfüllt) —

Satiated desire is therefore the *universal that has returned to itself*—it has *individuality* immediately in itself; — the theoretical return—of sense to itself merely produces the *lack* in what is *universal;* whereas the [universal] return of individuality does the same thing, but in a positive way. This thing {*In the margin:* inner organ. Vessel, blood, system—*heart*, brain, and digestion—the entire organism modeled in this fashion} that is lacking is filled with itself—it is a doubled individual. Sexuality—(a) ideality, both the same—universal, genus, (hearing)— (b) and both autonomous—(lack of

Es tritt der unmittelbare gestaltete Organismus, und der innere fürsichseiende einander gegenüber; beide aber nicht mehr als unvollendete Seiten des Ganzen, sondern als vollkommene. — Kontraktion des ganzen Organismus, ein einfacher Typus desselben—Exkretion des Ganzen—(a) Testikeln, System der lymphatischen Gefäße als Gehirn—und (b) Penis, Herzmuskel—Gehirn und Fürsichsein—Weibliche Uterus entspricht der Prostata, die im Manne bloß Drüse ist—sein Empfangen, einfaches Verhalten, ist entzweit in das produzierende Gehirn—und das äußerliche Herz. (Ibid.)

pure self is now filled). — The immediately configured organism and the [organism that has] inner being-forself confront one another; yet both no longer as incomplete sides of a whole; rather, as complete. — Contraction of the entire organism, a simple type of it—excretion of the whole—(a) testicles, system of the lymphatic vessels as brain—and (b) penis, heart muscle—brain and being-for-self. — The female uterus corresponds to the prostate, which in the male is a mere gland—his conceiving, simple comportment, is split into the productive brain—and the external heart.

Hegel's comparison of the penis to the heart in diastole, and of the testicle to the productive, receptive brain, hence his *doubling*, *redoubling*, or *sundering* of the genital function—that is, the entire question of *Entzweiung* and *das Entzweite*—will be discussed in what follows. For the moment, it is clear that Hegel places special emphasis on these members of the male—especially the genital member itself, the external or, as Hegel will soon say, the *sundered* heart. The reference to *hearing*, at first so strange, has to do with the *voice* that Hegel hears in every animal when it is dying—and singing its swan song (*JS*, 157). Why the swan song is heard at the precise moment when the genus is being achieved through genital union is an arresting question: it is as though the universal will be heard only in the cry of pain, the pain of critical illness, which is perhaps merely echoed in the throes of sex. Hegel continues:

(Ihre Vereinigung ist das Verschwinden der Geschlechter—einfache Gattung ist geworden. (Assimilation als Absorbtion, Exkretion, und Nutrition entspricht der Sensibilität, Irritabilität und Reproduktion)

Krankheit ist Sukzession der Prozesse; diese kann der Organismus nicht aushalten; es tritt die Gattung, das Allgemeine ihnen gegenüber; —das Tier stirbt; Tod des Tiers Werden des Bewußtseins; es ist das Allgemeine,

(Their unification is the disappearance of the sexes—become simple genus.[)] (Assimilation as absorption, excretion, and nutrition corresponds to sensibility, irritability, and reproduction)

Illness is succession of the processes; the organism cannot withstand them; the genus, the universal, now comes to confront them; —the animal dies; death of the animal the becoming of consciousness; it is the universal

das die Prozesse geschieden in sich ertragen, sich analysieren kann; der Raum, worin sein Leben ausgelegt besteht—als Glieder, die einfache Prozesse an ihnen selbst—oder Prozesse, die unmittelbar ruhende allgemeine sind.) (*JS*, 159–60)

that bears the processes separately in itself and that can analyze itself; the space in which its life perdures as interpreted—as members—the simple processes in themselves—or processes that are immediately at rest, are universal.)

Here Hegel identifies the tripartite Brownian structure (sensibility, irritability, reproduction) with his own analysis of assimilation, which can be interpreted in terms of the three moments of absorption, excretion, and nutrition. A hasty outline of illness highlights the *succession* of processes in the animal—illness as the flattening out of once harmonic processes into a one-dimensional (and terminal) sequence—as the core of the mortal problem.[6] The principal thesis of the mature system, which moves from philosophy of nature to philosophy of spirit, appears almost without a breath in this phrase of the Jena lectures, a phrase without copulative: "Death of the animal the becoming of consciousness." Presumably articulating this dying and becoming is the song of the swan, sung without verse or refrain, without succession, in one instant.

Even more astonishing, however, is the way in which consciousness will follow the tack of the illness that spawns it. For just as illness exhibits itself in the *temporal succession* of organic processes, once the simultaneous give-and-take of animal organization has collapsed into the final ticking away of the hours and minutes, when life has become the sheer *Nacheinander* of a time that is just about up, so too does consciousness exhibit itself as "the universal that bears the processes separately in itself and that can analyze itself." No wonder consciousness loves to analyze things to death: that is what it is born to do. That is the sickness that gives rise to it. In chapter II, as we follow Hegel more closely in his analysis of the baneful force of illness, we will have to return to this troubling gestation—and contagion—of consciousness.

Now that the outline of sexuality and demise has been run through, Hegel's detailed treatment of the dialectic of genitality begins. And it begins with the type:

Geschlechtsteilen, männlichen und weiblichen, liegt derselbe Typus zum Grunde—nur daß in den einen oder den anderen der eine oder der andere

The same type serves as the ground for both male and female genitalia— except that in the one or the other this or that part constitutes what is essen-

Teil das Wesentliche ausmacht; bei dem Weibe notwendig das Indifferente, bei dem Manne das *Entzweite*—Gegensatz—dort der *Uterus;* diesen an den männlichen Teilen zu entdecken, hat die meiste Schwierigkeit gemacht; ungeschickterweise den Hodensack dafür genommen; da doch die *Testikeln* sich bestimmt als das dem weiblichen Eierstock Entsprechende ankündigen {*Am Rande:* Schubert Seite 185, in Heuschrecken, *Gryllus verruccivorus,* die großen Ovarien aus ähnlichen bündelweis gerollten Eierleitern bestehend ähnlich—*Breme,* die Hoden sind nicht nur in ihrem Umriß ganz ebenso gestaltet als die gröberen, größeren Eierstöcke; bestehen auch aus fast eiförmigen, länglichen, zarten Bläschen, die mit ihrer Basis auf der Substanz der Hoden aufstehen, wie Eier an einem Eierstocke. Vegetabilische Verknoten}, [der] in vielen Tieren—eine Reihe Bläschen ist; nicht aus dem begrifflosen Entsprechen, sondern der Unterschied, der durch den Begriff gesetzt ist— (*JS,* 160)

tial. With woman, this part is necessarily the undifferentiating; with the male, the *dirempted* part—the opposite—; in the former case, the *uterus.* It was exceptionally difficult to discover the uterus among the male parts: the scrotum erroneously taken to be that part. However, because the *testicles* assuredly announce themselves as what corresponds to the female ovaries, which in many animals prove to be merely a series of tiny blisters, {*In the margin:* Schubert, p. 185. In grasshoppers, *gryllus verruccivorus,* the large testicles are bundles of vesicles rolled together; likewise, the large ovaries are similarly rolled bundles of egg clusters. — *The gadfly:* the testicles are not merely formed in the same way, as rather coarse and large ovaries, but they also consist of almost egg-like, oval-shaped, delicate blisters that are attached by their base to the substance of the testicle, like eggs on an ovary. In the vegetable world, nodes} [the testicles correspond] not on the basis of some nonconceptual correspondence but through the distinction that is posited by the concept[.] —

That the same *type* grounds both male and female *human* genitalia demonstrates the *conceptual* destiny of the human species. That there is a specialization of *parts* demonstrates *either* that human sexuality permeates the human species, creating a *habitus* and a *Naturell* for male and female that (presumably) extend to the realm of spirit proper, *or* that human sexuality remains animal, failing always and everywhere to achieve the enduring genus, the perdurant universal. If permeation is the rule, it should come as no surprise that female introversion and male extroversion are expressed socially, culturally, and legally as well as genitally. If permeation fails, in spite of all these expressions of genital difference in the realm of objective spirit, it should not surprise us that the perdurant universal will be found in terminal illness alone—the terminal illness that spawns consciousness, theory, and conceptual anaylsis.

Hegel's sources for the "indifferent" or "undifferentiated" part are no doubt many. He has doubtless been inspired by Schelling's concept of the "state of indifference": in 1799 that state has to do with unmagnetized earth, dead matter, and the lowliest of potencies; by 1809 it has to do with the God of love and longing, the God of languor, hence with wom(b)anly matters. Perhaps Hegel is even agreeing with his enemies—such as Friedrich Schlegel—when he establishes this most powerful of synecdoches, declaring the matrix to be the undifferentiated part, the part that is pregnant with the undifferentiated whole that is woman. For Schlegel has Julius celebrate Lucinde's undivided wholeness—she is "one and indivisible *[Eins und unteilbar]*," and Julius would be happier than Hegel to discover the sexual terrain that reveals Lucinde's mysterious wholeness.[7] What is highly unlikely, however, is that Julius would choose the womb as the particular organ that expresses Lucinde's indivisibility and intensity. Indeed, where Lucinde is concerned, Julius seems content to wander, whereas Hegel insists on finding the focus. How odd it is, furthermore, that Hegel should designate that part to which a new life first attaches itself—a new life, a new identity, a *different* person—as the *undifferentiated* part. What could be more self-differentiating, at least where every mother's son and every mother's daughter is concerned, than the womb?

Derrida has noted the anomaly or the paradox of the female "undifferentiated" part: although the female part never strives to differentiate itself in Hegel's sense, that is, never strives to turn to the outside, and thus is as far from spirit as anything could be, it is *toward* that unity, *toward* that proximity to self, *toward* that *Ganz-bei-sich-sein*, that spirit will always tend. Every masculinism is a fugitive, frustrated feminism.[8] The male "dirempted" part, *das Entzweite*, a familiar word in both the Novalisian and Schellingian systems, is a passive participle that dreams of being an active voice verb, even an infinitive. In its eagerness to carry out the task of difference, to be itself *die differente*, the dirempted part is turned to the outside, in some way doubled or halved (the prefix *ent-* is notoriously ambiguous), and well-nigh sundered. Except that Hegel does not say "well-nigh." He says that the part, the member, the penis, is (at least according to one reading of the prefix) *sundered, cut in twain*. The suggestion of the twofold in *Ent-zwei* at first makes one think of the paired testicles, if not the female lips; yet those suggestions are equally false. For the testicles, even in the grasshopper, are morphologically and functionally related to the ovaries, which are enclosed, *ganz-bei-sich*, behind the gut wall of the female. No matter how difficult it is to understand precisely how the sundered or doubled part assumes the double function of male genitality, which should be brain *and* heart, innard *and* member, gland *and* tool, we cannot fail to note that the male part, the differentiating part, does precisely what the concept does in and for a rational system: conceptual determination and analysis is differentiation, distinction, movement to the outside. And this is what the heart in diastole does, at least when it drops from the rib cage and the gut wall and is almost expelled from the body.⁹

At this point in Hegel's text, the search is still under way for the corresponding part in the male of the female undifferentiated part, which, ironically, serves as a kind of anchor or Archimedian point for the analysis of the universal type:

[D]er Uterus sinkt daher im Manne zur Drüse, zur gleichgültigen Allgemeinheit herunter; er ist die Prostata im Manne—Dies hat Ackermann an seinen Hermaphroditen sehr gut gezeigt; er hat einen Uterus, bei sonstigen männlichen Formationen; aber dieser Uterus ist nicht nur an der Stelle der Prostata, sondern die *conduits éjaculateurs traversent la prostate et s'ouvrent séparement dans l'urètre au fond d'une lacune appellée verumontanum;* Ausführungsgänge des Samens gehen durch seine Substanz und öffnen sich an der *crista galli* in die *uretra* (Harngang). Die weiblichen Schamlippen enthalten die Hoden; —die Mittellinie des *Scrotums* dagegen ist gespalten, und bildet die *vagina.* Man versteht auf diese Weise die Umbildung beider Geschlechtsteile vollkommen. — (*JS*, 160–61)

Thus in the male the uterus sinks to the level of a gland, to indifferent universality; it is the prostate in males. — Ackermann has demonstrated this quite convincingly in his hermaphrodites: they have a uterus along with the usual male formations; yet not only is the uterus in the place of the prostate, but also "the ejaculatory tubes cross through the prostate and open separately onto the urethra at the base of a gap called the *verumontanum.*" The ejaculatory tubes of the semen pass through the substance of the prostate and open onto the *crista galli* in the urethra (the urinary tract). Female lips contain the testicles; — the seam of the scrotum, however, is split, forming the vagina. In this way one can understand perfectly the transformation of both genital parts. —

Precisely where—or whether—Hegel's description of Ackermann's hermaphrodites stops in the above lines is difficult to say. Yet that is irrelevant for purposes of spirit, which in a sense is universally hermaphroditic, or hermaphroditically universal, whatever the spiritual tinctures of the male and female *Naturelle*. The prostate, sinking to the level of a mere secreting gland, loses its elevated status as a reproductive organ and joins the lowly excretory system, as it were. Its sinking status recapitulates the strange conjoining of the highest and the lowest systems of animal life, a conjunction that itself recapitulates the strange excursion of spirit to the outside, exterior, and extrinsic in general. How fitting, therefore, even though Hegel does not say so, that the prostate is the seat of disease and death for so many males.[10]

However, we now leave the prostate behind and turn to the testicle, the forgotten half of male genitality, the doubled but not quite sundered half, and in some sense the productive yet inactive brain of the operation:

Wie im Manne der *Uterus* zur bloßen Drüse herabsinkt, so dagegen bleibt der männliche Testikel im Eierstocke eingeschlossen, tritt nicht heraus in den Gegensatz, wird nicht für sich, zum tätigen Gehirne, und der Kitzler ist im Weibe das untätige Gefühl überhaupt; das hingegen im Manne das tätige Gefühl {*Am Rande:* Blutergüsse weibliche—entsprechen der männlichen Bluterfüllung}, das aufschwellende Herz, Bluterfüllung der *corpora cavernosa* und der Maschen des schwammigen Gewebes der Uretra — Der Mann ist also das Tätige—dadurch daß diesen Unterschied seine Tätigkeit hat; das Weib aber ist das Empfangende {*Am Rande: Verdauung* nach außen gekehrt {{*Daneben:* metaphorisches Hingeben des Herzens und Seele an das Weib}} —Weib die Milch der Brust; —Mann, Bartwuchs äußere Bedeutungslosigkeit; abgestumpfte Waffen}, weil sie in ihrer unentwickelten Einheit bleibt. (*JS*, 161)

Just as in the male the uterus sinks to the level of a mere gland, the male testicle, for its part, remains enclosed in the ovary [of the female]; the testicle does not emerge and enter into its opposite, does not become for-itself, does not become an active brain. And the clitoris in woman is inactive feeling in general; in contrast to it, we have in the male active feeling {*In the margin:* Female menstruation—corresponds to engorgement in the male}, the upswelling heart, engorgement of the *corpora cavernosa* and the network of spongy tissue in the urethra. Thus the male is the active one—by virtue of his activity possessing this distinction. But the woman is the one who conceives {*In the margin: Digestion* turned to the outside {{*Next to this:* the metaphorical surrender of heart and soul to the woman}}; —woman, milk of the breast; man, beard growth, outer insignificance; weapon reduced to stubble}, because she remains in her undeveloped unity.

Hegel's insistence that the testicle (like its morphological and functional counterpart, the ovary) does not "emerge" sounds oddly pathological, as though referring to an incomplete gestation of the male fetus, or a failed adolescence. What is decisive for this poor brain, which, even though it is productive, is not an *active* brain, is the failure to "enter into its opposite." (To be fair, however, only in Leonardo Da Vinci's early drawings does the penis make it that far—all the way to its proper opposite, which ostensibly is not the vagina but the womb. If in fact the penis enters into its opposite in the *vagina*, then the latter is its functional—and perhaps also morphological—complement. Yet where and how does the vagina figure in Hegel's text, apart from that redoubled and undone scrotal seam in Ackermann's hermaphrodites?) Such entry into the opposite is defined as the for-itself, which, beyond the in-itself, must advance into exteriority and otherness in order to return to itself. Where does this occur? In the realm of *thought*, presumably, in the activity of the active *brain*. In the realm of the genital, however, the testicle does not succeed in becoming an active brain and has to take lessons from the upswelling heart. (To be sure, when one considers the testicle as productive of semen, or the ovary as the port of embarkation for the egg, both sperm and egg being eventually destined for the outside, these "inactive brains" seem considerably less lethargic than Hegel asserts them to be.) With regard to the testicle/brain and penis/heart parallels, Hegel may be thinking of the similarity of glandular tissue in brain and testicle, as of unstriated muscle in the heart and glans; yet the configuration of the tissue would in turn only mirror the movement and function—the differenting—of the organs in question.

The fact that the clitoris *(der Kitzler)* is now mentioned is strange, unless it is the morphological similarity of the clitoris to the "*active* brain" (which, to repeat, is not the testicle but the other male part) that makes the transition, or—and this is more likely—unless the negative reference to the "active" ("does not become an active brain") induces this reference to a (masculine gendered) agent, to wit, "the tickler," that is nevertheless entirely passive. Ironically, as befits the one who is the irony of the community,[11] the tickling agent is, Hegel assures us, "inactive feeling in general," although he does not give us an account of what this "in general" means, nor why he attributes to that organ so much generalizing importance and yet so little activity. What it is that actively feels the clitoris receives no comment either; perhaps Hegel would like us to think that it is the active brain that does this feeling? In any case, the inactivity of woman, already fully embodied in the synecdoche of her undifferentiated, purely receptive organ, her passivity now corroborated by the inactive clitoris, extorts the marginal note from Hegel on menstruation—blood loss—in the female and the contrasting accretion of blood in the male member, the "upswelling heart," the heart in diastole, the hyperoxygenated and hyperactive brain. In order to feel the full impact of the contrast, it would be necessary to review all the references to warm-bloodedness in Hegel's philosophy of nature.[12] The female genitalia constitute the scene of blood loss, and if woman is the flower of nature, that is because she is anemic.

Yet what about this upswelling heart and active brain on which Hegel places so much emphasis? Are we right in thinking that it has less to do with the *glans*, itself too susceptible to passive agitation, too much an eye and a mouth, than with the shaft? What about this part that is most properly a member, a *Glied*, turned to the outside? What about its aerial feats, its mobility and putative autonomy, its *movement* to the outside?

The network of spongy tissues in the urethra certainly deserves comment here, if only because Gaston Bachelard, in *L'air et les songes*, cites the *spongy* as that which the aerial type of poet or thinker cannot abide.[13] Hegel says nothing about the possibility that the spongy tissues will not function, will not retain the blood, will not enable the (well-nigh) sundered part to make its aerial move across space. Fortunately, male activity is guaranteed in the tautology or speculative statement according to which such activity possesses the distinction as such—precisely because the male member, *das Entzweite*, does what the concept does. The male member is Hegel's adaptation of Novalis's primal telegraph or semaphore: the original prosthesis of mouth, tongue, and eye, a prosthesis that is not as sensitive and passive as these receptive organs but made of sterner stuff, the original tool or organ of spirit. The dialectic of genitality thus functions as a microcosm of the logic of the concept—and not merely as one microcosm among many, since the entire analysis of nature culminates in genitality and the sexual relation. One might object that the woman is the one who conceives *(das Empfangende)*, not in the sense of logical grasping, but in the sense of sensibility and receptivity, in other words, as a result of her "undeveloped unity." Yet if her capacity to conceive is a sometime thing, and if Hegel will soon deprive her even of the privilege of conception, what gives him such confidence in the spongy wings of the heart? Are not they too receptacles of sorts? Are not they too sometimes a sometime thing? The concept does not countenance failure, however, and so, with lowered eyes and humbled heart and benumbed brain, my commentary continues.

Two further marginal notes strike us here, the first defining the milk of the breast as digestion "turned to the outside." Here the breast mirrors *das Entzweite*, not only morphologically but also functionally, or at least hydraulically. By contrast, the male secondary sex characteristics—the weapon that is reduced to stubble and television ads—are of relatively little consequence. Most intriguing, however, is this "metaphorical surrender of heart and soul to the woman," located in the text next to the reference to the breast. It is as though this surrender *(Hingeben)*—a word that is otherwise associated with the surrender of the woman rather than the man—of heart and soul (upswelling heart and active brain?) interrupted in some way the triumphant march of the sundered organ; it is as though the "digestion turned to the outside" in woman marked a kind of Novalisian sensibility and sensuality that defeats or deflates the male organ, bringing the mouth or mouths—the organ of *Empfängnis*, as Hegel calls it, the organ of reception or conception—once again to the fore. But to continue:

Die Empfängnis ist die Kontraktion des ganzen Individuums in die einfache sich hingebende Einheit {*Am Rande: Feuer, Wasser*, einfache Vorstellungen—so die organische Natur, nicht *analysiert* in ihre abstrakte Momente—Zerlegen ins Chemische— unsägliche Kleinlichkeiten; —sondern ihre Kraft eben *allgemein;* nicht *Säure, Kali*, ohne sich abzustumpfen}, in seine Vorstellung; der Samen, die einfache physische Vorstellung—ganz Ein Punkt, wie der Name, und das ganze Selbst. . . . (*JS*, 161)

Conception is the contraction of the whole individual into simple self-surrendering unity; {*In the margin: Fire, water*, simple representations—thus organic nature, not *analyzed* into its abstract moments, not dissected into chemical components, unutterable minutiae; —rather, its power is precisely *universal;* not *acids, bases*, reduced and without edge.} contraction into the representation of the individual; seed, the simple physical representation—altogether one point, like the name, and the entire self. . . .

Hegel here refers to the powerful analysis in Goethe's *Metamorphose der Pflanzen* of the contraction (*Zusammenziehung* in Goethe; here *Kontraktion*) that interrupts the expansion or dilation, that is, growth, in the plant. Contraction "into simple self-surrendering unity" seems to suggest the womb, the organ of undivided unity, in which (or at least in the vicinity of which) conception takes place. As we will soon see, however, Hegel will displace the contraction of conception; *Empfängnis* will occur elsewhere, as will the traditionally female *Hingebung* or surrender, and with surprising consequences. Meanwhile, the marginal note suggests that an elemental, chemical analysis is out of place here; perhaps Hegel is responding to that note in Kant's *Anthropology*, which moves from a discussion of acids and bases to sexual reproduction among human beings; perhaps he is responding to the tendency in Schelling to search for a unified (albeit bipolar) chemical and electromagnetic theory for organization. Yet let us return to the main body of the passage: contraction of the individual into a single, unified representation occurs in and as the male's surrender of seed or semen, which is altogether one point— "like the name, and the entire self." The reference to the *name* is strange, except perhaps to complete the patro-andro-phallo-centric structure that has been unfolding from the start: the name of the new individual will be passed along through the line that carries the surrendered seed of the father, ejaculated in the name of the father, who now, out of his own mouth, conceives the child. *Conception too belongs to the male*, even if *das Weib ist das Empfangende*.[14]

— Empfängnis nichts anderes als dies, daß Entgegengesetzte {*Am Rande:* Teil ist *Mittel*, wesentlich die Vermittlung}, diese abstrakten Vorstellungen, zu Einer werden. {*Am Rande:* Jedes Organ *dient*, aber zugleich wird dasselbe auf einfache Weise zu Stande gebracht (*Embryonen* leben; Notwendigkeit irgend einer Funktion wird widerlegt durch den Fall, wo diese Funktion nicht statt hat—) der Unterschied der Teile ist, daß diese Anstalten nicht einfacher—Maschinen können vereinfacht werden, und sind um so vollkommener—nicht so der Organismus; Wirklichkeit ist diese Momente heißt nichts {{*Daneben:* zur Materie Beweis}} so entwickelt zu haben; das bloße Resultat ist nichts—wie Glauben an einen geometrischen Lehrsatz}

Conception nothing other than the becoming-one of these counterposed parts {*In the margin:* The part is a *means;* essential is the mediation}, these abstract representations. {*In the margin:* Each organ *serves*, but at the same time each one is brought to pass in a simple way (*embryos* are alive; the necessity of any function is refuted by the case in which this function does not occur—). The distinction of the parts is that whatever is instituted does not become simpler—machines can be simplified and are the more perfect on account of this—the organism not so. Actuality is these moments, which means that nothing {{*Next to this:* toward a proof of matter} commands it to have developed in this way; the mere result is nothing—it would be like believing in an axiom of geometry}}

Much in this passage is obscure. The gist of it seems to be a reaffirmation of the contribution of both male and female to the living, highly complex embryo, the development of which is anything but a geometric demonstration or mechanical simplification. At all events, the cycle of reproduction has now closed, and Hegel summarizes the entire matter in what follows:

So hat der tierische Organismus seinen Kreis durchlaufen; er ist nun das geschlechtslose Allgemeine, das befruchtet ist; es ist zur absoluten Gattung geworden. Diese ist der Tod *dieses* Individuums. Niedrige tierische Organismen sterben unmittelbar nach der Begattung; {*Am Rande:* Geschlechtsverhältnis ist Totalität — *Gattung,* (a) *Dieselbigkeit* des Ganzen vollkommene Einheit an sich —(b) Gegensatz; Realität der Gattung, selbständige Individuen, die unmittelbar begehrend sind, d. h. denen die *Gattung* Zweck ist *die Existenz* der *Gattung.* Aber das tierische *Selbst* als solches ist nicht als solches ihre Existenz; sie zerfällt an ihm in drei Seiten (a) *Kind,* in sich vollkommenes Ganzes—*unmittelbar* daseiend (b) Ganzes, als Bewegung—in die nicht unmittelbare Einheit; Auseinandertreten der zwei *Selbst* am *Eins;* sein Resultat (c) Tod—die reine *Negativität;* unmittelbares *Nichtsein.*} wie die Blütenteile, die reine Eingeweide, keine Individuen sind; höhere Organismen erhalten sich noch, haben höhere Selbstständigkeit, und ihr Tod ist der entwickelte Verlauf an ihrer Gestalt. (*JS,* 161–62)

Thus the animal organism has passed through its cycle; it is now the genderless universal that is fructified; it has become absolute genus. The latter is the death of *this* individual. Lower animal organisms die directly after mating; {*In the margin:* Sexual relation is totality—genus: (a) *selfsameness* of the whole, perfect unity in itself—(b) opposite; reality of the genus, autonomous individuals who are immediately desirous, that is, individuals for whom the genus is the goal and who take the *universal* to be outside themselves {*Inserted:* interiority *in-itself* is *not* yet in *them*}; their mating is the *existence* of the *genus.* Yet the animal *self* as such is not as such its existence; in that self, existence breaks down into three sides: (a) *child,* a whole, perfect in itself—*unmediatedly existent;* (b) the whole as movement—into the unity that is not unmediated; diverging of the two *selves* in the *one;* its result; (c) death—pure *negativity;* unmediated *nonbeing.*} just as the parts of a blossom, its pure innards, are not individuals; higher organisms survive longer, possess a superior autonomy, and their death is the fully developed course of their configuration.

It seems as though Schelling's dream of a *sexless* universal has now been fulfilled, a source of duplicity found that is not itself twofold. That dream culminates in the death of the individuals involved in the sexual relation. For the individuals remain desirous: they have not yet wholly interiorized their sense of belonging to a genus. The animal self has as its moments the child, mating adults, and death. What must become clear in the following is the transition from (b) to (c), that is, from the movement of gender and genital divergence from the sexual rejoining to the inertia of death. "Higher organisms survive longer," to be sure. Yet what does their superior autonomy have to do with the permeating *habitus* of sex and gender? For even the flowers are now granted innards, though not the separation of the sexual parts into independent individuals. Are the *soi-disant* higher organisms still merely cluttering the stage? And what is the relation of illness to the "fully developed course" of the human configuration? Hegel begins to broach these difficult questions in the following transitional passage—on his way to the dire theme of illness and the dialectic of death.

| | |
|---|---|
| Er ist das Werden des Individuums zur Gattung (a) der noch unwirklichen, des Kindes, aber daseienden einfachen Einheit des Allgemeinen und der Individualität; (b) der nicht *wirklichen*, sondern abstrakt seienden; im Tier ist dies noch nicht vereinigt, daß die *wirkliche* Gattung unmittelbar als einfachallgemeine, als abstrakte da ist; sondern beides fällt auseinander; das Allgemeine hat die Form der Individualität, und wo sie diese ablegt, und als Gattung ist, ist sie unwirklich, nicht Subjekt, und zerfällt in die Extreme der in sich *beschlossenen* totalen Gattung, und der abstrakten *seienden; Begriff* und *Sein* getrennt, und das *wirkliche* Leben, das ihre Mitte ist, steht zwischen diesen Extremen. (*JS*, 162) | It is the individual's way of becoming the genus (a) of the still nonactual, of the child, nonactual yet existent, the simple unity of the universal and of individuality; (b) of the not *actual*, but abstractly existent; in the animal, this is not yet unified—the *actual* genus is immediately there as the simple-universal, as abstract; rather, the two diverge; the universal has the form of individuality, and whenever it divests itself of this individuality, and is as genus, it is nonactual, not subject, and it splits into the extremes of the total genus, which is *closed in* on itself, and of the abstract *existent*. *Concept* and *being* separate, and *actual* life, which is their midpoint, stands in between these *extremes*. |

When concept and being split, life is caught in between two extremes. But not for long, at least as far as the living individuals themselves are concerned. When individual existences fail to grasp the concept, *be* the concept, a second turn awaits them—a turn to the *inside*.

# CHAPTER ELEVEN

# Turned to the Inside

## THE DIALECTIC OF DEATH

$S$idereal pox, a leprosy of stars, a rash of celestial proportions—we have heard Hegel on the stars of the night sky. Schiller's and Beethoven's *Sternenzelt* is actually an *Ausschlag*, not quite the *Aussatz* of leprosy, but an irruption of ruddy pustules all the same. We have yet to hear him on krill and plankton, on the phosphorescent slime of the sea, which he compares to the nocturnal sidereal profusion. Although the rash of stars is no more sublime than the rash on a man's face or a swarm of flies (9: 81), the explosion of life in the sea cannot be taken so lightly—precisely because pox, leprosy, rash, and irruption all make sense only on the scene of life, which the snotgreen sea introduces, as though to emphasize at once the abundance and squalor of the living.[1]

The sea is everywhere amniotic, nurturing and parturing life, *gebärend* (9: 364). Sailors tell of the *blossoming* of the sea in the warm summer months; yet they are not speaking the sentimental language of flowers. "In July, August, and September the sea becomes impure, turbid, slimy . . . ," says Hegel, and such murkiness and impurity are the sure signs of the rampant geometry of life: "The sea is filled with an infinite amount of vegetable points, threads, and planes; there is a tendency to irrupt into plant life *[eine Tendenz zum Ausschlagen ins Vegetabilische]*" (ibid.). The phosphorescence of these creatures turns the sea into a living mirror of the night sky, except that the argent tain of the oceanic mirror is ooze. Hegel seems uncertain whether the sea blossoms with "a longer life" or a merely "momentary existence." In any case, the shimmering light of the sea, like the flickering gas lanterns on "Unter den Linden" in Berlin, shines with infinitely greater brilliance than all the scintillant stars. It is the mark of spirit, says Hegel, as though anticipating Heidegger's remark in "Building Dwelling Thinking," which seeks to resist the spirit of Hegel, that it turn night into day—not that it gape at the stars and ponder morality.[2] And yet the turbid sea, the *impure* sea, is septic: it is as though life begins with corruption and stench—for the sea does stink, Hegel assures us. Its "army of stars," its battalions of fluorescent squid and octopus, swim in the "indifferent womb" of the sea, the Melvillean sea that rolls on as it rolled five thousand years ago; these legion sea creatures eventually swim themselves to death, melting into the fishy element out of which they emerged (9: 364: *zerschwimmen schnell wieder in das Element*). Novalis says that water is the fish among stones, Hegel that the fish go watery. If the phosphorescence of the brine seems to betray an interior light, we must remember that it is also the light of the will-o'-the-wisp, the ghostly light of rotting wood and swamp. If every drop of water contains a universe of infused life, as Leibniz was convinced it did, each cosmic drop nevertheless dissolves into universal liquidity (9: 365: *in das Allgemeine wieder zerfließen*). As Thales and Anaximander must have noticed, god and thorny fish alike struggle to *escape* the womb that bears them; and as Ferenczi too realized, the sea is the source of *catastrophe* for everything that is born of it, which is everything that lives. The sea animal struggles onto the land—fish gasping on the strand, trying to think of themselves as amphibians—but the land itself emerged from the sea and will one day sink back into the sea, so that the bootless struggle goes on, no matter what the arena. Every force of nature is a dire force. The emergent land, forged by Vulcan and wrested from Neptune, bears the scars of its birth in water and fire. The forces that shape it too are dire forces. Even in the gigantic granitic mountain ranges we find "horrid traces of a frightful rending and destruction" (9: 347). And the calcium flakes that one discovers on high mountain slopes do not derive from the oyster shells dropped by careless picnickers, as Voltaire supposed, but from the skeletons, exo- and endo-, born of the sea but stranded on the heights now that the rest of the sea creature has reverted to water (9: 346).

As Hegel proceeds to the world of vegetation proper, the precariousness of life never passes from his field of vision. Plants are always thirsty. Like aliens, or frogs in the alchemical emblem, they have attached their mouths to the breast of Earth and will not desist. The spiral tubes within their green and fleshy stems draw by capillary action the "organized juice" of the soil. There is something crudely direct about their nourishment. Plants—blossoms apart—are gutless. They suck (9: 406). Eventually, they desiccate and die: "The plant, like the animal, kills itself eternally *[tötet sich ewig selbst]*, by opposing itself to being" (9: 408). As the animal becomes arthritic, the plant becomes woody. Both calcify. The fats of the plant coagulate, the oils crystallize, the sugar crystals harden. The plant is not warm-blooded but is ready now to produce warmth (ibid.). As with all nature (all nature in Hegel's eyes), the plant is ready for the Phoenix-fire that will release its final essences—the fragrance of burning potato plants on a field in November, the smell of a beechwood fire in the December hearth, both lit by the hand of man.[3]

Before we abandon the plant world to conflagration, however, we should take a closer look at vegetable assimilation, the sucking action of the plant. Hegel calls it *"immediate infection"* (9: 381). No doubt Hegel means by *infection* what Goethe meant by *intussusception*. Neither refers explicitly to pathology, even though today *intussusception* is a name for an invaginated section of bowel, bowel that begins to turn inside out and consume itself, calling for surgery. *Infection* as we know it is what we heard Schelling call *Ansteckung*, catching a cold, for example, by being invaded and contaminated by a bacillus or virus, or, as Schelling would have called it, an *animalcule*. Yet the infectious sucking of plants is not as innocent as it may seem. For all assimilation in vegetable and animal organization is, as Novalis, Schelling, and Hegel all observe, a kind of poisoning. And that is what makes such organization spiritual. Hegel declares *Infektion* "the infinite power of life," and explains:

> The living is something fixed and determined in-and-for-itself. Whatever it touches chemically on the outside is immediately transformed by this contact. The living therefore immediately overcomes the insolence by which it works its effects chemically and preserves itself in this contact by means of an other. The living immediately poisons this other, transforms it, as spirit does when it intuits something, transforming it and making it its own. For that something is *its* representation. (9: 402–403)

As it was for Novalis and Schelling, poisoning for Hegel is not so much the accidental ingestion of something that harms us but the attack by the ingesting party, without which no poison could work its deleterious effects. The seemingly innocent sucking by the plant transforms the minerals of the Earth into "organized juices," the juices into greenery, and if some of this greenery is foxglove and buttercup, poinsettia and hemlock, no Socrates should be surprised. Whether every Socrates is prepared to admit that his or her spiritual representation poisons what it claims to represent "objectively" or "neutrally" we may fairly doubt, however.

Such infection, as the simplest process of ingestion, later appears on the scene of animal life as well (9: 480–81). There too it reveals a feigned immediacy, behind which a complex transformation is in process. Part of that complexity is the *reversibility* of all assimilation, whereby one *becomes* what one *eats*, poisoning the other but taking it in for the good health of the self. For the ingestion of otherness *infects* the being that is in-and-for-itself. The living being *lets the other in*, and so *lets itself in for* otherness and exteriority *(Einlassen mit dem Äußeren)*. The sucking alien, as horrendous and as invulnerable as it may appear, is always sucking in its death along with its life. To let the other in, to let oneself in for the other, is the *negative* of subjectivity as organism. Portnoy complains that his mother watches like a hawk over every single bite he puts into his mouth. Yet she knows that infection is always rife, and that eating is ultimately dire.

Nor should we forget the implications of infection for plant reproduction. Inasmuch as reproduction in plants is a mere extension of assimilation, it makes sense that the pollination of a plant be regarded, as we have already heard, as "a *poisoning* of the pistil" (9: 425). Nevertheless, it is intriguing that Hegel should cite so often in these pages the famous Italian botanist Spallanzani, who plays a role, if I am not mistaken, in both E. T. A. Hoffmann's "Der Sandmann" and Nathaniel Hawthorne's "Rappaccini's Daughter." In the first tale, the eyes of Olimpia, the wooden puppet, are the fiery source of Nathanael's ardor and eventual death—for her hands and lips are cold and her voice rings like glass. In the second tale, Rappaccini's daughter infects the perfume of the purple orchid, imbibes it in some spiritual way, the orchid in turn infecting both her and her lover. Both tales are dire allegories that Hegel would have spurned as Monday's Children, if not Sunday's, for he could not have disowned or denied them entirely. Given such allegories, it makes sense that Hegel's very first addendum on assimilation in the animal organism should refer to *illness*. For illness is itself the mirror image of assimilation, and both of them touch upon sex: "The process directed toward the outside," Hegel begins, his expression *nach außen* fore-shadowing the active, masculine, phallic process that we examined earlier. Here, of course, the matter in question is the ingestion of food. "The process directed toward the outside is the *real* process, in which the animal no longer makes its own nature into its inorganic, as it does when it is ill . . ." (9: 464). It is as though the initial model for illness is self-assimilation, auto-ingestion, intussusception in the pathological sense. If assimilation embraces reproduction, however, at least in the vegetable organism, then Hegel may be driven to speculate on an automatism of genitality and sexuality lying universally at the core of illness. If illness is like eating oneself, consuming oneself, perhaps it is also like making love to oneself.

That is exactly what Hegel claims in his early *Realphilosophie*. Only hints of the relevant material remain in the *Encyclopedia* (see the addendum to §371). Rather than taking up these later hints, which are also hints concerning Schellingian *Hemmung* or inhibition,[4] let us instead revert once again to the more detailed account in the 1805/06 lecture course. We shall pick up Hegel's text where we left off at the end of chapter 10, with the separation of *concept* and *being* in animal (and human) reproduction. For the discussion of illness begins with this very separation. Once again we will examine the German text along with an attempted translation:

| | |
|---|---|
| Die Individualität in ihrem sich Aufheben entzweit sich in diese beiden Extreme; die Bewegung zum Ersten haben wir gesehen—die Bewegung zum Anderen ist die Krankheit, die zum Tode führt; —der Organismus, der vom Selbst verlassen; stirbt aus sich, an sich selbst. — Eigentliche Krankheit, insofern sie nicht absterben ist, ist der äußerliche, existierende Verlauf. — Die Notwendigkeit des Todes besteht nicht in einzelnen Ursachen, wie überhaupt nichts im Organischen; gegen einzelnes gibt es immer Hilfe; es ist schwach, es ist nicht der *Grund*. {*Am Rande:* ohne äußere Ursache; daß das Äußere Ursache sei, liegt selbst im Organismus.} Dieser ist die Notwendigkeit des Überganges der Individualität in die Allgemeinheit; denn das *Lebendige* ist als lebendig; die Einseitigkeit des *Daseins* als Selbst — Die Gattung ist die Bewegung, die sich aus dem Aufheben des *einzelnen* | Individuality in its self-cancellation splits into these two extremes; the movement toward the first [i.e., the concept] we have already seen—the movement toward the other [i.e., being] is illness, which leads to death. The organism, abandoned by the self, dies from out of itself, dies in itself. — Genuine illness, to the extent that it is not demise, is the external, existent course. — The necessity of death does not consist in particular causes. Nor does anything else in the organic realm. With respect to particulars one can always seek aid. Rather, the organic is weak, it is not the *ground*. {*In the margin:* without extrinsic *cause;* that the extrinsic is a cause itself lies in the organism.} This ground is the necessity of the transition of individuality to universality. For the *living* is as living; the one-sidedness of *existence* as self. — The genus is the movement that comes to be out of the canceling of the |

seienden *Selbsts* wird; und in dasselbe zurückfällt—*Seiende* Einzelne geht darin zu Grunde—*Sein*, diese Abstraktion, die in ihr Gegenteil übergeht. (*JS*, 162–63)

*particularly* existent *self* and falls back upon that same canceling of self. — In this movement, the *existent* individual goes to its ground [i.e., perishes: *geht darin zu Grunde*]. *Being*, this abstraction that passes over into its opposite.

The opposite of being is, of course, nothing. The separation of concept and being is called a split or sundering, *sich entzweien*, the word that is used to name the differentiating part, the *conceptual* part, as it were, of the male. Movement toward the concept will no doubt be the key to the otherwise mystifying coming-to-be of consciousness out of the death of the animal; for its part, the movement toward the other, that is, toward being, entails illness and death.[5] The organic is labile not because of particular susceptibilities but because it is not its own ground; its movement is therefore a going to the ground, a *zu Grunde gehen*, a perishing. (It is perhaps worth noting that the discrepancy between organism and being-a-ground is paralleled in Heidegger's *Being and Time:* the finitude of Dasein consists in its not being a ground, its being groundless, abyssal; whether in Heidegger's view the *organism* sustains any relationship to ground, however, is a more complex question.)[6] That the organism is susceptible to the external and extrinsic is, we recall, a corollary of the *pharmaceutical principle* of illness: a poison functions as such only when an organism seeks to organize it, that is, ingest it, only to discover that it is unassimilable.

We may summarize Hegel's argument thus far by saying that one-sided individuality must pass over to universality and that it will do so successfully only by moving toward the concept—beyond all genus and species—in thinking consciousness. Insofar as it insists on doing so as animal existence, individuality passes into the abstract opposite of abstract being. Lifeless individuality is nothing at all.

At this point in Hegel's text (all of which I cannot reproduce here, only the most telling parts), the discussion of illness and death proper, if one can say so, begins. Hegel discusses the general enervation of old age and death. When it comes to illness as such, he falls back on the Brownian structures of sensibility and irritability, and above all, for reasons Schelling has demonstrated, on the *proportion* or *disproportion* between these. If health is proportion, and illness disproportion, the question remains as to how sensibility and irritability can diverge. Hegel takes the disproportion between sensibility and irritability to be, in effect, a split between the *existing* organic self, on the one hand, and the *universal* self, the grasped self of the concept, on the other. In a marginal note he writes: "Health is *proportion* of the organic self to its existence; or the fact that, as *one*, it does not diverge into two *selves;* —*existing* self, *universal* self — *How is its existence susceptible of such disproportion?* — According to the concept, we have seen the necessity of this. — Now grasped in the opposition" (*JS*, 163n. 2). The "opposition" here referred to is the sexual opposition, in which *both sides* of the relation—regardless of the vaunted privilege of the differentiated male—fail to sustain a universal relation to the genus. The upswelling heart and modest brain of the male are ultimately as ineffectual as the undifferentiated part and inactive feeling in general in achieving such a universal relation. What Hegel will now go on to contemplate is the force of that redoubled opposition, the male and the female, in any given individual, whether man or woman—a redoubled opposition that will define divergence, disproportion, deviation, and illness as such. Whereas Schelling hoped to reach a universal, sexless sphere by such redoubling, Hegel will understand the redoubling in a strictly pathological sense. Perhaps Novalis is the thinker who is best prepared to think these two redoublings—the divine and the pathological—as one. Be that as it may, for Hegel, each human individual will prove to be sick with sex.

Health is equilibrium between the organic and anorganic. From the point of view of the organic, one can say that health is equilibrium between *being* and *self.* When the self as a determinate force is split, its being becomes increasingly subject to the sway of *external* powers, the *real*, which impinges on it as its negative. It is in this precarious split between being and self that a second split, a second doubling—to wit, the sexual opposition *within* every man and woman—proves to be fatal. We resume with Hegel's text (after an omission of fifty-three lines):

*Übelsein, Selbstgefühl*, wie Begierde, Gefühl des Mangels, d. h. es ist sich selbst als *Negatives;* es bezieht sich *auf sich* als Negatives, dies Mangelnde ist es Selbst, und es ist sich als Mangelndes; {*Am Rande: Verdauungsfieber*—Verdauung des *Ganzen*} nur daß bei der Begierde dieser Mangel ein ÄUSSERES

*Being sick, self-feeling*, like desire, a feeling of lack; that is, it is itself as *negative;* it relates itself *to itself* as negative. The one who lacks is its self, and it is its self as lacking {*In the margin: Digestive fever*—digestion of *the whole*}. It is only that with desire the lack is an EXTERNAL one, or a lack that is not

ist, oder das selbst nicht gegen sein *Gestalt* als solche gerichtet ist; in der Krankheit aber ist das negative Ding, die Gestalt. Krankheit[7] ist also eine Disproportion zwischen *Reizen* und *Wirkungsvermögen*—dies ist die wahre Bestimmung — Dies sind wahre Gegensätze, Reize, die Form des Daseins; {*Am Rande: abstrakte Momente*} (*JS*, 164–65)

directed against its very *configuration*. In illness, however, the negative thing is the configuration. Illness is thus a disproportion between *stimuli* and *efficacity*. This is the true determination [of illness]. These are true opposites, stimuli, the form of existence; {*In the margin: abstract moments*}

The sense here seems to be that what used to be felt as a lack in the individual self, whether ostensibly male or female, led that self *to the outside*, that is, induced the individual self to seek fulfillment in another. Now the lack comes home to roost. The marginal note seems to compare it to intussusception in the pathological sense, whereby the intestine begins to swallow itself in autoperistalsis. The configuration *[Gestalt]* of the organism, according to the mature system, is the very first moment of its realization, its growth and filling out, the moment that Hegel recounts prior to both assimilation and reproduction. Because the lack affects the very *figure* of the organism, and because the dialectic has now turned *inward*, the result will be fatal for the individual. Once again Hegel defines the disproportion that causes illness as a disproportion between external stimuli and internal capacity—in Brown's, Novalis's, and Schelling's language, between sensibility and irritability. It now remains for Hegel to descry in these an explicitly sexual connection, a connection for which the dialectic of genitality has prepared us:

[D]er Organismus kann über seine Möglichkeit gereizt werden, weil er ebensosehr *ganze* Einheit der Möglichkeit, Substanz, und Wirklichkeit des Selbsts, ganz unter der einen und der anderen Form ist; jenes theoretischer Organismus, dies praktischer. Der Geschlechtsgegensatz trennt dies, verteilt dies an zwei organische Individuen, *Wirksamkeit*, und *Reize;* das organische Individuum selbst beides, und dies ist *die Möglichkeit seines Todes an ihm selbst;* daß es selbst unter diesen Formen auseinander tritt; im Geschlechtsgegensatze sterben unmittelbar

The organism can be stimulated beyond its possibility, because it is equally as much *the whole* unity of the possibility, substance, and actuality of the self, entirely under the one or the other form; the former is the theoretical organism, the latter the practical. The sexual opposition separates this, divides this into two organic individuals, *efficacity*, and *stimuli;* the organic individual itself is both, and this is *the possibility of its death in its self,* the possibility that under these forms it diverges from itself. In the sexual opposition, only the specialized sexual

nur die ausgesonderten Geschlechts-
glieder—die *Pflanzenteile*. Sie sterben
hier durch ihre Einseitigkeit; nicht als
Ganze; als Ganze sterben sie durch
den Gegensatz der Männlichkeit und
Weiblichkeit, den jedes an ihm selbst
hat. — Wie bei der Pflanze die Stamina
zum passiven Fruchtboden aufschwillt,
die passive Seite des Pistills zum
gebährenden, so ist nun jedes Individuum selbst die Einheit beider Geschlechter; dies aber ist sein Tod; es ist
*nur Individualität*, dies ist seine wesentliche Bestimmtheit; nur die Gattung
ist in *Einer* Einheit, in einem *Eins*, die
Einheit vollständiger Individualitäten
ist, —als Selbst, nicht nur als Gattung
in seinem inneren Begriffe. Möglichkeit der Krankheit ist, daß das Individuum dies beides ist—im Ge-
schlechtsverhältnisse hat es seine
wesentliche Bestimmtheit *nach außen*
aufgegeben, insofern es sie im Ver-
hältnisse ist; itzt an sich selbst, sich
gleichsam mit sich selbst begattend.
(*JS*, 165)

members immediately die—the *parts of
the plant*. They die because of their
one-sidedness, not as wholes; as wholes
they die because of the opposition of
masculinity and femininity that each
one has in itself. — As in the case of
plants, where the stamens swell to become the passive basis of the fruit, the
passive side of the pistil becoming the
part that bears the fruit, just so, every
individual is now itself the unity of the
two sexes; but this is its death; it is
*mere individuality*, this is its essential
determinacy; the genus alone is in *one*
unity, in a *One*, the unity of a complete
whole. In individuality, this movement of both is the course that cancels
them, and its result is consciousness,
the unity that is in and for itself the
unity of the two complete individualities—as a self, not merely as a genus in
its inner concept. The possibility of
illness is that the individual is both of
these—in the sexual relation it has
surrendered its essential determinacy
*to the outside*, inasmuch as it is in relation; now, in itself, it is mating with
itself, as it were.[8]

The organic individual itself, at some undisclosed point (namely,
the point that leaps *inward* to another point, thus producing the line
of illness and demise), now becomes both sexes, both the stimulating
female and the active, irritable male; instead of being thoroughly
permeated and imbued with one side of the sexual opposition, the self
now becomes both, "and this is *the possibility of its death in its self*, the
possibility that under these forms it diverges from itself." Readers of
Hegel are accustomed to thinking of *one-sidedness* as the fatal flaw that
forces the dialectic to abandon all its figures one by one and move on
to others. Now, however, it is the *two-sidedness* of the self that proves
fatal. "Every individual is now itself the unity of the two sexes; but
this is its death." Novalis's poetics of the baneful has prepared us for
a move from the theory of illness to a theory of love, but Novalis took
that move to be an advance or ascent: "Every illness is perhaps the
necessary *commencement* of the more intense conjunction of two

creatures—the necessary beginning of love" (*Werke*, 2: 628). Now, however, what Novalis called "the closer conjunction of lovers" occurs *in one individual;* it occurs in and as the very figure of fatality.

Hegel's sexual analysis of illness, strange on its own terms, is also disconcerting for a time such as our own, which prides itself on the discovery of the endocrinological and hormonal spectrum, that is, the graduated scale of masculinity and femininity in any given individual—so that sexual identity is less a univocal genital destiny than a multifaceted and therefore always hazy gender identity. Further, gender identity is inculcated as much by nurture as by nature, inscribed as much by culture as by birth, and, some would aver, even a matter of free choice. The pride of an enlightened and emancipated twentieth-century conception of sexual identity—namely, the spectrum of imbricated identities—is, for Hegel, the very mystery of disproportion and death. Insofar as the individual organism can be stimulated by the outside, it is receptive, *conceptive,* as it were— female; insofar as the individual organism can move to the outside and alter its environment, achieving effects on the outer world that stimulates it, and thus differentiating that world, it is active—male. Insofar as the individual organism is bisexual, two selves in one, it is destined for death.

One might have hoped that this achievement of an intrinsically unified sexuality in one organism would resolve the problem of the turn to the outside, the problem of letting oneself in for the external, which is the secret of toxicity and death. Yet the toxin is already within: the stimuli (or charms, *Reizen*) that disturb the equilibrium of the active individual work their effects from within, usurping the very function of irritability. It is as though when we become terminally ill we mimic Hoffmann's Nathanael, gazing through the spyglass of our own *Perspektiv* at the utterly charming, endlessly stimulating Olimpia, who is nothing other than Nathanael's projections onto dead wood—which is what he too soon shall be. One might have hoped that this fusion of both sexes into one individual would put a halt to the wicked infinity by which, generation after generation, each individual is invariably but one half of the genus, a wretched σύμβολον of the whole, never more than that. But no, the fusion itself is illusory, driving every Nathanael and every Clara to his or her or its individual death.

As Freud well knows, it is the excessive quantity of *inner* unbounded energy that is so detrimental to the organism. And so it seems to Hegel. Yet the mystery that Freud also puzzles over in his 1895 *Entwurf*, the puzzle of the origin of *quality*, that is, the origin of *consciousness* out of primary process—this mystery, too, Hegel confronts as forcefully as he can. He announces, as though it were perfectly clear simply because the ascetic tradition has always insisted on it, that the death of the individual organism, which is due to the presence of both male and female sexualities in it, itself *produces* consciousness: "In individuality, this movement of both is the course that cancels them *[der Verlauf, der sie aufhebt]*, and its result is consciousness *[und dessen Resultat das Bewußtsein ist].*" It is as though, in the higher organism that is the human being, sexuality so permeates the individuals that it kills their bodies proleptically, deadens them ahead of time, while they are still alive, and this (gradual? sudden?) dying of or to or by sexuality, this *mortification* of the flesh, illumines the pristine light of consciousness. Whereas the mating of animals—including the human variety, the "perfect" variety—produces one-sided individuals into infinity, the proleptic fusion of male and female in each of the one-sided individuals produces consciousness—along with (or after?) the illness and death of the conscious individual.

One would like to know more about this genesis of consciousness from the death of the one-sided animal that acts as though it were two-sided—and thus is fatally ill. Is that the story told in Hegel's *Phenomenology of Spirit*, at least at the point where consciousness becomes *self*-consciousness by passing through the universal liquid medium of *life*, the medium of *desire?* Yet does the *Phenomenology* account for this thoroughly permeating sexuality that underlies consciousness itself, even at the most natural level—the consciousness of sensuous certainty? Finally, does the *Phenomenology* offer an account of the most telling configuration of consciousness, namely, the one that is born of terminal illness? Is terminal illness the spume of infinity, flowing from the absolute's cup on the Place of the Skull? These questions cannot be readily answered. And they certainly cannot be answered here. They would require a new reading—an infectious or contagious reading—of Hegel's early masterwork.

Yet there is a more awkward question still, as Hegel now reverts to the nosology of bisexuality. For the thorough permeation of one individual by the two sexes produces consciousness only by first inducing death—which does not function proleptically. The immediate result of bisexuality is that the organism mates with itself—and that such introverted sexuality is its death, and this death its consciousness. The order of implication must somehow also be a genetic order: first, self-mating, illness, and death; second, consciousness. The light of consciousness is Phoenix-fire, rising from the pyre of male and female in any given human individual. A pyre—no longer a Novalisian calyx or a Schellingian conjugal bed—on which sexual duplicity is burned. When the organism turns on itself in an interior way, when it eschews the search for its completion on the outside, even though that search too was ultimately futile, it makes itself sick, sick unto death. Now, fumbling with itself, pawing itself, it is engaged in a kind of desperate autoerotic necrophilia: "Now, in itself, it is mating with itself, as it were."[9]

Perhaps we need not follow in detail Hegel's account of the organism's final divergence from itself, its *auseinandertreten*, in illness. That divergence is expressed in the organism's desire to mate with itself, to turn utterly inward in ardor and longing. The mirror of this narcissistic preoccupation is of course the inward-turning reflection into self, which is consciousness as self-consciousness. Or, to put it the other way around, which Hegel—for reasons—does not, the consciousness of self mimics this impossible but feverish mating of self with self; the mind attempts to attune its solar and lunar selves, to bring its rational, receptive, and proprioceptive selves into harmony at last. Not only does consciousness assimilate the world, poisoning whatever offers itself to representation, stinging it, paralyzing it, and sucking it dry; consciousness now takes the inward turn and, doubling up on its male and female bodies, poises itself to mate with its stimulating inner self alone. Consciousness of self is the attempt, as Matthew Arnold has Empedocles say, "To see if we will poise our life at last."[10] A phenomenology of (self-)consciousness would have to see itself as the foreplay, the coitus, the orgasm, the slumber, and the reawakening of desire in this ineluctable narcissism; it would have to present *(darstellen)* this autoeroticism that gives itself out phenomenologically as an autonoesis. A phenomenology of the shapes of consciousness would have to experience such autoeroticism not as merely *natural* consciousness but as the sole consciousness there is, the conscious, presentational "we" of phenomenology, the multisexed "we" that will have arisen from the burning bed and charred calyx of the mortified self. The very feverishness of the individual's frustrated self-mating, however, intimates something about the final crisis of the phenomenological illness, the crisis that is announced by *fever*. We take up Hegel's 1805/06 Jena lectures once again (after an omission of thirty-two lines):

Die {*Am Rande: Drittes Stadium;* dem RUHIGEN *allgemeinen* Selbst gegenüber wird das Ganze als unterscheidende *Bewegung, Fieber.*} eigentliche Konstitution der Krankheit ist nun, daß {*Am Rande:* Der Organismus setzt sich als Ganzes gegen die Bestimmtheit; —er als *Ganzes* wird ein Bestehen, die einzelne krankhafte Affektion verwandelt sich in *das Ganze,* das in Bewegung gerät; —schlägt sich in den Kreis der Notwendigkeit auseinander; weil es Kreis, das Ganze.} der organische Prozeß sich nun in dieser befestigten Gestalt verläuft, in diesem Bestehen, d. h. daß die Prozesse eine *Aufeinanderfolge* bilden; und zwar die allgemeinen Systeme auseinandergerissen, nicht unmittelbar eins sind, sondern diese Einheit durch die Bewegung, Übergehen des einen in das andere darstellen. *Fieber,* dies ist denn die eigentliche reine *Krankheit,* oder der kranke individuelle Organismus, der sich *befreit* hat, von seiner *bestimmten* Krankheit, {*Am Rande:* eben weil er das Ganze krank macht} wie der gesunde von seinen bestimmten Prozessen; Fieber ist also das reine Leben des kranken Organismus; zugleich als dieser Fluß der Funktionen, ist es die *Bewegung,* die Fluidisation derselben, so daß durch diese Bewegung zugleich die Krankheit, eben das Fixieren einer Funktion aufgehoben wird, die Krankheit verdaut wird; es ist ein Verlauf in sich, und gegen seine *unorganische* Natur gekehrt, Verdauung von Arzneimitteln. (*JS,* 167)

{*In the margin: Third stage:* in contrast to the CALM *universal* self, the whole becomes a distinguishing *movement, fever.*} The genuine constitution of illness is that the organic process, now in its firmly established configuration, in its perdurance, runs its course; {*In the margin:* The organism posits itself as a whole in opposition to determinacy; —as a *whole* it becomes perdurant, its particular morbid affection transforms itself into *the whole,* and this illness *of the whole* is at the same time *a healing,* for it is the *whole* that begins to move; —it shatters itself as it slips into the circle of necessity; because it is a circle, the whole.} that is, the processes constitute a *sequence;* —indeed, the general systems are torn apart, are no longer immediately one; their unity is presented only through movement, through the transition of the one into the other. *Fever,* then, is the genuinely pure *illness,* or the sick individual organism that has *liberated* itself from its *determinate* illness {*In the margin:* precisely because fever makes the whole ill}, in the way that the healthy have liberated themselves from their determinate *processes;* fever is thus the pure life of the sick organism. At the same time, as this flux of functions, it is the *movement,* the fluidization of these functions, so that through this movement the illness—precisely the fixating of a function—is canceled, the illness is digested; illness is a course in itself and is turned against its *inorganic* nature; digestion of pharmaceuticals.

Here we arrive at the notion of *sequence*, which Hegel earlier described as that which the individual organism cannot withstand. In illness the organic process as a whole *runs its course*. One cannot help but think of the sequence of developmental stages in Schelling's *First Projection*, although in Hegel the sequence induces death, not the absolute. Unless, for both thinkers, these are one and the same. All the systems that go into producing an organism—the respiratory, assimilatory, circulatory, urogenital, and so on—find themselves in flux, melting into one another in the way that the tiny sea creatures melt back into the elemental ocean. This ocean, however, appears on the brow of the dying one. The one in agony finds himself dissolving, going elemental, freed at last from the fixations of his particular affliction; indeed, his morbid affection has by now become an affection for his inner opposite sex. The one in agony—perhaps he is in a military hospital in Djakarta, dying of inflammatory fever—perspires away his and her life alike, exhaling not only his and her disease, but also his and her mortal coil as such. Shattering all fixated, one-sided identities, the one in agony finally succeeds in following the logic of the concept. At last the action of *Aufhebung*, so recalcitrant to the understanding, can be grasped, at least insofar as *cancellation* may be understood as *relieving*. Fever relieves the fixation caused by illness. It makes the particular malady an illness of the whole; it is the good health of the dying individual. Fever accompanies the movement of the whole as it breaks out into (not out of) the vicious circle and becomes a distinguishing movement. Fever is the unspoiled life of the sickness in the individual; it is also convalescence, since the one in agony will soon be cured of what ails him and her. Fever marks the *crisis*, the moment of total divorce, the ultimate separation, the final excretion. The dying manwoman consumes by fire the inorganic nature of his and her illness, and the digestion *of* or *by* pharmaceuticals to which Hegel refers (*Verdauung von Arzneimitteln*) is as much the consumption *of* the individual *by* the medicaments as the reverse. Thus the entire metaphorics of health and illness melts and swirls in indeterminacy, in imminent immanent crisis—mating with itself, as it were. And that foundering metaphorics takes the logic of the concept with it.

In the final pages of his analysis of the organic realm in the philosophy of nature, Hegel refers several times, and always emphatically, to the *crisis*. The problem with chronic illness, of course, is that it postpones the crisis. Chronic illness produces no fever—until the time of the organism is up. Doctors speak of a fever *breaking*, and it is this critical *fracture* that they anxiously await; or, in modern times, they try to keep fever from reaching the critical point, the threshold, at which it—or the patient—might break. Hegel is not interested in quelling the crisis, however, inasmuch as the crisis—the burning fever—is the whole, the undifferentiated burning matrix from which spirit will be born: "The *crisis* is the organism that has become master of itself" (*JS*, 168); and "*Crisis* is digestion in general, and at the same time an excreting" (ibid.). Again, the mastery of the organism in crisis lies in its self-mating, self-digesting, and self-excreting activity, all the automatisms that are soon to be stilled and fulfilled in death, so that the only efficacious automatism—that of cogitative consciousness—can be born. Whereas prior to the point of crisis fever is *"insidiously lingering,"* all the processes of the digesting and excreting organism now become "untethered," each process "operating for itself alone," although the battlefield that the organism has become in the civil war of life will soon reverberate to silence.[11]

At the end, or at least the end as we possess it, inasmuch as the holograph of Hegel's early lectures on nature philosophy breaks off with the words *Die Krise*, Hegel brings together the two moments of illness and death as he is thinking them here—the moments of internalized sexuality and of fever. After an omission of fifty-seven lines of text, we present here the final lines of the extant manuscript of the Jena philosophy of nature:

Wie zuerst *der Gegensatz von Männlichkeit und* Weiblichkeit *unüberwunden* in den Organismus fiel, so bestimmter der Gegensatz dieser *abstrakten Formen* des Ganzen, die im Fieber auftreten, oder des Ganzen in diesen Formen gesetzten, Abstraktionen, die mit dem Ganzen erfüllt sind—*die Individualität* kann *ihr Selbst nicht so verteilen,* weil es nicht ein allgemeines ist. (Der *empfindende* Organismus ist nicht zugleich der Schauder des Fieberorganismus, der in sich selbst alle seine Teile in der Einfachheit des Nerv aufgelöst, in die einfache Substanz zurückgehen fühlt. — Der begehrende ist ebenso gegen Äußeres gekehrt; er ist nicht die Hitze, das Fürsichsein, welches sich selbst der Gegenstand, und nach der *eigenen*

Just as *the unovercome opposition of masculinity and* femininity first overwhelmed the organism, the more determinate opposition of these *abstract forms* of the whole that emerge in fever [now overwhelms it], or the opposition of the whole that is posited in these forms, these abstractions that are filled with the whole. *Individuality* cannot *divide up its self in this way,* because it is not a universal. (At the same time, the *receptive* organism is not in itself the shudder of the fever-ridden organism, all of whose parts dissolve in the simplicity of the nerve, so that it feels itself regressing into simple substance. — In the same way, the desirous organism is turned toward the external; it is not the heat, the being-for-self, which is itself the

Substanz und Wesen begehrt, die sich selbst das Negative ist. — Die Krise (*JS*, 169)

object, and which desires its *own* substance and essence, which is itself its negative. — The crisis

Hegel's manuscript breaks off here. Or, to give the *fatum libellorum* its due, these are the last pages of the *Naturphilosophie* manuscript that have survived. Down to its final words, the sexual opposition, the ardent opposition of masculinity and femininity, overwhelms the organism in the way that fever will ultimately consume it. The heat that wants its own substance and essence—that is what once seemed to be reserved for animal life, at least the warm-blooded variety, but also for plant life, as its sugars and fats harden into fuel. In the end, however, the fever within, which turns each sex to the other in exhalations of love, will turn against them both. For they will have already contaminated one another before they ever meet. Male and female are contagion to one another, whether their contact be external or internal, whether they collide in sex or languish in sickness, whether their anastomosis be by word of mouth or genital orifice or phantasm. Arising from such contagion, to be sure, is consciousness—spirit proper, as it were. Yet one must wonder whether spirit retains the mark of its birth in the sweat of its brow and the involuted exhalations of its sexes.[12]

What was Hegel about to say concerning "the crisis"? What does he know of the crisis—the regression to simple substance, the hyperaesthesic nerve, raw sensibility, the inactive brain? Does he think of it in the way that Schelling will soon think of it, namely, as the ultimate divorce of good from evil in the ground of God? Or does he think of the crisis in terms of its duplicitous products, consciousness and death—death first, consciousness second? Or does he come to see that this sequence, like every other sequence, is itself illness and death, and that the crisis must rather be a matter of simultaneity, with the Siamese twin(s) of death and consciousness, consciousness and death, inseparably joined? So that his doctrine of consciousness will always have to wait upon the practice of dying and being dead? So that his practice of consciousness will always mean the death of anyone who seeks to understand it? What a triumph that would be . . .

# CHAPTER TWELVE

## *Conclusion*

A  TRIUMPH  OF  ASHES

$\mathcal{T}$he secret of finitude, in Hegel's view, is the outerdirectedness of life. Life turns outward in order to replenish itself by eating, and it eats what nature puts in front of it. "For the [living] individual, inorganic nature is something presupposed, merely found there; in this consists the finitude of the living" (9: 464). Life also turns outward in order to reproduce itself sexually, to replace itself with the following generation, and although this outward turn may seem to be a more fecund one, the results are much the same. Whether in eating or in sex, it all comes down to craving: "The practical process [once again, of assimilation] is, to be sure, an alteration and a cancellation of external anorganic nature with respect to its autonomous material subsistence; yet it is a process of unfreedom, because the organism in its animal craving *[Begierde]* is turned to the outside *[nach außen gekehrt]*" (9: 472). Even when the process of unfreedom turns to the inside, with the sexual opposition in the sick individual feverishly elaborating his and her death, the problem of the process as a whole can be defined in terms of its exterior and extrinsic tendency. And now that the word *freedom*, or *unfreedom*, has fallen, Hegel allows himself a brief disquisition on human pain and on what Novalis calls the *baneful*, a disquisition we ought to follow here at the end of our investigation.[1]

Not even in acts of practical willing are human beings free, notes Hegel, inasmuch as precisely in such acts there is a relation to the *real*, something in and of the outside world. Rather, only in the rational will, the theoretical will, is the human being free. In acts of the practical will, the human being feels that he or she is dependent, not truly for-self; something other, something negative, is necessary for it, beyond the merely contingent. "That is the unpleasant feeling of need," Hegel comments (9: 472). He continues:

> The problem of the three-legged stool is the problem that is in us. It is already a problem with life itself, yet there it is relieved [aufgehoben], because life knows its barriers as a lack. It is thus a privilege of higher natures to sense pain; the higher the nature, the more unhappiness it feels. The great human being has a great craving; and he has the drive to relieve that craving. Great deeds arise solely out of the profound pain within our heart of hearts [Gemüt]. The origin of the baneful, etc., has its solution here. (Ibid.)

It is strange that the featherless bipeds should, at the end, be brought back to the riddle of the Sphinx: the three-legged creature that never achieves poise and balance appears to know less than life itself, which at least "knows its barriers as a lack." The higher the nature, the greater the misery. Those who clutter the stage are not happy. They are in pain, and they cannot stop craving. Human craving, *Begierde*, surpasses even the animal's feral urge. Nothing will sate it. The heart of hearts, the labyrinth of the human mind, the untranslatable *Gemüt*, no longer takes heart in its confrontation with raging seas, howling blizzards, or towering cliffs. Its storms and its heights are within, and from them there is no refuge, no relief. What then does it do with an outside that forever taunts it with reflections of its own finitude? It lights a fire, ignites the extrinsic, and watches the outer nature burn.

Nature is the hull or empty husk, the chaff, its ethereal oils and sugar crystals now fuel for the fire of spirit. Nothing that lives is of the measure of spirit, nothing vegetable, nothing animal: all of it taken together and weighed in the balance is *unangemessen*. It does not measure up. The idea must therefore "break through the circle" of life, must not allow its encompassing third to be merely a differently sexed and partial individual. For even a third that amalgamates both sexes is lethal. The idea therefore calls upon death to relieve the individual and establish the species once and for all: the genus *as thought* is immortal, the existent universal, to which the mortal is always inappropriate.

> This is the *transition of the natural* [des Natürlichen] *into spirit*. Nature has completed itself in the living and has made its peace, by inverting itself [umschlägt] to something more elevated. Thus spirit has gone forth out of nature. The goal of nature is to kill itself and to break through the husk of

its immediacy and sensuousness; as Phoenix, to burn itself, in order to emerge rejuvenated as spirit from this exteriority. (9: 538)

A philosophy of nature does not merely want to lose nature but to reconcile itself to nature, says Hegel. Yet that reconciliation can only be a liberation from nature (9: 539: *Befreiung von der Natur*), an acquiescence or active participation in its suicide, a willingness to ignite it and watch it burn. Reconciliation occurs only through the insight that nature is—if we may listen once again to that one desperate voice in *The Apprentices at Saïs*—the frightful mill of death. Yet it is, in Hegel's putatively reconciliatory view, a mill that grinds itself away to ash. Triumphant idealism celebrates spirit as the wake of the living. For only in the fires of the funeral pyre can the contagion of life—the infection, the contamination, the poisoning, the polluting—be purified. Purification is pyrification. And the only spiritual voice that is left at the end is the one that bears and masters the fires of reduction, the voice that intones:

> *Ich bin der Geist, der stets verneint!*
> *Und das mit Recht; denn alles, was entsteht,*
> *Ist wert, daß es zugrunde geht.*

> I am the spirit, who always negates!
> And rightly so; for everything that comes to rise
> Is worthy of its own demise.[2]

There are other, less furious spirits, of course, where nature is concerned. Among these are Novalis and Schelling, who are not driven to proclaim the suicide of all nature. Both see the dire forces of nature as clearly as Hegel does. Yet neither thaumaturgic nor tormented idealism ignites the philosophic holocaust. It is true that Novalis sees the hierarchy of forms in nature as marked by death— the death of the stone being the life of the plant, the death of the plant the life of the animal. In Novalis's final reflections, God himself appears as the most compact metal, the most dense matter, the deadest of dead materials, whereas life-giving air is "of the devil." It is also true that Schelling at times dreams of a final purgation of sex and an ultimate convalescence from life—in death. Yet neither Novalis nor Schelling mortify nature and naturalness in order to obliterate the debt of the death we owe to nature, not even when the forces of life are most dire. They work at their magic, they labor over their torment. It is curious that the triumphant philosophy, the philosophy that triumphs over its opponents and over nature and life as well, speaks with the voice of death, promotes the program of death. Curious also that in our time the voices of life—a life in dire straits, to be sure, but still, a life—are all but unheard in academic circles. A culture continuously in terror of the body, the body that haunts the bearer today as it haunted our puritan forebears, a culture inventive of new ways to hold the others at bay and to keep the self in sterile isolation, will doubtless always find the voice of death more congenial. Yet if other voices have risen in more recent times—those of Nietzsche, Merleau-Ponty, Irigaray, Cixous, Blanchot, and Derrida, to name only a few—surely the voices of Schelling and Novalis will not be muted forever.

However, is there not something puerile in this opposition of Novalis and Schelling to Hegel? Is it really a matter of removing the laurels from Hegel's furrowed brow and hoary head, distributing them elsewhere? Is it really a matter of prosecuting Hegel for arson? Or is it instead a matter of learning to read Hegel, along with Hegel's greatly underestimated contemporaries, in a new way? If the latter, then it is surely something that has been going on for a long time, at least since Kojève and Hyppolite. If this be conceded, I would say only that Hegel's philosophy of nature is perhaps a privileged place for learning this new kind of reading. For nowhere is the system of reason so at peril as it is here; nowhere is it so difficult to see the necessity of its advances; nowhere does it seem so exposed to contingency and accident, nowhere does its dialectical legerdemain seem such a transparent sleight of hand. Indeed, this is what Hegel himself—or one of the Hegels—tells us in his lectures on the philosophy of nature.

What we notice in Hegel's philosophy of nature is actually something that happens throughout his system, whether in the logic, the aesthetics, the philosophy of history, or the philosophy of right: the detailed analyses, which become more telling and more compelling precisely as they become increasingly detailed and get closer to the ground, as it were, never quite manage to advance from one analysis to the next as the system demands. The student of the system is forced to move on because every temporary outcome or result is summarily declared "one-sided, bloodless, and abstract," even though the student finds it multifaceted, concrete, and gory. Nevertheless, the system demands that one go on, abandoning the splendid accidental booty that may have fallen to one's reading, surrendering it for the sake of the larger picture—which is of course the picture of a maudlin and somewhat jaded but otherwise entirely predictable Christendom. The larger picture, however, is never as rewarding as the bits and scraps, nooks and crannies, accidents and windfalls of the text. Hegel is a thinker not because he sees to it that his system always triumphs but because he is always biting off more than his system can chew, because he is always exposing his system to chronic indigestion—and even to poisoning. Or, to move from assimilation to reproduction, because he is always seeking that perfect polymorphic otherness out there in the world. There is admittedly a sense in which he will always want to cover his tracks and hedge his bets, will always want to insist on his capacity to swallow it all and embrace everything in the name of spirit, that he will restrict his economy forever. Yet the system's excreta, the logic's effluvia, the recalcitrant moments, the *caput mortuum* that will not be buried but keeps popping up like Finnegan, and all the ones that got away—the procession of these *faux pas* is what exhibits the greatness of the system. The splendor in Hegel's case as well, and not only in Schelling's or Novalis's, lies in its failures. Its triumph is always a triumph of ashes.[3]

Schelling fails always more awkwardly, more visibly, more painfully than Hegel does. Schelling does not cover his tracks nearly so well, and his bets are always desperate and extravagant: they lead him into bankruptcy. Instead of a monism of spirit, a fatherly One, Schelling again and again confronts duality and duplicity. For him, the word *dialectic* is equivalent to trumpery and deception: it is the logician's trick, the sophist's fancy footwork, designed to distract the system from its perpetual demise. There are moments when the collapse seems to be accepted too complacently, as when Schelling too declares death the cure for a life that always cuts us in twain. Yet these moments always pass, as Schelling insists on the cut, the sundering, the divorce, the crisis—and may the rational system take the hindmost. At times, perhaps most of the time, the *pathos* of the Schellingian system is tragic. The reader is in an operation theater, observing surgery on a patient who, however maudlin and jaded, is still alive. It is a surgery in which the origin of all things is being vivisected. All the cuts and plunges Schelling makes are necessary ones, but they go deeper and deeper, and the patient—call him or her God, or the One, or Homogeneity—begins to hemorrhage. Schelling calls out for sutures and clamps, works feverishly to staunch the bleeding, ties every knot he knows how to tie, but we observers know that his patient will soon be a shade and that we will have entered into the end.

After such Hegelian and Schellingian dramas, Novalis's story can only seem tame, and Novalis himself bemused. He seems capable of dreaming on as the world about him goes up in smoke. An impoverished aristocrat, a Quixote, he seems to dabble in science and philosophy until his untimely end puts an end to his education. One can even understand Hegel's inability to resist the temptation to mock Novalis's lights—those lungs that hollowed out—as though Novalis were a character in *The Magic Mountain*. The more we read Novalis's astonishing notebooks, however, whether early on in his *Fichte-Studien* or later on in his *Blütenstaub, Logologische Fragmente*, and *Allgemeine Brouillon*, the more complex becomes the network of his studies. They never form a system proper, nor even a loosely bound encyclopedia; but the energy of the particular analyses and the scope of them all begin to stagger us. I have said little or nothing in this volume about Novalis's hieroglyphics, semantics, and graphematics; about his understanding of tragedy, fable, and fairy tale; about his critical reading of Goethe's *Wilhelm Meister* or his notes to Friedrich Schlegel's *Ideas*. Especially for English-speaking readers, there are uncharted worlds awaiting exploration.

Yet we have seen enough to conclude that Novalis too knows of ashes. His devotion to wisdom, to Sofie, is a devotion to (the) death. We must worry about him, as we worry over Walt Whitman on the shoreline, rapt to "that low and delicious word."[4] Novalis does not always dream or brood, however; he inspects, as a superintendent of mines ought. And even if his initial project is to advance from the ego, through the not-I, to God, he sails beyond all ontotheology and metaphysics of origins to a thought of contagion and contamination, a thought of complexities far beyond contradiction and confident dialectical advance. His thaumaturgic idealism is as much a pathology as an epistemology, as much an experience of something that is happening to him as a project. In this way, he is a thinker for times long after him, times such as ours, which have all but forgotten him— until a hurried reading such as this one grants time for an initial infection, needing only a prolonged incubation period.

The early Hegel, the young Schelling, and a Novalis who never had time to grow old and systematic: these are among the figures in a history of contagion, which is perhaps a segment of that history of *inhibition* mentioned earlier. One must regret the absence from these pages of Hölderlin, Hamann, Schlegel, Jean Paul, and so many others in the rich tradition of German Romanticism and Idealism. One can only hope that the seed of contagion that flourished in all these thinkers of the past will flourish in our own time, inasmuch as ours is a time in which the dire forces of nature still have something to show us.

# NOTES

## INTRODUCTION

1. See the pseudo-Goethean text in *Naturwissenschaftliche Schriften*, ed. Rudolf Steiner, 5 vols. (Dornach, Switzerland: Rudolph Steiner Verlag, 1982), cited throughout by volume and page; for the present quotation, see 2: 5–7.

2. See Johann Wolfgang von Goethe, *Metamorphose der Pflanzen* (1790). I have used the illustrated edition by Rudolf Steiner, 6th ed. (Stuttgart: Verlag Freies Geistesleben, 1992), citing it by paragraph number in the body of my text. The *Metamorphose* appears in the *Naturwissenschaftliche Schriften* (cited in note 1, above), at 1: 17–59.

3. Immanuel Kant, *Kritik der Urteilskraft*, Akademieausgabe B (1793), ed. Gerhard Lehmann (Stuttgart: Philipp Reclam Verlag, 1966), ix. I shall cite the third *Critique* as *KU*, either by paragraph (§) or by page number of the Akademieausgabe edition, located in the lower inner margin of the Reclam edition.

4. I shall cite Novalis by volume and page in the body of my text, according to the following edition: Novalis, *Werke, Tagebücher und Briefe*, ed. Hans-Joachim Mähl and Richard Samuel, 3 vols. (Munich: Carl Hanser Verlag, 1987), with particular reference to vol. 2, *Das philosophisch-theoretische Werk*. I have also checked my quotations against the historical-critical edition initiated by Paul Kluckhohn and Richard Samuel and revised in 1981 by Richard Samuel and Hans-Joachim Mähl (Stuttgart: Verlag W. Kohlhammer, 1981), vols. 2 and 3. Virtually nothing of Novalis's theoretical scientific-philosophical work has appeared in English up to now. The State University of New York Press is now advertising a book entitled *Novalis: Philosophical Writings*, edited by Margaret Mahony Stoljar, scheduled for publication in 1997. The book will contain many of Novalis's philosophical and aesthetic writings; from the description, however, it seems that little of *Das allgemeine Brouillon* will be included. One can only hope that a second volume is now in preparation, since Novalis's scientific and medical notes are of major importance for contemporary Continental thought.

5. See Friedrich Wilhelm Joseph von Schelling, *Schriften von 1799–1801* (Darmstadt: Wissenschaftliche Buchgesellschaft, 1975), 1–268, a photomechanical reprint of the 1858–1859 edition by Karl Schelling, published by J. G. Cotta. I will cite Schelling's *Erster Entwurf* as *EE*, followed by page numbers, in the body of my text.

6. For the Jena lecture course I have referred to Georg Wilhelm Friedrich Hegel, *Jenaer Systementwürfe III: Naturphilosophie und Philosophie*

*des Geistes*, ed. Rolf-Peter Horstmann (Hamburg: Felix Meiner Verlag, 1987), cited as *JS*, followed by page numbers, in the body of my text.

7. On this and every aspect of Novalis's scientific interests and labors, the extraordinary monograph by John Neubauer merits careful study—I have profited from it countless times while preparing the first part of my own book: see John Neubauer, *Bifocal Vision: Novalis' Philosophy of Nature and Disease* (Chapel Hill: University of North Carolina Press, 1971). See also the extraordinarily detailed accounts by Johannes Hegener, *Die Poetisierung der Wissenschaften bei Novalis, dargestellt am Prozeß der Entwicklung von Welt und Menschheit: Studien zum Problem enzyklopädischen Welterfahrens* (Bonn: Bouvier Verlag Herbert Grundmann, 1975), and Theodor Haering, *Novalis als Philosoph* (Stuttgart: Verlag W. Kohlhammer, 1954); on the *encyclopedic* project of Novalis's *Das allgemeine Brouillon*, see Hegener throughout, along with Haering's excellent treatment, 57–70; on Novalis's view of nature as fundamentally organic, see Hegener, 404–54, and Haering, 567–86. Finally, see Lydia Elizabeth Wagner, *The Scientific Interest of Friedrich von Hardenberg (Novalis)*, doctoral diss. (Ann Arbor, Mich.: Edwards Brothers, 1937), for an early yet still very useful account of science in Novalis's career.

8. I await with enthusiasm the publication of Anna Vaughn's translation of, and research into, this crucial early text of Schelling's, the *Timaeus* commentary. The German text appears now in F. W. J. Schelling, *"Timaeus" (1794), Schellingiana*, vol. 4, ed. Hartmut Buchner (Stuttgart: Frommann-Holzboog, 1994).

9. See Novalis's *Werke*, 1: 211. I have referred to much of this material, especially involving the first kiss and the system of the mouth, in chapter 9 of my *Infectious Nietzsche* (Bloomington: Indiana University Press, 1996), 180–86. I apologize for the inevitable repetition.

10. On the theme of *lifedeath* in post-Freudian metapsychology, see, above all, Jacques Derrida, "Spéculer—sur 'Freud,'" in *La carte postale de Socrate à Freud et au-delà* (Paris: Aubier-Flammarion, 1980), 275–437; translated by Alan Bass as *The Post Card: From Socrates to Freud and Beyond* (Chicago: University of Chicago Press, 1987), 257–409. See also David Farrell Krell, *Daimon Life: Heidegger and Life-Philosophy* (Bloomington: Indiana University Press, 1992), chap. 7, "Lifedeath: Heidegger, Nietzsche, Freud." It is clear to me that the entire present project, focusing as it does on *contagion*, is inspired by Derrida's deconstruction of the major oppositional pairs, categories, mythemes, and philosophemes in the Western intellectual tradition(s). One is not surprised to find references to *contamination, contagion*, and even *contagium* in the 1976 *Glas*, where Hegel and Jean Genet confront one another; see Jacques Derrida, *Glas* (Paris: Galilée, 1974); translated by John P. Leavey Jr. and Richard Rand (Lincoln: University of Nebraska Press, 1986); see also John P. Leavey Jr., *Glassary* (Lincoln: University of Nebraska Press, 1986), 203, for a listing of the references. Nor is one surprised to find allusions to contamination and contagion everywhere in "Plato's Pharmacy," first published in 1968 and revised in 1972; see Jacques Derrida, *Dissémination* (Paris: Seuil, 1972), 69–197, esp. 172; translated by Barbara Johnson as *Dissemination* (Chicago: University of Chicago Press,

1981), 61–171, esp. 149: "According to a pattern that will dominate all of Western philosophy, good writing (natural, living, knowledgeable, intelligible, internal, speaking) is opposed to bad writing (a moribund, ignorant, external, mute artifice for the senses). And the good one can be designated only through the metaphor of the bad one. Metaphoricity is the logic of contamination and the contamination of logic." Yet as far back as the 1967 *Of Grammatology*, the fundamental themes of deconstruction have turned about the issue of contagion. When in that book Derrida refers to Nietzsche, whose genealogy of oppositional thinking—in *Beyond Good and Evil* and *On the Genealogy of Morals*—is important for my own work on contagion, he (Derrida) writes of *la virulence de la pensée nietzschéenne* (32); throughout the *Grammatology*, it is a matter of the putative *nocivité de l'écriture*, as experienced from Plato through Rousseau to Saussure (61); if writing is Rousseau's "dangerous supplement," that is because it infects the writing-of-the-heart, and thus is nothing less than the *menace de mort* (347); finally, that mortal menace is rooted in nature, and Rousseau's nightmare is expressed in the question as to whether *le manque de la nature est* dans *la nature* (364); so that, in effect, these textual matters touch on the very nature of nature. See Jacques Derrida, *De la grammatologie* (Paris: Minuit, 1967); translated by Gayatri Chakravorty Spivak as *Of Grammatology* (Baltimore: Johns Hopkins University Press, 1974).

There is some sense in which my preoccupation with contagion in Novalis, Schelling, and Hegel takes up quite *literally* the deconstructive preoccupation with *metaphoric* contamination. It is not that I take Romanticism and German Idealism to be the *literal, historical origin* of the *metaphoric* deconstruction of mutually contaminating opposites in texts; yet I *am* struck by a philosophical thinking—two centuries old now—that expands its focus from contagion as a force of nature to the farthest reaches of ontotheology, if only to recoil from the full consequences of contagion. For it remains true that the structures of the absolute in Novalis, Schelling, and Hegel are not yet altogether moribund. Yet it is also true that those structures are infected and will succumb.

Finally, there is a sense in which my interest in contagion is driven by apparently strictly extratextual concerns. Who can deny that the human race is today threatened on all sides by more virulent viruses and microbes than have ever flourished before? The mutant, highly resistant strains of bacteria that produce tubercular and other infections; the new forms of malaria and other tropical diseases that appear to thrive on what used to kill them; the adaptive variation and resilience of influenza viruses; and, most menacing of all, the upsurgence of the human immunodeficiency viruses (HIV) and the advanced immunodeficiency syndrome (AIDS); all these seem to be taking with excessive literalness what one had hoped was either a strategy for reading or a positive cry for change—Zarathustra's cry that the human being is something that must be overcome. No doubt, the dire forces of nature of which I am writing here, the dire forces that have not yet shown us the worst, touch on the textual *and* the living in a way that terrifies us— and calls on us to think.

11. This work has been published in an English translation as *Ideas for a Philosophy of Nature* by Errol E. Harris and Peter Heath (Cambridge: Cambridge University Press, 1988).

12. See the reference to Schelling's treatise in David Farrell Krell, "The Crisis of Reason in the Nineteenth Century: Schelling's Treatise on Human Freedom (1809)," in *The Collegium Phaenomenologicum: The First Ten Years*, ed. John Sallis et al. (Dordrecht: Kluwer Academic Publishers, 1988), 16, 30.

13. Hegel, *Theorie Werkausgabe*, 9: 13; that is, Georg Wilhelm Friedrich Hegel, *Werke in zwanzig Bänden* (Frankfurt am Main: Suhrkamp Verlag, 1970), cited in the body of my text by volume and page. For the Jena lecture course, see note 6, above.

14. The *philosophical* fate of the philosophies of nature of Novalis, Schelling, and Hegel is perhaps a shared fate. Even the most triumphant of the three plunges into ignominy and oblivion when the topic of "nature" is raised. Yet there are signs of a Schelling renaissance, and a Novalis renaissance cannot be far behind. Indeed, there are even some signs that Hegel's philosophy of nature is receiving new and creative attention—after decades of neglect. Dietrich von Engelhardt notes that since 1830 only fifty studies of Hegel's philosophy of nature have appeared, only five of these on chemistry; further, of the 15,500 courses in philosophy given at universities in the Federal Republic of Germany between 1945 and 1970, only two were devoted to Hegel's philosophy of the natural sciences; no more than twelve involved any reference to it at all. One wonders what the calculation would be for Schelling and Novalis. One *knows* what the calculation would be in the English-speaking philosophical world. See Dietrich von Engelhardt, "Das chemische System der Stoffe, Kräfte und Prozesse in Hegels Naturphilosophie und der Wissenschaft seiner Zeit," in Hans-Georg Gadamer, ed., *Stuttgarter Hegel-Tage 1970: Vorträge und Kolloquien des Internationalen Hegel-Jubiläumskongresses*, published as *Hegel-Studien*, supplement 11 (1974): 125–39; see also Michael John Petry, "Hegel's Philosophy of Nature: Recent Developments," *Hegel-Studien*, 23 (1988): 303–26, esp. 305. In spite of the relative dearth of material on Hegel's philosophy of nature, see Wolfgang Neuser, "Sekundärliteratur zu Hegels Naturphilosophie (1802–1985)," in M. J. Petry, ed., *Hegel und die Naturwissenschaften* (Stuttgart: Frommann-Holzboog, 1987), 501–42. See also in the same volume Neuser's very useful survey of Hegel's library holdings in the natural sciences, "Die naturphilosophische und naturwissenschaftliche Literatur aus Hegels privater Bibliothek," 479–99. For an account of the neglect of Hegel's philosophy of nature in the English-speaking world, see Gerd Buchdahl, "Hegel's Philosophy of Nature," *British Journal for the Philosophy of Science* 23 (1972): 257–66.

## 1. THE FIRST KISS

1. Friedrich Hölderlin, *Hyperion, oder der Eremit in Griechenland*, letter 11 of part 1, in *Sämtliche Werke und Briefe*, ed. Michael Knaupp, 3 vols. (Munich: Carl Hanser Verlag, 1992), 1: 649–50.

2. Adolf Beck, ed., *Hölderlins Diotima Susette Gontard: Gedichte—Briefe—Zeugnisse* (Frankfurt am Main: Insel Verlag, 1980), 63.

3. Novalis, *Werke*, 1: 211; cf. Klingsohr's account of Chaos in *Heinrich von Ofterdingen*, part 1, chap. 9; 1: 348. Johannes Hegener, *Die Poetisierung der Wissenschaften bei Novalis* (cited in note 7 to the introduction), 491, emphasizes the importance of this "death mill" passage in *Lehrlinge;* see his entire discussion (487–96) of nutrition and assimilation in Novalis.

4. On ashes in the thought of Derrida, see above all *Feu la cendre* (Paris: Des Femmes, 1987); translated by Ned Lukacher as *Cinders* (Lincoln: University of Nebraska Press, 1991).

5. Martin Heidegger, "What Is Metaphysics?" in *Basic Writings*, revised and expanded edition by David Farrell Krell (San Francisco: HarperCollins, 1993), 110.

6. See Plato, *Timaeus* 33b–d. Timaeus explains that the Earth was created as a globe containing all things, hence without need of sense organs—indeed, without need of organs of any kind: "[N]or would there have been use of organs by the help of which he might receive his food or get rid of what he had already digested, since there was nothing that went from him or came into him, for there was nothing besides him. By design [ἐκ τέχνης] he was created thus, his own waste [φθίσις] providing his own food and all that he did or suffered taking place in and by himself." Timaeus does not appear to be bothered by the contradiction of this equation of food and waste—in a globe that for essential reasons neither ingested nor excreted.

7. Friedrich Schlegel, *Lucinde* (Stuttgart: Philipp Reclam Verlag, 1979), 17.

8. My thanks to Elizabeth Hoppe, who provided our graduate seminar on Novalis at DePaul University in 1993/94 with a recording of Mozart's song. Special thanks, too, to Bernie Mizock, M.D., who participated regularly in the seminar and provided indispensable guidance to the entire group on all matters physiological, biochemical, anatomical, and surgical.

9. See Martin Heidegger, *Was heißt Denken?* (Tübingen: Max Niemeyer Verlag, 1954), esp. part 1; and *"Der Weg zur Sprache,"* in *Unterwegs zur Sprache* (Pfullingen: Günter Neske, 1959), 241, 265.

10. *Teplitzer Fragmente; Werke*, 2: 407. The theme of the eucharist, of eating as an act of gratitude and commemoration—the theme that is about to be broached—has its classical source in the seventh of Novalis's *Spiritual Songs*, entitled "Hymn"; see *Geistliche Lieder; Werke*, 1: 188–90. Once again, our religious preferences may call upon *us* to alter the liturgy and the ritual of Novalis's alimentary religion—to make of Novalis's text what he himself will call a *genuine* trope. The only thing of which we may be certain is that these liturgies will engage mouths and hands and senses—that they will be both sensual and spiritual in a way that only a thaumaturgic idealism can teach us.

11. Milk plays an important role in Novalis's pharmaceutical principle. Consider the following note: "If milk and the demulsifying agents serve as antidotes, diminishing the effects of toxins in organs, they can be such only to the extent that the toxins augment those organs—and this would be their so-called *involutive* effect" (*Das allgemeine Brouillon; Werke*, 2: 576).

12. *Freiberger Studien, Physikalische Fragmente; Werke,* 2: 453; cf. the following from *Das allgemeine Brouillon; Werke,* 2: 498: "The philosophy that allows nature to proceed from minerals to mankind is the theory of fire with regard to nutrition, positive combustion; the philosophy that lets things unfold in the reverse direction is the theory of secretion with regard to fermentation, negative combustion." Novalis's nourishing philosophy remains a thinking of excrement. Perhaps recollecting the account of the self-sufficient universe in Plato's *Timaeus,* with which we began, Novalis asks, "Could someone survive by devouring his excrement?" Later he asks, "Should not *filth* lend itself to being used again?" (*Das allgemeine Brouillon; Werke,* 2: 504; 680). Freud and Derrida would concur: the recurrent dream of philosophers involves saving not only the appearances but also the disappearances—the scraps, the waste. As we shall see in part 3 of the present book, Hegel too shares this dream.

13. See the long note in *Das allgemeine Brouillon; Werke,* 2: 521–22, from which I extract the following: "The risible is not *biting.* Laughter is a cramp. The cause of laughter must therefore be a sudden release of tensed attention—originating by means of a contrast. Similarity with electrical sparks. The genuine comic must have an earnest and dignified appearance when he makes a joke. (Irony, parody, travesty—costume is a major component of the ridiculous. Plays on words. Ridiculous questions and answers. Anecdotes. *Scenes.* Shakespeare. The Italians. Aristophanes. Wit *of the common people. Caricatures. Hogarth. Lichtenberg.*) . . . *Laughter*—a cure for hypochondria. However, hypochondria can also originate from excessive joking and laughter. . . . Weeping and laughing, *with all their modifications,* thus pertain to psychic life in the way that eating and defecating belong to the life of the body. Weeping constitutes the arterial system—laughter the venous system."

14. On the *Ordo amoris,* see Max Scheler, *Von der Ganzheit des Menschen: Ausgewählte Schriften,* ed. Manfred Frings (Bonn: Bouvier, 1991), 3–32.

15. Novalis, *Werke,* 2: 675. Cf. Martin Heidegger, *Die Grundbegriffe der Metaphysik: Welt—Endlichkeit—Einsamkeit,* Martin Heidegger Gesamtausgabe, vol. 29/30 (Frankfurt am Main: Vittorio Klostermann, 1983), 7. This volume has been translated by William McNeill and Nicholas Walker as *The Fundamental Concepts of Metaphysics: World, Finitude, Solitude* (Bloomington: Indiana University Press, 1995).

16. On the drama of the thunderstorm in nature, in which liquid rain and fiery lightning rejuvenate the Earth, see Schelling's *Ideas for a Philosophy of Nature* (cited in note 11 to the introduction), 108, and *Von der Weltseele,* in *Schriften von 1794–1798* (Darmstadt: Wissenschaftliche Buchgesellschaft, 1980), 623. For Hegel's text on baptism in *The Spirit of Christianity* (1798–1800), see the *Theorie Werkausgabe,* 1: 391.

17. The account of Mary Magdalene in Hegel's *The Spirit of Christianity,* written precisely at the time when Novalis was writing the notes we are considering here, is discussed in David Farrell Krell, *The Purest of Bastards: Works of Mourning, Art, and Affirmation in the Thought of Jacques Derrida* (University Park: Pennsylvania State University Press, forthcoming), chap. 8.

18. See Hegel, *Theorie Werkausgabe*, 12: 120–29; see also David Farrell Krell, "The Bodies of Black Folk: Kant, Hegel, Du Bois, and Baldwin," in Kevin Miles, ed., *The Academy and Race: Toward a Philosophy of Political Action*, (Lanham, Md.: Rowman and Littlefield, forthcoming).

19. On the debate concerning whether the note portends suicide or promises further philosophical engagement, see the helpful commentary by the editors of Novalis's *Werke*, 3: 330–31. My thanks to Bob Vallier, who reminded me of this passage, but who, alas, told only half the story.

## 2. A POETICS OF THE BANEFUL

1. See Anni Carlsson, *Die Fragmente des Novalis* (Basel: Verlag Helbing & Lichtenhahn, 1939), 6, 200, and all of chapter 9, on "magical idealism." Carlsson analyzes Novalis's notes in the context of "the Romantic fragment" in general and in contrast to the demands of the aphorism. Her conclusions are sober yet affirmative: "The spirit improvises, but its force carries it sufficiently far for it to grasp its problems in a genuine way—though not far enough to solve them" (6). For the "literary Saturnalia" to which Novalis wants to invite us we need to learn a new patience, for we will be given *profiles of thoughts* rather than the fully developed thoughts themselves (200). The disadvantages are, alas, clear. The advantages are the possibilities of exponential expansion, logarithmic reduction, and a rapid and complex combinatorics—which we shall discuss in a moment.

Lore Hühn has shown convincingly that the Romantic fragment—and especially the fragmentary writing of Novalis and Schlegel—is anything but a literary affectation or conceit. It is rather the kind of writing that responds to a historical-philosophical datum. For what Fichte's doctrine of the imagination had demonstrated was that a truly scientific system can never articulate and found its own ground; it can only hover or oscillate (*schweben*) with a certain "in-between" realm of virtually endless positings and negatings. In other words, the Romantic fragment responds to the irrefragable disappearance of the *fundamentum*. The fragment can now only project itself upon actuality by means of the magic of the imagination. Indeed, it can only project itself on the basis of the fleeting projection by which it itself is projected and in which it *hovers*. What traditional metaphysical philosophy sees as a failure, namely, the incapacity to flee the swamp of representational positings for the solid ground of positive speculation, the inability to escape from the toils of *Reflexion* to a calm and lasting grasp of the absolute, Romantic writing recognizes as its only hope for success: what perdures in and for the Romantic fragment is the "in-between," which is the realm of something like "differencing." Lore Hühn calls such differencing "the *incitamentum* of the entire process" (574). The process to which she is referring, I might add, is common to both poetic art and the science of nature. Indeed, the Romantics hover in the expectation that nature herself will prove to be such a process and that the imagination will become her chosen one, the fitting recipient of her contagion. See Lore

Hühn, "Das Schweben der Einbildungskraft: Zur frühromantischen Überbietung Fichtes," *Deutsche Vierteljahrsschrift für Literaturwissenschaft und Geistesgeschichte* 70, no. 4 (December 1996): 569–99.

2. See the introduction to Georges Bataille, *L'érotisme* (Paris: Union Générale d'Editions, 1972 [first published by Minuit in 1957]), esp. 17, 22, 27; and Maurice Blanchot, *L'entretien infini* (Paris: Gallimard, 1969), esp. 1–11, 228, 230, 235. On the fragmentary writing of *Novalis*, see Eckhard Heftrich, *Novalis: Vom Logos der Poesie* (Frankfurt am Main: Vittorio Klostermann Verlag, 1969), chap. 2, "Orphic Science: Encyclopedics and Experiment." Heftrich shows that Novalis's scientific and theoretical writing, especially in *Das allgemeine Brouillon*, is not a "collection of fragments" but something both less and more. Less, because it is a compilation of materials for future use, raw materials whose law of organization (as Novalis himself concedes) is "contingent" and "alien." More, because Novalis conceives of encyclopedics as the art of constructing a scientific organon of all the sciences and all the genres of writing (26–28). Heftrich understands the nature of experiment in terms of the Kantian Copernican Revolution in philosophy, so that in his view Novalis's encyclopedics fulfills the most stringent cognitive requirements set by modern philosophy (29–37).

3. Martin Dyck argues that mathematics serves as the "spinal cord" of Novalis's scientific writings as a whole, not by preponderating over other areas of inquiry but by being the method or the language of inquiry as such: "In his fragments on mathematics Novalis is concerned with an extension of this science beyond its usual domain and with its elucidation in broad contexts of art, life, and thought. . . . He regards mathematics as the ideal science and intends to use it as a unifying principle in his contemplated universal encyclopedia of knowledge." On logarithms as such, Dyck writes: "Logarithms had been invented by Napier about two hundred years before Novalis studied mathematics. Logarithms had enabled mathematicians to carry out elementary arithmetical operations much quicker than by the usual processes. . . . Novalis suggests that the ideal, proper language would resemble a system of logarithms in its capacity of simplifying and accelerating mental processes." See Martin Dyck, *Novalis and Mathematics: A Study of Friedrich von Hardenberg's Fragments on Mathematics and Its Relation to Magic, Music, Religion, Philosophy, Language, and Literature* (Chapel Hill: University of North Carolina Press, 1960); for the quotation on the "spinal cord," see 1; for the long quotation on the extension of mathematics, see 93; on the particular relevance of mathematics for *Enzyklopädistik*, see chap. 4, 75ff.; for the quotation on logarithms, see 82. See also John Neubauer, "Zwischen Natur und mathematischer Abstraktion," in Richard Brinkmann, ed., *Romantik in Deutschland: Ein interdisziplinäres Symposion* (Sonderband der *"Deutschen Vierteljahrsschrift für Literaturwissenschaft und Geistesgeschichte* (Stuttgart: J. B. Metzlersche Verlagsbuchhandlung, 1978), 175–86, which places special emphasis on combinatorics, logarithms, and exponentials: potentiation is not merely an exertion of Aristotelian δύναμις or the medievals' *potentia* but a combination of and with oneself; potentiation is precisely a series of "confrontations with the self" (177), a raising to the

powers that expresses "the inner power for creative self-assertion" (178). Finally, for a concise account of these mathematical issues, see Theodor Haering (cited in note 7 to the introduction), 541–52, esp. 550–52.

4. William Butler Yeats, "The Tower," in *Collected Poems* (New York: Macmillan, 1956), 197.

5. John Brown, *Elementa medicinae*, translated by the author in *The Works of Dr. John Brown*, ed. William Cullen Brown (London, 1804). See the full-length commentary by Thomas Henkelmann, *Zur Geschichte des patho-physiologischen Denkens: John Brown (1735–1788) und sein System der Medizin* (Berlin: Springer-Verlag, 1981). See the helpful pages of Neubauer, *Bifocal Vision*, 23–30. See also Johannes Hegener, *Die Poetisierung der Wissenschaften*, 458–63, and Lydia Elizabeth Wagner, *The Scientific Interest of Friedrich von Hardenberg (Novalis)*, 35–46 (both cited in note 7 to the introduction). Although his context is Schelling, Richard Toellner too shows how widespread John Brown's influence was in German medicine early in the nineteenth century; see Toellner, "Randbedingungen zu Schellings Konzeption der Medizin als Wissenschaft," in Ludwig Hasler, ed., *Schelling: Seine Bedeutung für eine Philosophie der Natur und der Geschichte (Referate und Kolloquien der Internationalen Schelling-Tagung Zürich 1979)* (Stuttgart: Frommann-Holzboog, 1981), 119–20.

6. In part two of the present book, we will hear Schelling lodge precisely the same complaint concerning Brown's failure to distinguish. However, Lydia Wagner shows that Novalis's perceptive critique of John Brown (see her dissertation [cited in note 7 to the introduction], 42–46) did not deter him from reverting to Brown's most avid German disciples in 1800, at the time of the onset of his own illness (86). On Novalis's critical reception of John Brown, see also Hans Fischer, "Die Krankheitsauffassung Friedrich von Hardenbergs (Novalis), 1772–1801: Ein Beitrag zur Medizin der Romantik," *Verhandlungen der Naturforschenden Gesellschaft* 56 (1945): 399–400.

7. Novalis's words, quoted by Gerhard Schulz, *Novalis in Selbstzeugnissen und Bilddokumenten* (Reinbek bei Hamburg: Rowohlt, 1969), 59. Early in the twentieth century, Egon Fridell noted that the perverse nature of Novalis's love for Sofie is bound up with his "odd and eccentric philosophy of illness." Fridell calls Novalis's a "Fichtean" love, in the sense that for Fichte the "not-I" is released by the "I" as a kind of "unconscious imagination" and "liberated object" that seems to stand over against the "I" as an autonomous phenomenon. In other words, the poet loves his projection and not the screen on which he is projecting—precisely in the way that E. T. A. Hoffmann's Nathanael loves Olimpia only when he gazes on her through his own *Perspektiv* (see note 8, below, on Hoffmann's *Der Sandmann*). See Egon Fridell, *Novalis als Philosoph* (Munich: Verlagsanstalt Bruckmann, 1904), 13, 85. Interestingly, Fridell is one of the first to see in Novalis's philosophy of illness the basis of a positive relation to Nietzsche (86). On Novalis's admittedly bizarre thought on the positive aspects of illness, see also the more detailed remarks of Theodor Haering, 508–16, esp. 513–15, and Johannes Hegener, 475–81 (both cited in note 7 to the introduction).

8. Novalis, *Werke*, 2: 679. Of the uncanny, Novalis writes: "It is strange

that in a well-wrought tale there is always something secret—something incomprehensible. The story seems to touch still unopened eyes in us—and we find ourselves in an altogether different world when we return from its realm" (2: 760). It is almost as though he had moved ahead in time in order to read E. T. A. Hoffmann's *Der Sandmann*, which undoubtedly "seems to touch still unopened eyes." For a more conservative view of the nature of Novalis's uncanny thaumaturgy, see Theodor Haering, 364–81. Finally, for a structuralist analysis of the fairy tale in Novalis's oeuvre, see Ulrich Gaier, *Krumme Regel: Novalis' "Konstruktionslehre des schaffenden Geistes" und ihre Tradition* (Tübingen: Max Niemeyer Verlag, 1970), chaps. 3–5.

## 3. Touching, Contact, Contagion

1. Novalis, *Werke*, 2: 423. For an account of the typographic model of sensation and memory, see David Farrell Krell, *Of Memory, Reminiscence, and Writing: On the Verge* (Bloomington: Indiana University Press, 1990), part 1.

2. On the essentially incomplete touched-touching paradigm, see Maurice Merleau-Ponty, *Le visible et l'invisible* (Paris: Gallimard, 1964), chap. 4; translated by Alphonso Lingis as *The Visible and the Invisible* (Evanston, Ill.: Northwestern University Press, 1968).

3. Novalis, *Werke* 2: 712. The precise relation of Novalis to Schelling remains a matter of debate. Early in this century, researchers tended to minimize Schelling's impact on Novalis, perhaps because "the anxiety of influence" was especially great when trying to establish Novalis as a thinker of the first order. Waldemar Olshausen, *Friedrich von Hardenbergs (Novalis) Beziehungen zur Naturwissenschaft seiner Zeit* (Leipzig: University of Leipzig, doctoral diss., 1905), 17, attributed "no thoroughgoing influence" to Schelling, not even to Schelling's *Ideen* and *Von der Weltseele*. The earlier work of Schelling was, Olshausen conceded, "supportive" and "stimulating," and Franz Hemsterhuis was even a "new and decisive stimulus" (16–17), but by and large it was a matter of showing Novalis's singular and unaided importance. Hermann Pixberg, *Novalis als Naturphilosoph* (Gütersloh: C. Bertelsmann, 1928), 33–41, argued that Novalis's relation to Schelling, at least after an initial infatuation with the 1797 *Ideen*, was principally one of opposition, *Gegnerschaft*. He suggested that Schelling ultimately had only "a *very slight* influence" on Novalis (41). He cited Henrich Steffens, a declared disciple (though not a student) of Schelling's, who complained that Novalis "does not want primal duplicity," but rather "a primal infinitism of nature" (Steffens, quoted by Pixberg at 41). Whether the influence is as slight as Olshausen and Pixberg wanted it to be, and whether Novalis's "infinitism" was ever anything other than a "primal duplicity," one may also fairly doubt.

4. On the prophetic role of the physician-artist, see Hans Fischer, "Die Krankheitsauffassung Friedrich von Hardenbergs (Novalis), 1772–1801: Ein Beitrag zur Medizin der Romantik," *Verhandlungen der Naturforschenden Gesellschaft* 56 (1945): 406–407. One of the most significant detailed readings

of Novalis's account of the physician as a prophet of the art of illness is Heinrich Schipperges, "Krankwerden und Gesundsein bei Novalis," in Richard Brinkmann, ed., *Romantik in Deutschland* (cited in note 3 to chap. 2), 226–42. Schipperges acknowledges that health and illness are *Grundphän-omene* with Novalis, not mere biographical or literary categories but matters of prime existential and theoretical importance. Schipperges interprets Novalis's view of illness as not only a "quarrel of organs" but also as the very secret of "individualization" (228–29). His discussion culminates in the question of what it means "to have become ill," and the impending threat of the "annihilation of death," whereby the genitive is oddly subjective as well as objective. On the relation of illness to the "art of living," see 234–36; on pharmacy as "the elementary science of man," see 237–41. Because it is not too much to say that Schipperges's article is one of the most important interpretations of health and illness in Novalis that we possess, it is quite striking, and quite disappointing, that the one phenomenon that is missing from his account is human sexuality, which, if I am right, stands at the center of Novalis's reflections on health and illness. In this respect, Schipperges follows the lead of Johannes Hegener and Theodor Haering, who, although they provide excellent accounts of Novalis's "infinitesimal medicine," the medicine practiced by the "artist of immortality," for which death is a kind of therapy (Hegener, 475–79; Haering, 508–16), leave eros and sexual relations out of account.

## 4. THE ARTIST OF IMMORTALITY

1. Novalis, *Werke*, 2: 717. On "inoculation with death" as the most radical therapy practiced by an "artist of immortality," see Lydia Wagner, 45–46; see also Theodor Haering, who provides a helpful discussion, 576–77; and, above all, see Johannes Hegener, 475–79 (all cited in note 7 to the introduction).

2. Novalis, *Werke*, 2: 550. For one of Novalis's more critical notes on John Brown, see 2: 606–607, which wonders, "Is *life* merely complex *excitation*, or is it a higher composition *[Zusammensetzung]*? Is excitation a composition of stimulation and reception?" Novalis finds that the Brownian system fails to shed much light on the nature of the stimulus as such (2: 615). He is on the trail of the principal weakness of the Brownian system, itself based on the theories and experiments of the Swiss physiologist Albrecht von Haller (1708–1777), whose *Dissertation on the Sensible and Irritable Parts of Animals* (1732) influenced several generations of scientists. The principal weakness of Brown's Hallerian theory, at least from the point of view of contemporary nosology, or classification of illnesses, is that the straightforward division of all illnesses into (hyper)sthenic and asthenic genuses falls back on a *monistic* conception of excitation; further, it pays no heed to the sundry anatomical or organ-based etiologies of illness. See Thomas Henkelmann, 66–67.

3. Novalis, *Werke*, 2: 654. Karl Heinz Volkmann-Schluck notes that

natural occurrences, in Novalis's view, generally cannot be reduced to either necessity or contingency alone. Rather, nature acts "necessarily-contingently." True, natural events cannot be traced back to universal causal laws; yet "blind, senseless accident does not prevail." Instead, occurrences in nature are guided by "mysterious relations, marvelous affinities," which it is the object of thaumaturgic idealism to discover. See Volkmann-Schluck, "Novalis' magischer Idealismus," in Hans Steffen, ed., *Die deutsche Romantik: Poetik, Formen und Motive* (Göttingen: Vandenhoeck & Ruprecht, 1967), 45–53; see 48–49 for the above quotations. Ulrich Gaier argues that in Novalis's theoretical writings contingency and accident always play a crucial role in the approximation to perfection; that the highest synthetic principles are therefore *krumme Regel*, that is, bent or crooked rules, by dint of which all theoretical construction must be *indirect*. See Gaier (cited in note 8 to chap. 2), 248. Gaier's study takes its inspiration from the following remarkable note in the third group of handwritten materials for *The Universal Sketchbook*: "Underlying every ideal is a deviation from the common rule, or a *higher* (crooked) *rule*. [¶] (Concerning straight and crooked rules.) [¶] (The moral law is a crooked rule.)" The very next note in *The Universal Sketchbook*, "Prejudices of the Scholars," which pertains to the issue of contingency and accident in the realm of "crooked rules," sounds an undeniably Nietzschean note—as do so many of Novalis's late notes. See Novalis, *Werke*, 2: 653.

4. I wish I had known about this passage before I wrote my chapter on the great magical realist of our time, Gabriel García Márquez. See David Farrell Krell, *Lunar Voices* (Chicago: University of Chicago Press, 1995), chap. 6.

5. *Werke*, 2: 820. These notes on the "compact metal" of divinity and the diabolical nature of life-giving air, while among the strangest in Novalis's oeuvre, are at the heart of the theme of the dire forces of nature. On the importance of oxidation and deoxidation in Novalis's chemistry, see Hans Fischer, "Die Krankheitsauffassung Friedrich von Hardenbergs" (cited in note 6 to chap. 2), 403–404. On the entire question of phlogistical and antiphlogistical theories at the end of the eighteenth century, see Dietrich von Engelhardt, *Hegel und die Chemie: Studie zur Philosophie und Wissenschaft der Natur um 1800* (Wiesbaden: Guido Pressler Verlag, 1976), sections 2.2 and 2.3.

6. Novalis, *Werke*, 2: 829. On the question of sin in the traditional Christian context, and also on the psychoanalytic parallel to Novalis's account of illness and death, see chapter 5 of Karl Theodor Bluth, *Medizingeschichtliches bei Novalis: Ein Beitrag zur Geschichte der Medizin der Romantik* (Berlin: Verlag Dr. Emil Ebering, 1934), esp. 44 and 49–51. Johannes Hegener, 458, also notes that for Novalis the Christ is principally a *physician*. One of the most important aspects of Novalis's consideration of illness in the context of Christianity and its doctrine of the soul emerges in his debate with Christian Wilhelm Hufeland. Novalis joins Kant in criticizing Hufeland's defeatism, affirming the capacity of the *will* to discipline and master the body. Such a capacity is essential for Novalis's "doctrine of the art of

life," which is the principal doctrine of an "artist of immortality." What needs to be stressed, however, is that unlike Kant, Novalis underscores the capacity of *belief* and even of *fancy* and the *imagination*—rather than the discipline of *reason*—for what he considers the higher form of hypochondria. On this entire question, see Hans Sohni, *Die Medizin der Frühromantik: Novalis' Bedeutung für den Versuch einer Umwertung der "Romantischen Medizin"* (Freiburg im Breisgau: Hans Ferdinand Schulz Verlag, 1973), 132–39.

## 5. FIRST PROJECTION: AN OUTLINE OF THE WHOLE

1. Friedrich Wilhelm Joseph von Schelling, *Erster Entwurf eines Systems der Naturphilosophie, zum Behuf seiner Vorlesungen* (Jena and Leipzig: Gabler Verlag, 1799). (See note 5 to the introduction for the edition I shall be using throughout these chapters.) A large number of commentators, among them Hermann Krings, Wolfgang Bonsiepen, Günter B. Risse, Nelly Tsouyopoulos, Werner Hartkopf, Joseph L. Esposito, and Alan White, affirm the importance of Schelling's 1799 *Erster Entwurf eines Systems der Naturphilosophie* among his works in this area. Krings notes that in the *First Projection* Schelling envisages his inquiry into the philosophy of nature as an autonomous inquiry, essentially independent of transcendental philosophy, although later, by the time of the "identity philosophy" of 1801, he views it as a subordinate component of a system of transcendental philosophy. See Hermann Krings, "Vorbemerkungen zu Schellings Naturphilosophie," in Hasler, ed., *Schelling: Seine Bedeutung* (cited in note 5 to chap. 2), 73–76. Bonsiepen, in his account of Hegel's critique of Schelling in the *Phenomenology of Spirit*, cites Schelling's *First Projection* as the single most important source for Schelling's early position. See Wolfgang Bonsiepen, "Zu Hegels Auseinandersetzung mit Schellings Naturphilosophie in der 'Phänomenologie des Geistes,'" in Hasler, ed., *Schelling: Seine Bedeutung*, 167–72. Risse calls the *Erster Entwurf* "a new and more lucid exposition," "more systematic and didactic" than the earlier works. See Günter B. Risse, "Schelling, 'Naturphilosophie' and John Brown's System of Medicine," *Bulletin of the History of Medicine* 50 (1976): 321–34. Nelly Tsouyopoulos notes that the young Schelling "established himself as one of the great philosophers—as is well known—with his *Projection*." See Tsouyopoulos, "Der Streit zwischen Friedrich Wilhelm Joseph Schelling und Andreas Röschlaub über die Grundlagen der Medizin," *Medizinhistorisches Journal* 13 (1978): 229. Hartkopf argues that the *First Projection* "is doubtless the major systematic work of this epoch in Schelling's writings, even if it does not succeed in producing the final integration into one system of all the starting points for a philosophy of nature." See Werner Hartkopf, *Studien zur Entwicklung der modernen Dialektik: Die Dialektik in Schellings Ansätzen zu einer Naturphilosophie*, Monographien zur philosophischen Forschung, vol. 102 (Meisenheim am Glan: Anton Hain Verlag, 1972), 57. Esposito's sole reference to the *Erster Entwurf* suggests that it "reflects Schelling's first effort to give systematic

clarity to the more haphazard work he had set out in the *Ideen* and *Von der Weltseele.*" Joseph L. Esposito, *Schelling's Idealism and Philosophy of Nature* (Lewisburg, Pa: Bucknell University Press, 1977), 87. Like Esposito, White argues that the *Erster Entwurf* represents Schelling's first significant "constructive account" (as opposed to an inductive demonstration of a number of the principles) of a philosophy of nature. Both the *Ideen* and *Von der Weltseele* are precisely such inductive accounts, whereas the *First Projection* tries to deduce, establish, and ground the fundamental principles of dynamism and polarity. See Alan White, *Schelling: An Introduction to the System of Freedom* (New Haven: Yale University Press, 1983), 50–54. Neither Esposito nor White, who alike hope to make Schelling's a triumphant idealism, take up the themes of sexuality, illness, or any other particularly potent duplicity in Schelling's *Erster Entwurf.* As for Werner Hartkopf, he does stress the importance of duplicity (and triplicity) for Schelling's dialectic of nature, yet he has little to say concerning the role of illness and death in the dialectics of the *Erster Entwurf.* Finally, I should note that Joseph P. Lawrence emphasizes the importance of Schelling's *Ideen*, though one might have expected him to deal principally with the *Erster Entwurf;* however, Lawrence's own thought-provoking book does not confront the crucial problems bound up with nature conceived of as a living organism until it does turn to Schelling's *First Projection.* See Joseph P. Lawrence, *Schellings Philosophie des ewigen Anfangs: Die Natur als Quelle der Geschichte* (Würzburg: Königshausen & Neumann, 1989), 72–73, 83–84, and elsewhere.

2. On Schelling's studies in Leipzig between April 1796 and August 1798, originally intended as preparation for his lessons as the tutor of two young German barons but soon all-absorbing for himself, see Günter B. Risse, "Schelling, 'Naturphilosophie,'" cited in note 1, above. Risse's article provides an excellent brief introduction into Schelling's contribution to the history of medicine in general. For an excellent account of the empirical research into medicine and the biological sciences taken into account by the young Schelling, see Dietrich von Engelhardt, "Die organische Natur und die Lebenswissenschaften in Schellings Naturphilosophie," in Reinhard Heckmann, Hermann Krings, and Rudolf W. Meyer, eds., *Natur und Subjektivität: Zur Auseinandersetzung mit der Naturphilosophie des jungen Schelling (Referate, Voten und Protokolle der II. Internationalen Schelling-Tagung Zürich 1983* (Stuttgart: Friedrich Frommann Verlag, 1985), 39–57. Von Engelhardt cites over 140 empirical researchers listed among Schelling's sources during the years 1797–1805. In another article, "Schellings philosophische Grundlegung der Medizin," von Engelhardt notes that Schelling's brother Karl Eberhard was himself a physician; Karl Eberhard supplied his brother with empirical data, and the two were in constant consultation. For this article by von Engelhardt, see Hans Jörg Sandkühler, ed., *Natur und geschichtlicher Prozeß: Studien zur Naturphilosophie Schellings* (Frankfurt am Main: Suhrkamp Verlag, 1984), 306. For another excellent account of the medical background prior to—and after—Schelling's activity, see Karl Eduard Rothschuh, "Naturphilosophische Konzepte der Medizin aus der Zeit der deutschen Romantik," in Brinkmann, ed., *Romantik in*

*Deutschland* (cited in note 3 to chap. 2), 243–66, esp. 245–51. For the importance of Schelling in the history of medicine generally, see Rothschuh's major work, *Konzepte der Medizin in Vergangenheit und Gegenwart* (Stuttgart: Hippokrates Verlag, 1978). Rothschuh writes: "One could take ... Schelling's philosophy of nature, on which the most important representatives of medicine during that era constructed their theories, as an altogether unromantic achievement, an achievement of the highest order, by an intellect proceeding by way of method" (385).

3. Klaus Düsing shows how important Spinoza's concept of substance was for both Schelling and Hegel during the years of their cooperative labors on the *Critical Journal* in Jena, 1801–1803. See Düsing, "Idealistische Substanzmetaphysik: Probleme der Systementwicklung bei Schelling und Hegel in Jena," in Dieter Henrich and Klaus Düsing, eds., *Hegel in Jena*, published as *Hegel-Studien*, supplement 20 (1980): 25–44, esp. 36. With regard to the Kantian Critical project, however, it remains true to say that the epistemological concept of receptivity is not at the heart of Schelling's appreciation of Kant's philosophy. Rather than any such notion from the theory of knowledge, Schelling is clearly focused on the future he sees for the Analytic of Teleological Judgment in the third *Critique*, for the 1786 *Metaphysische Anfangsgründe der Naturwissenschaft*, and perhaps also for Kant's final reflections on the realm of nature in the *Opus posthumum*. In this last regard, Reinhard Lauth has shown that Kant's *Opus posthumum* conceives of the Earth and all nature in organismic terms, much in the way that Schelling is conceiving it by the time of the *Erster Entwurf*. See Lauth, "Der Unterschied zwischen der Naturphilosophie der Wissenschaftslehre und Schellings von zwei charakteristischen Ansatzpunkten des letzteren aus erläutert," in Heckmann et al., eds., *Natur und Subjektivität* (cited in note 2, above), 211–28; see esp. 202–203.

4. According to Jean-Louis Vieilliard-Baron, the essential dualism and duplicity of Schelling's concept of matter, and hence of the *construction* of matter, owes everything to two principal sources. First, Kant, in his *Metaphysische Anfangsgründe der Naturwissenschaft* (1786), had defined the very concept of matter in terms of the opposed forces of attraction and repulsion. Second, Jacobi, in his *Letters to Moses Mendelssohn on the Doctrine of Spinoza* (1789), had presented the dualistic views of Giordano Bruno in *On Cause, the Principle, and the One* (1584), in which Bruno argues that potency (Schelling's *Potenz*) is both passive, hence human, and active, hence divine. Thus for Schelling (and for Hegel as well), matter is both chemical and ethereal, both finite and absolute. See Vieilliard-Baron, "La notion de matière et le matérialisme vrai selon Hegel et Schelling à l'époque d'Iéna," in Dieter Henrich and Klaus Düsing, eds., *Hegel in Jena* (cited in note 3, above): 197–206. Perhaps what I am here calling *dualism* and *duplicity* would be better designated as *polarity*. On the importance of polarity in Schelling's philosophy of nature, a polarity that is also crucial for Novalis's theories and, indeed, for all Romantic thinkers, see Sohni, *Die Medizin der Frühromantik* (cited in note 6 to chap. 4), 45–47 and esp. 147–51.

5. *Hemmung* is a word that is used commonly by the time Novalis,

Schelling, and Hegel are writing. Friedrich Schlegel, in *Lucinde*, published in 1799, uses the word the way we use it today: he criticizes those "lackeys of the intellect," such as philosophers, who "inhibit every bolder flight of fancy." (See *Lucinde*, 17.) On Hegel and *Hemmung*, see part three of the present book and note 4 to chapter 11. For Novalis on *Hemmung*, see *Werke*, 2: 124, which presents a note that makes the same point that Schelling has only now made about inhibition as activity: "Inhibited activity can be inhibited only through activity. That which inhibits is the object—the inhibited—the state. . . ." With regard to this note (from February–March 1796), along with the opening pages of Schelling's *Erster Entwurf*, written and published in 1799, one should of course search for the common source in Fichte's philosophy—for Novalis's and Schelling's principal terms (including *absolute Tätigkeit, Hemmung, Produktivität*, etc.) are also the principal terms of Fichte's theoretical and practical philosophy from the outset. The task of demonstrating this remains for a future undertaking; allow me here to supply only three brief indications.

First, it is clear that Fichtean *Tätigkeit*, as the positing activity of reason and the productive imagination, and *Hemmung*, as the equiprimordial inhibition of reason, are the key features of Fichte's philosophy from the 1794 *Grundlage der gesamten Wissenschaftslehre* and the 1795 *Grundriß des Eigenthümlichen der Wissenschaftslehre* onward. See Johann Gottlieb Fichte, *Grundlage der gesamten Wissenschaftslehre (1794)* (Hamburg: Felix Meiner Verlag, 1961); see also the discussion by Johann Eduard Erdmann, *Philosophie der Neuzeit: Der deutsche Idealismus* (Reinbek bei Hamburg: Rowohlt, 1971), 52–60; and Reinhard Lauth, "Der Unterschied" (cited in note 3, above), 211–28, esp. 214 and 226. Moreover, the term *Hemmung* arises precisely at the point (in §5 of the *Wissenschaftslehre*) when "a difficulty . . . threatens to upset our entire theory" (*Grundlage*, 182). Fichte confronts the difficulty that "the intelligence is not to be an essence outside the ego; it is to be the ego itself, that which poses its own limitation" (*Grundlage*, 183). Fichte hopes to avoid any naive appeal to an object or a product as the source of such inhibition, and he hopes to show that there can be a "restitution of the inhibited *[gehemmtes]* striving" in consciousness (ibid.). His worst nightmare, however, is that there is something within intelligence itself that "inhibits the activity containing the primal ground of all consciousness" and that such inhibition and its source "would never come to consciousness" (ibid.). Schelling sees and struggles against that nightmarish possibility for the intelligence of nature—in the night during which more than the cows would all be black.

Second, and more narrowly, Nelly Tsouyopoulos argues that both Schelling and his physician-friend Andreas Röschlaub owe the initial steps taken by their theory of illness (which will be crucial in the chapters to follow) to Fichte's synthesis of the *Ich* and *Nicht-Ich* in the 1794 *Wissenschaftslehre*. See Nelly Tsouyopoulos, "Schellings Krankheitsbegriff und die Begriffsbildung der Modernen Medizin," in Heckmann et al., eds., *Natur und Subjektivität*, 273. Reinhard Lauth, "Der Unterschied," and Nelly Tsouyopoulos, "Schellings Krankheitsbegriff," show that it is the *synthesiz-*

*ing activity* of theoretical consciousness as such, and the irreducibly *practical* nature of that activity (due to the experience of *resistance, barrier,* and *inhibition*), as developed in Fichte's doctrine, that provide Schelling with his starting point in the *Erster Entwurf.*

Third, and finally, one might cite several passages from the third and final part of Fichte's popular text, *Die Bestimmung des Menschen,* which offers a broad-based sense of *absolute activity,* one that embraces both the theoretical and practical projects. Even though *Die Bestimmung* was published in 1800, a year after Schelling's *First Projection,* it still exhibits something of Fichte's growing emphasis on *Tun, Tathandlung,* and *Tätigkeit,* deed and activity, in the moral realm. For Fichte's use of these words is increasingly devoted to the sphere of ethicality and practical philosophy, as Schelling's own use too will soon be, at least after 1806. In the 1800 *Bestimmung des Menschen* Fichte writes: "There is in me a drive to absolute, autonomous self-activity. Nothing is more repulsive to me than to be merely in an other, for an other, and by virtue of an other: I want to become and to be something for myself and by virtue of myself. I feel this drive as only I can perceive myself; it is indivisibly united with the consciousness [I have] of myself." Johann Gottlieb Fichte, *Die Bestimmung des Menschen (1800),* ed. Theodor Ballauff and Ignaz Klein (Stuttgart: Philipp Reclam Verlag, 1962), 107. Later, in an account of the will in Book Three of *Die Bestimmung,* Fichte refers to "the deed," *die Tat,* as "a certain movement of matter, the first link in a material chain that extends through the entire system of matter" (147). From the earliest days of his involvement with Fichte's thought, Schelling was obsessed, I believe, by nothing other than this "movement" throughout the "system of matter," which is both infinitely productive and self-inhibiting. On the importance of Schelling's relation to—and liberation from—Fichte, see Claus-Artur Scheier, "Die Bedeutung der Naturphilosophie im deutschen Idealismus," *Philosophia naturalis* 23 (1986): 389–98.

6. Schelling enters the following note into his outline: "If one considers nature as object to be *real,* and as having originated not by evolution but by *synthesis* (and we have no alternative from the empirical standpoint), atomism is necessary, whether it be mechanical or dynamic. — In the transcendental view to which speculative physics ultimately elevates itself, everything is entirely transposed."

7. On the *decomposability* of matter in relation to Schelling's "dynamic atomism," see Reinhard Löw, "Qualitätenlehre und Materiekonstruktion: Zur systematischen Aktualität von Schellings Naturphilosophie," in Hasler, ed., *Schelling: Seine Bedeutung* (cited in note 5 to chap. 2), 101. The apparently arcane problem of the (in)decomposability of matter has everything to do with the crucial problem of the construction of matter—the problem that lies at the beginning and end of the "Outline of the Whole." Löw confirms that the key question for the construction of matter—and what he calls the doctrine of quality—is that of the relation of organic to anorganic or inorganic matter. Schelling's question, in Löw's words, is: "How must matter be thought (construed) if the puzzling nexus between organic and inorganic matter is to be explained?" (99).

8. Allow me once again to refer to the forthcoming book by Anna Vaughn on Schelling's *Timaeus* commentary, and also to cite a forthcoming work by John Sallis on Plato's *Timaeus*. See now the remarkable inquiry by Jacques Derrida, *Khôra* (Paris: Galilée, 1993). With regard to "formless liquidity," Schelling would have found corroboration for his view of it, and thus indirectly for his view of the χώρα of Plato's *Timaeus*, in Goethe's scientific observations. Doubtless, it was Schelling himself who influenced Goethe in this regard. See Goethe's 1824 "Grundzüge allgemeiner Natur-betrachtung," §§9–16, in Johann Wolfgang von Goethe, *Naturwissenschaft-liche Schriften* (cited in note 1 to the introduction), 1: 426–29. Whether Goethe ever fulfilled his promise of 1820 to render a full account of his debt to Schelling (and others), I do not know; see Goethe, *Naturwissenschaftliche Schriften*, 1: 30. Günter B. Risse (cited in note 1, above), 321–24, offers an excellent account of the early years of the relationship between Goethe and Schelling.

9. In his 1798 *Von der Weltseele*, Schelling had already ascertained the fundamental dualism in nature as a duality of opposed sexes: "This relation-ship [i.e., the relationship of "divine identity"] is represented solely in the opposition and unity of the sexes." See F. W. J. Schelling, *Von der Weltseele* (cited in note 16 to the introduction), 430. Concerning that fundamental dualism, Dietrich von Engelhardt writes, "We must assume that there is an original dualism, an original polarity, in the identity of nature." See von Engelhardt, "Prinzipien und Ziele der Naturphilosophie Schellings—Situ-ation um 1800 und spätere Wirkungsgeschichte," in Hasler, ed., *Schelling: Seine Bedeutung* (cited in note 5 to chap. 2), 78. Von Engelhardt traces the consequences of such dualism, and of the "inhibition" it implies, for a monism of "absolute activity," without speculating on the specifically sexual opposition that underlies Schelling's sense of dualism. He also extends his remarks to Schelling's theory and practice of medicine (80–81), although he does not see that illness exposes the absolute itself to contagion. Eventually we shall have to compare to Schelling's analysis that of Hegel in his *Enzyklopädie*, §370, on the superiority of the *Gattung*—conceived of as a *logical* genus—over the individual. One should also compare Martin Heideg-ger, *The Fundamental Concepts of Metaphysics: World, Finitude, Solitude* (cited in note 15 to chap. 1), 386, and Heidegger, *Beiträge zur Philosophie (Vom Ereignis)*, Martin Heidegger Gesamtausgabe, vol. 65 (Frankfurt am Main: Vittorio Klostermann, 1989), 277, for a disconcertingly similar analysis.

10. Immanuel Kant, *Kritik der reinen Vernunft*, ed. Raymund Schmidt (Hamburg: Felix Meiner Verlag, 1956), A 832–33, B 860–61, for this and the following references; translated by Norman Kemp Smith as *The Critique of Pure Reason* (New York: St. Martin's Press, 1965).

11. With regard to Kant's antitechnical architectonic of pure reason, which seems to be based more on reproductive τίκτειν than on any form of technology, allow me to mention my *Archeticture: Ecstasies of Space, Time, and the Human Body* (Albany: State University of New York Press, 1997). The first and fourth chapters of the book deal with the problem of χώρα in Plato's *Timaeus;* the second chapter deals with space and time in Kant, Hegel, and Heidegger.

12. Perhaps I may be permitted to refer once again to my earlier article on Schelling, itself based on a presentation to the Collegium Phaenomenologicum a decade ago: see "The Crisis of Reason in the Nineteenth Century: Schelling's Treatise on Human Freedom (1809)," cited in note 12 to the introduction. On *Die Weltalter* in relation to Schelling's early *Naturphilosophie*, see Joseph P. Lawrence (cited in note 1, above), 166–203. No doubt, readers will find that I am considerably less optimistic than Lawrence is about the success of Schelling's later efforts to offer an account that rescues both nature and the absolute—though I am as convinced as Lawrence is about the importance and even the grandeur of Schelling's attempt, which in the "Crisis" article I call (in Faulkner's words) "his most splendid failure." If I may express matters here in the form of a mystery, I would say that the most *successful* moments of Schelling's essentially *tormented* meditation occur early on in the 1811 draft of *Die Weltalter*, in those formulations (later withdrawn from publication) where the "loving tone" of the narratives that pass from divine Father to Son are interrupted by the multiple faces and facets of the *feminine*. These are the earliest moments in Schelling's own narrative of "the past": the wrath and tenderness *(Zorn/Zartheit)* of the absolute before it masculinizes itself and engenders itself (but whence?) a Son; the Battle of the Amazons embroidered on God's footstool, which is the fecund Earth; the charming attractiveness *(Anziehung)* that precipitates all Creation out of the primal Chaos *(jenes göttliche Chaos)* of darkness and night, when the Earth first became fruitful and when the first existent proves to be a *Doppelwesen* of "the most tender embodiment"; the Age of Gold, Oil, and Balsam, in which every beginning proves to be a *Dualisierung*, and when the doubling and redoubling of every beginning produces anxiety rather than a Son. The words I have cited here appear in the first half of the first impression (1811) of *Die Weltalter: Fragmente*, ed. Manfred Schröter (Munich: Biederstein und Leibniz, 1946), 10–53. And if all this does indeed exceed the scope of our present inquiry, it remains nonetheless true that nothing in Schelling's archetictonic thought can ever be disconnected from the rest.

13. Schelling notes: "Inasmuch as the subordinate forces of both universal and organic nature already presuppose an original heterogeneity, a cause is postulated that *brings forth* [hervorbringt] heterogeneity (out of homogeneity); the cause of universal magnetism is posited, initially as a mere hypothesis, as occupying such a site." As we have seen, however, it is precisely this problem of the "presupposed original heterogeneity" that torments Schelling's idealism. Magnetism is merely one name—though a persistent one—for that torment.

14. *Erster Entwurf*, 220; very similar wording appears at 240. Alan White (cited in note 1, above) has recognized the importance of this passage; he cites it in his brief discussion of Schelling's text (53–54). Günter B. Risse (also cited in note 1, above) observes: "For Schelling, this polarity was one of the deepest insights into organic nature in general. Within such a dualism, sensibility or receptivity was considered to be the most developed and noblest member of the pair" (331). Yet the fatal flaws within this most developed and noblest duplicity, the flaws of sexual opposition and fatal illness, mar the putative infinite activity that Schelling sees behind all

duality and duplicity. They haunt and torment his system, which cannot reply to the questions of *Whence?* and *Whither?* and *Wherefore?*

15. Immanuel Kant, *Anthropologie in pragmatischer Hinsicht (1798)*, ed. Wolfgang Becker (Stuttgart: Philipp Reclam Verlag, 1983 [first published in 1798]), 101 n.; Akademieausgabe, 178 n.

## 6. Sexual Opposition, Inhibition, Contagion

1. William Harvey, *Anatomical Exercises on the Generation of Animals, etc.*, in *The Works of William Harvey, M.D.*, translated from the Latin by Robert Willis, M.D. (London: Sydenham Society, 1847; New York: Johnson Reprint Corporation, "The Sources of Science," no. 13, 1965), 321–22, cited in my text as *AE*, followed by page number. Schelling first cites Harvey's work in the *Erster Entwurf* at 60. A letter from Schelling to Hölderlin, dated "Jena, August 12, 1799," suggests that these references to Harvey's work on generation are hardly incidental to Schelling's general scheme; the significance of sexuality for the *First Projection* can scarcely be exaggerated: Schelling describes his upcoming inaugural course at Jena as a whole as "some lectures on *the organic relationship of the sexes.*" See Friedrich Hölderlin, *Sämtliche Werke und Briefe* (cited in note 1 to chap. 1), 2: 803. For a detailed description of Harvey's *De generatione animalium*, see Jörg Jantzen, "Physiologische Theorien," in F. W. J. Schelling, *Historisch-kritische Ausgabe: Ergänzungsband zu Werke Band 5 bis 9*, ed. Hans Michael Baumgartner, Wilhelm G. Jacobs, and Hermann Krings (Stuttgart: Frommann-Holzboog, 1994), 566–668. Jantzen rightly emphasizes the importance of the *ovum* for Harvey, but he does not seem to recognize the importance for Schelling's *Erster Entwurf* of Harvey's concept of generation by *contagium*—the process by which the egg is (as we post-Leeuwenhoekians and post-Spallanzanians say) *fertilized*.

2. See chapter 4 of my *Infectious Nietzsche* (cited in note 9 to the introduction) for the source, and a sampling, of Melville's story.

3. *Erster Entwurf*, 73n. 1. On the importance of the organism's activity in the phenomenon of poisoning, see Nelly Tsouyopoulos, "Schellings Krankheitsbegriff," in Heckmann et al., eds., *Natur und Subjektivität* (cited in note 2 to chap. 5), 280–81. With regard to Schelling's reference to the invisible boundary between medicament and poison, that is, to Schelling's pharmacology, see Dietrich von Engelhardt, "Schellings philosophische Grundlegung der Medizin," in Sandkühler, ed., *Natur und geschichtlicher Prozess* (also cited in note 2 to chap. 5), 315. The invisibility of that boundary is confirmed, if only reluctantly, by historians of pharmaceuticals: Dieter Oldenburg notes that for the Romantic conception of pharmaceuticals in general there is a "fluid transition from foodstuffs, to pharmaceuticals proper, to poisons"; see Oldenburg, *Romantische Naturphilosophie und Arzneimittellehre* (Braunschweig: Pharmaziegeschichtliches Seminar der Technischen Universität Braunschweig, doctoral diss., 1979), 34.

4. Among Novalis's notes in the *Universal Sketchbook* is one that reads

simply "Concept of infection *[Ansteckung]*" (2: 499). Like Schelling, Novalis is interested in diseases (such as smallpox) that are endemic to entire peoples, in "humoral pathology," and in the entire "unworked field" of the history of medicine (2: 500).

5. *Erster Entwurf,* 48. Dietrich von Engelhardt notes the importance of the division of each species into two genders—the "opposed directions" essential to the perfection of each product or stage of development in nature; see von Engelhardt, "Die organische Natur," in Heckmann et al., eds., *Natur und Subjektivität* (cited in note 2 to chap. 5), 49.

6. *Erster Entwurf,* 63n. 2. Dietrich von Engelhardt notes the central role played by the "point of inhibition" in Schelling's thought; see von Engelhardt, "Schellings philosophische Grundlegung der Medizin," in Sand-kühler, ed., *Natur und geschichtlicher Prozess* (cited in note 2 to chap. 5), 307. Compare Schelling's *Hemmungspunkt* with all the many "points" in Hölder-lin's theoretical essays of these same years; see Krell, *Lunar Voices* (cited in note 4 to chap. 4), chap. 2, "Stuff • Thread • Point • Fire: Hölderlin's Dissolution."

7. In the *Anthropology* (cited in note 15 to chap. 5), Kant writes: "What might be the cause of the fact that all the known organic creatures reproduce their kind solely by means of the unification of two sexes (which one then calls the male and the female)? Surely we cannot assume that the Creator, merely on account of some eccentricity, and simply in order to devise an arrangement on our earthly globe that pleased him, was only playing, as it were; rather, it seems that it must be *impossible* to enable organic creatures to originate through reproduction from the matter of which our globe consists in any other way than by founding two sexes to that end. — In what obscurity does human reason lose itself when it undertakes, even by way of surmise, to ground here its lineage?" (Akademieausgabe, 177–78 n.). I first discussed this Kantian text (in the context of Nietzsche's *The Gay Science,* in "The Crisis of Reason in the Nineteenth Century" (cited in note 12 to the introduction), 14–15.

8. Hans Querner, "Das Phänomen der Zweigeschlechtlichkeit im Sys-tem der Naturphilosophie von Schelling," in Hasler, ed., *Schelling: Seine Bedeutung* (cited in note 5 to chap. 2), 139–43, confirms that for Schelling bisexuality is "a central presupposition for the explanation of the phenom-ena of organic nature" (139). It may be wise to recount the basic features of Schelling's analysis once again, this time with Querner's help. According to Querner, even the "postulate of unity," that is, what we have been calling Schelling's *monism,* must be explained, not in *spite of,* but in *terms of, Zweigeschlechtlichkeit.* For by the time of *Von der Weltseele* (1798) Schelling is identifying the bipolarity of gravity/lightness and darkness/light in terms of female and male, respectively. Only in the *Erster Entwurf* is a detailed analysis of bisexuality offered, moving from the absolute as unconditioned activity, via inhibition, to the finite product in all its stages of development, *Entwicklungsstufen.* The key transitional term, according to Querner, is *Gestaltung,* the formation of the individual products themselves. Such formation occurs through the "opposed and mutually limiting actions of

nature" (140). It is in the context of formation that the *entgegengesetzte Richtungen* represented by the bipolar sexes emerge: they are derived, argues Querner, from a transformation of the paleoanthropological and anatomical theories of Johann Friedrich Blumenbach (1752–1840). In his *On the Natural Varieties of Mankind* (1775), Blumenbach had accounted for the development of species—including the human—in terms of a *Bildungstrieb*, a "formative drive." (For a detailed account of Blumenbach's *Bildungstrieb*, see Jantzen, "Theorie des Bildungstriebs," in Schelling, *Historisch-kritische Ausgabe*, ed. Baumgartner et al. [cited in note 1, above], 636–68.) Schelling takes the process of *Gestaltung* to be the essential mechanism of the *Bildungstrieb*, and formation is always the result of an initial separation and eventual conjunction of "counterposed tendencies." Precisely how the sexual opposition enables *Gestaltung* and the *Bildungstrieb* to work their effects Schelling is unable to say: there is as yet, of course, no explicit theory of evolution through accidental variation and sexual selection, no theory of genetic mutation, variation, and inheritance. The only explanation proffered by Schelling seems to proceed *ex negativo:* each stage of development is incomplete until its *two* avatars, which have been following *entgegengesetzte Richtungen*, conjoin (141). Nor is there an explicitly drawn parallel between embryology and morphogenesis in general—although Schelling seems to be presupposing something like this when he refers to the empirical data of botany and zoology. Indeed, Schelling's *First Projection* is crying out for such theories. Finally, with regard to the proximity of sexual opposition, unification, and the death of the individuals, Querner notes it (141) without discussing it in any detail. Yet the torment of idealism occurs when the perfection of *Gestaltung* runs full-speed into illness and demise. Sexuality is the site of *contagium* as *illness*, the site of the bridge to death.

### 7. The Bridge to Death

1. Sigmund Freud, *Aus den Anfängen der Psychoanalyse*, ed. Ernst Kris (New York: Imago, 1950), 381; see Krell, *Of Memory, Reminiscence, and Writing* (cited in note 1 to chap. 3), chap. 3, esp. 112. Detlev von Uslar, "Die Aktualität Schellings für Tiefenpsychologie und Psychotherapie," in Hasler, ed., *Schelling: Seine Bedeutung* (cited in note 5 to chap. 2), 163–66, notes the propinquity of Schelling to Jung, no doubt due to the historically mediating writings of Carl Gustav Carus, Eduard von Hartmann, and Arthur Schopenhauer. Von Uslar emphasizes the importance of Schelling's view of dream life and the unconscious, but I would place considerably more stress on the propinquity to Freud, especially to the *Trieblehre* and the difficult question of the dualism of drives in Freud's late metapsychology. I would argue that if Schelling is close to Jung it is because they both make trouble for Freud's exquisite dualism—Freud's intense and legendary desire, his drive, to separate off the erotic from the death drives. The expression *lifedeath*, used throughout the present volume, is meant to contribute to that trouble for Freud entirely in the spirit of Schelling's tormented idealism.

2. Aristotle, *On the Soul,* 413–14, 421–23, and 435, takes up the aporia of the organ and medium of touch, that is, σάρξ, "flesh." I have referred to the Loeb Classical Library edition throughout, translated by W. S. Hett (Cambridge: Harvard University Press, 1975).

3. *Erster Entwurf,* 87–88n. 3; 90–91n. 2. On Schelling's critique of Brown in the *Ideen* and *Von der Weltseele,* recantation of the critique in the *Erster Entwurf,* and later reinstantiation of the critique, see Nelly Tsouyopoulos, "Schellings Krankheitsbegriff," in Heckmann et al., eds., *Natur und Subjektivität* (cited in note 2 to chap. 5), 270–71. In these pages Tsouyopoulos also clarifies the often very confusing Brownian terms *receptivity (receptivitas, Empfänglichkeit), sensibility, irritability (irritabilitas), excitability (incitabilitas, Erregbarkeit,* itself resulting from the *combination* of sensibility and irritability). Erich Mende, "Die Entwicklungsgeschichte der Faktoren Irritabilität und Sensibilität in deren Einfluß auf Schellings 'Prinzip' als Ursache des Lebens," in *Philosophia naturalis* 17 (1979): 327–48, offers a detailed account of the theory of irritability in the history of medicine from Haller and Brown to Schelling's 1797 *Ideen.* See also Dietrich von Engelhardt, "Schellings philosophische Grundlegung der Medizin," which offers a detailed account of Schelling's concept of excitability (that is, of sensibility/irritability) and reproduction; in Sandkühler, ed., *Natur und geschichtlicher Prozess* (cited in note 2 to chap. 5), 310–11; on John Brown's system in general, see 315–16. For a brief but excellent introductory account of Brown and Schelling, see Günter B. Risse (cited in note 1 to chap. 5), esp. 325–34. Finally, for detailed information on the essential *background* to John Brown's theory of irritability and sensibility, especially on Haller and Blumenbach, see once again the extensive study by Jörg Jantzen, "Physiologische Theorien," in Schelling, *Historisch-kritische Ausgabe,* ed. Baumgartner et al. (cited in note 1 to chap. 6), 375–498.

4. Georg Simmel, in *Lebensanschauung: Vier metaphysische Kapitel* (Munich: Duncker und Humblot, 1918), 109 n., argues that God can be rescued only if we go back to Schelling's notion of *Indifferenz* or Spinoza's "infinite attributes," drawing the full consequences of their arguments by *depriving God of life.* In short, only God's death—his being, as Novalis put it, as dense as the most compact metal—can keep him "alive." For a discussion of Simmel, see Krell, *Daimon Life: Heidegger and Life-Philosophy* (cited in note 10 to the introduction), 94–95.

5. In my view, the most interesting pages of this second section are *EE,* 116–18, where Schelling begins to discuss the fundamental forces of expansion and contraction, forces that were central to Goethe's natural science and that will be essential to Schelling's future account of the potencies in the 1809 treatise *On Human Freedom* and the later *Ages of the World.* This analysis culminates in a *trialism,* beyond dualism, in Schelling's search for the common source of organic and anorganic nature (see also *EE,* 163, 193, 199, 214).

6. *Erster Entwurf,* 159, 218. It would be interesting to compare what Schelling does with the famous principle of identity—both here and in later texts such as the *Stuttgarter Privatvorlesungen* of 1810—to Heidegger's treat-

ment in "Der Satz der Identität," *Identität und Differenz* (Pfullingen: Günter Neske, 1957), 9–30.

## 8. THE ULTIMATE SOURCE OF LIFE

1. Johann Wolfgang von Goethe, *"Grundzüge"* (1824), in *Naturwissenschaftliche Schriften*, 1: 424; discussed in the introduction, above.

2. On Schelling's account of the pathology of hypersthenic and asthenic disease, see the helpful diagram and detailed explanations of Nelly Tsouyopoulos, "Schellings Krankheitsbegriff," in Heckmann et al., eds., *Natur und Subjektivität* (cited in note 2 to chap. 5), 274–77. According to Tsouyopoulos, Schelling's greatest achievement is to unite the aspects of excitability (that is, sensibility and irritability conjoined) to an account of reproduction—in the sense of the regeneration of tissue—and to understand illness as a disturbance in such reproduction. Disturbances occur, for example, in the systems of secretion—on which, as we have seen, Novalis too had placed so much emphasis. As we have also mentioned, the pathology of excitability is discussed in terms of deviation *(Abweichung)* from the norm, in such a way that the sequence of stages in nature's development itself appears to be pathological. (For further discussion, see note 5, below.)

3. *Erster Entwurf*, 231. Dietrich von Engelhardt notes the importance of this threshold below which stimulation dare not fail, this "minimum of sensibility," for Schelling's Brownian-Röschlaubian theory of illness; see von Engelhardt, "Die organische Natur," in Heckmann et al., eds., *Natur und Subjektivität* (cited in note 2 to chap. 5), 48.

4. See Dietrich von Engelhardt, "Schellings philosophische Grundlegung der Medizin," in Sandkühler, ed., *Natur und geschichtlicher Prozess* (cited in note 2 to chap. 5), 313, and Günter B. Risse (cited in note 1 to chap. 5), 330. Even though von Engelhardt and Risse emphasize that illness is a natural phenomenon and a fundamental appearance of life itself, a *Lebenserscheinung*, they do not draw the consequence that life itself may be a phenomenon of illness and deviation. To be sure, Schelling too resists drawing that consequence; yet every strand of his argumentation ties the knot between life and illness. Nor is it enough to respond to Schelling's notions of a life wrested from nature against her will, a life that struggles against nature only to destroy itself, by appealing, as Werner Hartkopf does, to some sort of parallel to Hegel's notion of "the cunning of reason" in world history; see Hartkopf (cited in note 1 to chap. 5), 82–83. For just as spirit's cunning in world history turns out to be a dialectic of either wickedness or stupidity or both, so do nature's and life's internecine battles disclose themselves as a dialectic of absolute self-destruction. *Absolute* self-destruction, however, includes the destruction of any and every system of reason.

5. I would like to conclude this section on Schelling by affirming that Nelly Tsouyopoulos's articles are the most informative and incisive articles on Schelling's theory of illness that I have found; see "Schellings Krankheitsbegriff," in Heckmann et al., eds., *Natur und Subjektivität* (cited in note

2 to chap. 5), 265–90; "Der Streit zwischen Friedrich Wilhelm Joseph Schelling und Andreas Röschlaub," *Medizinhistorisches Journal* (cited in note 1 to chap. 5); and "Schellings Konzeption der Medizin als Wissenschaft und die 'Wissenschaftlichkeit' der modernen Medizin," in Hasler, ed., *Schelling: Seine Bedeutung* (cited in note 5 to chap. 2), 107–16. Tsouyopoulos has clearly recognized the importance of the 1799 *Erster Entwurf* in Schelling's natural-philosophical oeuvre as well as the significance of the theory of illness developed there for 1) Schelling's entire philosophy of nature and 2) the history of medicine generally. With regard to this last point, Tsouyopoulos is not alone. Richard Toellner, "Randbedingungen zu Schellings Konzeption der Medizin als Wissenschaft," also in Hasler, ed., *Schelling: Seine Bedeutung*, 117–28, is in fundamental agreement with her; he notes that Schelling helps modern medicine to escape "its theoretical cul-de-sac," that is, to overcome the impasse of an empiricism devoid of theoretical principles (117). In "Schellings Konzeption," Nelly Tsouyopoulos shows that Schelling's conception of medicine is fundamentally *semiotic* in nature, employing symptomatology not only for diagnosis but also for purposes of therapy (108–109). Schelling's semiotic view—one that we might also quite readily attribute to Novalis—counters the prevailing view that illness is "unnatural" with a more holistic approach. Her considered assessment of Schelling's achievement is quite positive: "Schelling's conception of medicine as a science contributed to the effort to overcome the . . . stagnation of medicine. The demand on medicine was actually quite clear: a scientific pathology would have to exhibit, on the one hand, an organic relation to pathology and, on the other hand, a principle of therapy that it could dispense" (111). She argues that Schelling's theory and therapy based on *excitability* fulfilled both conditions. Her "Schellings Krankheitsbegriff" and "Der Streit" are equally affirming. If her studies consistently end on an optimistic note—the positive contributions of Schellingian theory to modern medical practice— that is because she values so highly Schelling's contribution to the history of medicine: in "Schellings Krankheitsbegriff" she takes his unified theory of excitability and reproduction to anticipate one of the most exciting areas of twentieth-century pathology, namely, Dr. Hans Selye's theory of stress. See Hans Selye, *The Stress of Life* (New York: McGraw Hill, 1956). If Schelling's resistance to his own fruitful discovery seems mysterious to Tsouyopoulos ("Krankheitsbegriff," 282), however, I hope to have shown that such resistance can be explained by the monstrous consequences to which Schelling's theory of illness must lead him—monstrous in the sense that his theory demonstrates that the ultimate source of life is the bridge to death and that the absolute is riven. According to Tsouyopoulos, the flaw that runs through Schelling's *Erster Entwurf* is the result of his attempt to accommodate two contradictory influences: first, Karl Friedrich Kielmeyer's theory of the sequence of stages in the development of life throughout nature, which had impressed Schelling as early as 1793; and second, the pathogenetic theory of Andreas Röschlaub, which Schelling had apparently discovered only in the middle of his 1799 lecture course (Tsouyopoulos, "Krankheitsbegriff," 268– 69). Röschlaub's theory, developed in the first volume of his *Untersuchungen*

*über Pathogenie* (1798), was itself based on John Brown's theory of sensibility-irritability-reproduction. Schelling embraced Röschlaub's Brownian theory, abandoning his earlier criticisms of Brown in his 1798 *Von der Weltseele* only to intensify those criticisms in later years (281–82); on the details of Schelling's break with Röschlaub in 1803, which weakened the influence of *Naturphilosophie* on the theory and practice of medicine in Germany, see Tsouyopoulos, "Der Streit," 229–46; see also "Schellings Konzeption," 112. For a brief stretch of time, according to Tsouyopoulos, Schelling was caught between the contradictory demands of ontology (von Kielmeyer) and pathology (Röschlaub). However, I would argue that what tormented Schelling was not only the difficulty of reconciling mechanism and biological dynamism, or empirical and teleological judgment, or the mystery of psychosomatic illness to either of these two oppositions, as Tsouyopoulos claims, but also the fundamental problem (that is, the pathologico-ontological problem) of excitability as such—the ultimate source of life itself. It is not that Schelling collapses back into a "Cartesian dualism," as Tsouyopoulos believes, nor that he merely succumbs to contradictory influences. If he consistently denounces the Brownian-Röschlaubian theory after 1800 it is because he already knows that the absolute will die on account of it. The *homeostasis* of Hans Selye's stress theory therefore cannot be identified with Schelling's concept of *Indifferenz*, as Tsouyopoulos avers ("Krankheitsbegriff," 284), because such *Indifferenz*, though later (in the 1809 *Treatise on Human Freedom*) to be identified as the abyssal source of the life of God, is the death of the organism. Schelling's problem is not the stress of life but the life of stress, indeed, the life of torment, in which, to repeat, the ultimate source *is* the bridge to death. Schelling's problem is *la vielamort*. Without end—except for the end that is reached in the death of absolute activity.

A final "note to a note," a mere anecdote, if I may, to conclude part two, "Tormented Idealism." In 1806 Friedrich Schlegel writes Madame de Staël, condemning the "insanity" and "absurdity" of Schelling's philosophy of nature. Schlegel is apparently no longer sensitive to the proximity of Schelling's views to those of his deceased friend, Friedrich von Hardenberg. Schlegel mocks Schelling as "a philosophical surgeon" and derides Schelling's skein of concepts as *"signes de l'agonie."* (On Schlegel's letter, see Dietrich von Engelhardt, "Schellings philosophische Grundlegung der Medizin," in Sandkühler, ed., *Natur und geschichtlicher Prozess* [cited in note 2 to chap. 5], 308.) Schelling doubtless *is* a philosophic surgeon; in this Schlegel is surely correct. However, Schelling's patient is hemorrhaging, and beginning to slip into the final throes of his death agony. Schelling's patient is the absolute in and of all philosophy. What other signs, then, could there be for a tormented idealism than *signes de l'agonie?*

## 9. NATURE'S SEDUCTIVE IMPOTENCE

1. The importance of the Jena materials for our topic is demonstrated, *ex negativo*, I believe, by the eight extant sets of student notes on Hegel's

Berlin lecture courses on the philosophy of nature from 1818 to 1828. The third part of the philosophy of nature, first called "organic physics," and later "organics," is not much altered from the first edition of the *Encyclopedia* in 1817 to the second edition of 1828, this suggesting that Hegel did not alter his views on organic nature much during the decade of his lecture courses on nature philosophy. The addenda to the final paragraphs of the philosophy of nature (as edited by Karl Ludwig Michelet) recapitulate the much earlier analyses of the philosophy of nature in the Jena *Realphilosophie* courses, thus indicating the supreme importance of the early Jena materials for Hegel's view of the organism, sexuality, genitality, health and illness, etc. See Wolfgang Bonsiepen, "[Über Nachschriften zu] Hegels Vorlesungen über Naturphilosophie," in *Hegel-Studien* 26 (1991): 40–54, esp. 48–49. With regard to philological matters surrounding the Jena texts, see Rolf-Peter Horstmann's introduction to the *Jenaer Systementwürfe III*, ix–xxxii; see also the articles by Heinz Kimmerle, "Dokumente zu Hegels Jenaer Dozententätigkeit (1801–1807)," and "Zur Chronologie von Hegels Jenaer Schriften," in *Hegel-Studien* 4 (1967): 21–99, 125–76, respectively.

2. For the reference to the trash of the system, see 9: 28: "Thus nature has been expressed as being the *dejection* of the idea from itself *[der* Abfall *der Idee von sich selbst]."* The apparently supplementary or even superfluous question of the trash of the system is actually the much-debated question of the relation of Hegel's philosophy of nature to his *Logic,* in both its greater and lesser forms, and we shall have to return several times to the trash of the system. (A reminder that the edition of the *Encyclopedia* that I am using throughout is volume 9 of the *Werke in zwanzig Bänden: Theorie Werkausgabe,* cited in note 13 to the introduction. I refer to this work in the body of my text by volume, followed by page number, in parentheses.)

3. A reminder that the edition of Hegel's *Realphilosophie* that I am using is the new historical-critical edition; see *Jenaer Systementwürfe III: Naturphilosophie und Philosophie des Geistes* (cited in note 6 to the introduction). I shall be focusing on excerpts from pages 159–69 of this "Philosophische Bibliothek" text (corresponding to the *Gesammelte Werke,* 8: 171–84), citing the "Philosophische Bibliothek" volume as *JS,* followed by page numbers, in parentheses in the body of my text.

4. Georg Wilhelm Friedrich Hegel, *Phänomenologie des Geistes,* ed. Johannes Hofmeister, 6th ed. (Hamburg: F. Meiner, 1952), 156–58. On the theme of dizziness and swindle, see my *Of Memory, Reminiscence, and Writing: On the Verge* (cited in note 1 to chap. 3), chap. 5.

5. The *Theorie Werkausgabe* cites only four references in Hegel's oeuvre to Novalis. Two of them appear in his 1828 review of Karl Wilhelm Ferdinand Solger's *Posthumous Writings,* where Hegel comments on the "hollow characters and situations" of Novalis's *Heinrich von Ofterdingen* (11: 215). Such hollowness Hegel attributes—ironically, cruelly—to Novalis's consumptive spirit, which, itself hollow, brings on his tuberculosis. The compulsion to think conducted "this beautiful soul" only to the level of languor *(Sehnsucht)* and abstract intellect; such "transcendental languor" is nothing more than a tubercular spirit *(die Schwindsucht des Geistes),* which

penetrated Novalis's body and thus determined his corporeal fate in a way that was consistent with his spirit (11: 267). Hegel repeats the phrase "consumption of spirit" in his lectures on aesthetics, where he takes Novalis's transcendental longing as a more noble counterpart of Schlegelian irony—more noble but every bit as ineffectual (13: 211). Finally, in his lectures on the history of philosophy, Hegel aligns Novalis with the other subjective idealists surrounding Fichte. Once again, the words "beautiful soul" and "languor" flow from Hegel's pen, which then adds these concluding phrases: "Extravagant subjectivity often leads to insanity. If it perdures in the thought, it remains caught up in the maelstrom of the reflective understanding, which is always negative toward itself" (20: 418).

On the basis of Lore Hühn's convincing argumentation, I would suggest that Hegel's bitter critique of Novalis and the Romantics in general, especially of Romantic *irony* and *languor,* his fulmination against the "unfulfilled infinity" and "restlessness" of Fichte and all the Romantics, arises from his terror in the face of the wicked infinity that in his view marks and mars all life, nature, and "naturalness." If Hegel growls that the Romantics are entangled in endless, bootless rotations of infinite becoming, and that their irony and languor inevitably prove to be the despicable and contemptible responses of an inadequate philosophical starting point, if, in other words, Hegel dreams of a triumphant return to a tranquil repose in the absolute, he must also inevitably subject life, nature, and naturalness to an infinite brushfire, to pyrification and incineration. In a sense, what our own inquiry will have shown is that life and nature themselves are the great ironists, the desperate and ultimately defeated lovers. It is they, and not merely the Romantics, that a philosophy of the absolute must persecute. See, again, the thought-provoking article by Lore Hühn, "Das Schweben der Einbildungskraft" (cited in note 1 to chap. 2), esp. 573–74, 581.

6. *Theorie Werkausgabe,* 9: 28. On the issue of the trash of the system as a problem of the *logic* of Hegel's philosophy of nature, see Martin Drees, "The Logic of Hegel's Philosophy of Nature," in Michael John Petry, ed., *Hegel and Newtonianism* (Dordrecht: Kluwer Academic Publishers, 1993), 91–101. Drees argues (100–101) that Hegel "did not always remember that 'it is an error on the part of the philosophy of nature to attempt to face up to all phenomena'" (*Encyclopedia,* §270, Addendum [9: 106]). Hegel's remark comes at the conclusion of a discussion of Kepler and Newton, yet it surely has an impact on his view of contingency and accident throughout nature, including the realm of "organics." Hegel notes: "Philosophy must take as its point of departure the concept. And even if it arrives at few results, one has to be satisfied with them. It is a confusion in philosophy of nature to want to turn to *[Face machen]* all phenomena. This is what happens in the finite sciences, where everything is to be traced back to the universal thoughts (the hypotheses). The empirical alone here corroborates the hypothesis; for this reason, everything has to be explained. Whatever is known by virtue of the concept, however, is clear for itself and stands firm; philosophy need not be disquieted by the fact that not all phenomena have been explained" (9: 106).

It may be, however, that if Hegel "fails" to remember his disclaimer, that failure has to do with the demands of a *comprehensive* system of reason, for which no mere disclaimer will suffice. See Arnold Vincent Miller, "Defending Hegel's Philosophy of Nature," in Petry, ed., *Hegel and Newtonianism*, 103–113: "There is, therefore, a truly *essential* relationship between the *Logic* and the *Philosophy of Nature*, and any appraisal of his natural philosophy must recognize the significance of his achievement in having developed into such a well-ordered system the categories in which we habitually do our thinking" (103). And again: "The subject matter of the *Logic* may be more abstract than that of the *Philosophy of Nature*, but the general teleological principles, the analysis and synthesis by means of which it is ordered, are precisely the same" (109). Against Miller, I would only suggest that the good order of the *Logic* is constructed upon the disorder of dire forces in (philosophy of) nature—attempting, but failing, either to absorb or to excrete them. Finally, although this is to anticipate: on the identity of sexuality, illness, and death as structures of *logic*—each of them being *concrete universal concepts*—see Wolfgang Jacob, "Der Krankheitsbegriff in der Dialektik von Natur und Geist bei Hegel," in Hans-Georg Gadamer, ed., *Stuttgarter Hegel-Tage 1970* (cited in note 14 to the introduction), 165.

7. *Theorie Werkausgabe*, 9: 35. It is intriguing to see how Hegel sometimes *uses* the notion of the "weakness of the concept in nature." When he sees the inconsistencies in Plato's *Timaeus*, he variously attributes those inconsistencies to 1) the theory (made popular by the philologist Wolf during Hegel's time) that the dialogue is but a compilation of Pythagorean views; 2) Plato's insufficient empirical background, which cannot meet the demands of his far-ranging reflection; but also 3) the weakness of the concept in nature herself. According to this third reason, if either Plato or Timaeus got nature wrong, she, nature, is herself to blame. See Jean-Louis Vieilliard-Baron, "L'interprétation hégélienne du *Timée*, ou la philosophie de la nature," *Revue de Métaphysique et de Morale* 81, no. 3 (July–September 1976): 376–95.

8. On the theme of the weakness of the concept in nature, as exemplified in the profusion of monstrosities, especially in the animal kingdom, and on Hegel's rejection of the great chain of being, that is, his rejection of the rational confidence in nature inherited from Aristotle and Leibniz, see Hans Querner, "Die Stufenfolge der Organismen in Hegels Philosophie der Natur," in Hans-Georg Gadamer, ed., *Stuttgarter Hegel-Tage 1970* (cited in note 14 to the introduction), 161–62. To be sure, this matter is closely related to Hegel's view of evolution in general and especially to his contrasting of evolution with emanationism. See Wolfgang Bonsiepen, "Hegels kritische Auseinandersetzung mit der zeitgenössischen Evolutionstheorie," in Rolf-Peter Horstmann and Michael John Petry, eds., *Hegels Philosophie der Natur: Beziehungen zwischen empirischer und spekulativer Naturerkenntnis* (Stuttgart: Klett-Cotta, 1986), 151–71, and Olaf Breidbach, "Hegels Evolutionskritik," *Hegel-Studien* 22 (1987): 165–72, for accounts of Hegel's critique of "evolution." Evolution is obviously not to be taken in a Darwinian sense here but

either as the "preformation" of individuals *in ovo* or of species in the divine mind, hence the very opposite of what we today take evolution to mean, or in the Lamarckian sense of the evolution of species through the inheritance of acquired characteristics. To the preformationist view, Hegel opposes the theological notion of *Emanation;* the latter, according to §249 of the *Encyclopedia,* has in Hegel's view distinct advantages over the preformationist-evolutionary view. To the Lamarckian view of species evolution, Hegel opposes his notion of the *stages* of spirit. Martin Drees, "Evolution and Emanation of Spirit in Hegel's *Philosophy of Nature," Bulletin of the Hegel Society of Great Britain* 26 (Autumn-Winter 1992): 52–61, argues against Wolfgang Bonsiepen (and in agreement with Breidbach) that Hegel is essentially an emanationist, rather than an evolutionist, in spite of his commitment to the development of spirit. In defense of Bonsiepen, it must be said that he too notes Hegel's opposition to biological evolution: Bonsiepen offers a close reading of Hegel's lectures from the winter semester of 1823/24, lectures that constitute a new "introduction" to his philosophy of nature. In these lectures Hegel counterposes his own (or Schelling's?!) conception of a sequence of "stages" in nature to the prevailing views of evolution, emanation, and biological or historical metamorphosis (152–53). Like Breidbach and Drees, Bonsiepen too recounts Hegel's rejection—in the strongest rhetorical terms—of biological evolution, which lies essentially beyond his imagination. Finally, on evolutionary *Zufall* and *Zufälligkeit,* especially with regard to contemporary discussions in the biological sciences of the invariance and mutation of genetic inheritance, see Vittorio Hösle, "Pflanze und Tier," in Michael John Petry, ed., *Hegel und die Naturwissenschaften* (Stuttgart: Frommann-Holzboog, 1987), 386–88. A final remark on accident and contingency: it seems to me—as it seemed to Schelling—that any effort to integrate nature into a system of reason must confront without conceptual sleight-of-hand the problem of nature's contingency; that is, such efforts must avoid statements like the following: "Contingency as such, the form that varies arbitrarily but remains consistent in itself, is accessible to reflection." See Olaf Breidbach, *Das Organische in Hegels Denken: Studie zur Naturphilosophie und Biologie um 1800* (Würzburg: Königshausen & Neumann, 1982), 270. Monstrosity is only rarely consistent with itself, especially when it varies arbitrarily; and if it ever *is* consistent, it is so only in order to tease systems of reason.

9. James Joyce, *Ulysses* (London: Bodley Head, 1960), 212. For the heaventree of stars, see 819.

10. There is, as far as I know, no literature on the nonrelationship of Hegel to Novalis. Yet the literature on Hegel and Schelling is as voluminous as it is depressing. Why depressing? Xavier Tilliette gives the answer: "Hegel's and Schelling's relations are forever star-crossed." By that Tilliette means that the mutual recrimination that began during the careers of both thinkers has continued unabated since their deaths. One must, he argues, avoid championing one thinker over another—a temptation to which I will succumb when I go on to call Hegel the "junior partner" on the *Critical*

*Journal* project. No doubt, Hegel, though Schelling's senior, is dependent on Schelling in institutional-philosophical terms: it was Schelling who enabled him to write his habilitation thesis, receive the *venia legendi* (the right to give lectures as a *Privatdozent*), and then to receive the call as Adjunct Professor. Yet from the Tübinger Stift days onward, Hegel, the "Old Man," as the others called him, was no one's intellectual junior partner. And so the debate has raged about who owes what to whom. Perhaps one may say that Hegel learned a great deal from Schelling when it came to the philosophy of nature and to the need to respond to Fichte; whereas Hegel taught Schelling much about the nature of speculation and the goal of a rational system of the absolute. See Xavier Tilliette, "Hegel in Jena als Mitarbeiter Schellings," in Dieter Henrich and Klaus Düsing, eds., *Hegel in Jena* (cited in note 3 to chap. 5), 12. On the early cooperation of Schelling and Hegel in Jena, see also Klaus Düsing, "Spekulation und Reflexion: Zur Zusammenarbeit Schellings und Hegels in Jena," *Hegel-Studien* 5 (1969): 95–128. Of course, the original and most extraordinary document of the close cooperation of Schelling and Hegel, along with Hölderlin, is the 1797 "Oldest Program toward a System in German Idealism." See my presentation of it in *Owl of Minerva* 17, no. 1 (Fall 1985): 5–19. Finally, for an account of Schelling's later criticisms of Hegel's philosophy of nature (as both a distortion of Schelling's own views and as a "logicizing" of nature), see Rolf-Peter Horstmann, "Logifizierte Natur oder naturalisierte Logik? Bemerkungen zu Schellings Hegel-Kritik," in Horstmann and Petry, eds., *Hegels Philosophie der Natur* (cited in note 8, above), 290–308.

11. For an explicit reference to Brown in the *Encyclopedia*, see 9: 437. For a discussion of Hegel's relation to the theories of John Brown, see Dietrich von Engelhardt, "Hegel's Philosophical Understanding of Illness," in Robert S. Cohen and Marx W. Wartofsky, eds., *Hegel and the Sciences* (Dordrecht: D. Reidel, Kluwer Academic Publishers, 1984), 126–27. In a more recent article, von Engelhardt offers a helpful discussion (and diagram) of Hegel's deployment of the Brownian system. As is always the case with Hegelian dialectic, the Brownian system is here brought to a kind of intussusception, inasmuch as sensibility, irritability, and reproduction function at each of the three stages: within sensibility, that is to say, within the nervous system, centered in the head, irritability and reproduction are also present and at work; within irritability, that is, the circulatory system, centered in the chest, sensibility and reproduction are also active; and in reproduction, that is, the digestive system, centered in the gut wall (stomach and intestines), sensibility and irritability are also present. See von Engelhardt, "Die biologischen Wissenschaften in Hegels Naturphilosophie," in Horstmann and Petry, eds., *Hegels Philosophie der Natur* (cited in note 8, above), 121–37, esp. 128.

12. Sandor Ferenczi, *Versuch einer Genitaltheorie*, in *Schriften*, ed. Michael Balint, 2 vols. (Frankfurt am Main: Fischer Taschenbuch Verlag, 1982), 2: 317–400; translated by Henry Alden Bunker as *Thalassa: A Theory of Genitality* (New York: W. W. Norton, 1968).

## 10. TURNED TO THE OUTSIDE:
### THE DIALECTIC OF GENITALITY

1. On the question of animal assimilation in Hegel, see Mark C. E. Peterson, "Animals Eating Empiricists: Assimilation and Subjectivity in Hegel's *Philosophy of Nature*," *Owl of Minerva* 23, no. 1 (Fall 1991): 49–62. Peterson takes as his starting point Hegel's apparently humorous references in the *Phenomenology of Spirit* to animals—which recognize the truth of sensuous certainty and express it by going out to devour sensuous beings. Peterson shows that attention to the account of assimilation in the *Encyclopedia* transforms the joke into a dialectical profundity. What he fails to consider is the question as to whether the animals in question include *human* animals, that is, whether human beings too (empiricists eating empiricists) express the truth of sensuous certainty when they eat. Nor does Peterson note that dialecticians as well as empiricists belong to the diet of certain carnivores. Nor, finally, does he take up the most important aspect of Hegel's little joke: just as assimilation involves a "poisoning" of the ingested materials, so does theoretical ingestion destroy what it takes in. For Hegel, the dialectician's chickens, after they go out to devour niblets of corn, always come home to roost. On the less jocular matter of the milk of the breast and the "gentle elevation" of the "moralized chest," see once again the remarks by Novalis cited in chapter 1. Inasmuch as, for Hegel, reproduction belongs to the system of assimilation, this particular elevation, turned to the outside, has beguilingly multiple senses.

2. Friedrich Schlegel, *Lucinde*, 14.

3. On the inadequacy of plants with regard to genuine interiority, and the paradoxical exclusion of vegetable life from the sexual sphere, see Hans Querner, "Die Stufenfolge der Organismen in Hegels Philosophie der Natur," in Gadamer, ed., *Stuttgarter Hegel-Tage 1970* (cited in note 14 to the introduction), 157–58.

4. On the problem of *Natürlichkeit*, see the "debate" on freedom between Karl Heinz Volkmann-Schluck, "Die Entäußerung der Idee zur Natur," in Hans-Georg Gadamer, ed. *Hegel-Studien*, supplement 1: *Heidelberger Hegel-Tage 1962* (1964): 37–44, and Dieter Wandschneider and Vittorio Hösle, "Die Entäußerung der Idee zur Natur und ihre zeitliche Entfaltung als Geist bei Hegel," *Hegel-Studien* 18 (1983): 173–99. Volkmann-Schluck devotes himself to the problem of the transition from *logic* to *philosophy of nature* in Hegel's system, conceived of as a system of and by "the absolute idea," focusing on the dilemma of the movement of the idea into nature as both *necessary* and *free* (41). Dieter Wandschneider and Vittorio Hösle try to argue against Volkmann-Schluck that the concept of freedom that needs to be employed in the question of spirit's self-externalization as nature is a highly complex one, and that it cannot be merely counterposed to some concept of necessity. Yet in their very ambitious and closely argued article, they themselves succumb to the stale, flat, and unprofitable view that nature is in the end merely "the vehicle of spirit's realization" (185). Such a vehicular

view makes nonsense of the question of freedom and necessity. Neverthe-less, in the context of this debate on freedom, Wandschneider and Hösle offer an excellent account of Hegelian *Natürlichkeit,* which they relate to the "contingent moments" that cause the purity of the system to be "veiled, deformed, and elliptical" (195). With perhaps unintended irony, they call such "natural factors" and "elements of accident" a kind of *Irritation.* Yet if irritability is the eminent sign of life for Hegel, as it is, then the moment of accident and contingency is itself the highest necessity of the life of spirit. If the *history* of spirit "is constantly crossed and frustrated by the inelimin-ability of the natural" (196), and no doubt it is, one must push on to the question as to how Hegel can repeatedly pursue the goal of its elimination, seeing in such elimination the triumph of spirit—rather than spirit's death without resurrection.

5. Once again, the passages from the *Jenaer Systementwürfe III: Natur-philosophie und Philosophie des Geistes (JS)* that I will be reproducing here appear at pages 159–69 of the volume cited, corresponding to the *Gesammelte Werke,* 8: 171–84. Note that in what follows I have moved Hegel's marginal notes back into the body of his text. I realize that this makes reading the text terribly difficult: one has to suffer endless irritating interruptions. Yet that seemed to me the only way to rescue Hegel's notes from my own footnotes. Hegel's marginal notes appear in fancy brackets {like these}. My own interventions in the quotations occur in square brackets.

6. When Hegel insists that illness—which we will discuss in greater detail in chapter 11—occurs as the *succession* of stages in the organism, he means that it shatters the unity and simultaneity of the organism's sundry systems. Malady usurps the function of organization as such, allowing the organism to break down into a number of discrete functions. See Wolfgang Jacob, "Der Krankheitsbegriff in der Dialektik von Natur und Geist bei Hegel," in Hans-Georg Gadamer, ed., *Stuttgarter Hegel-Tage 1970* (cited in note 14 to the introduction), 169.

7. Friedrich Schlegel, *Lucinde,* 17.

8. See Jacques Derrida, *Glas* (cited in note 10 to the introduction), 130A/113A.

9. *Das Entzweite* is itself, to repeat, the differing, differentiating part. Thus it is not merely one "part" for or of Hegel. The action of *Entzweiung,* which we have seen everywhere in Schelling's philosophy of nature, ex-presses the very fate of totality in the system. It is the origin of everything in Hegel that can be called life, need, drive, striving, craving, or desire. On all these matters, see Konio Kozu, *Das Bedürfnis der Philosophie: Ein Überblick über die Entwicklung des Begriffskomplexes "Bedürfnis," "Trieb," "Streben" und "Begierde" bei Hegel,* published as *Hegel-Studien,* supplement 30 (1988): 104, and elsewhere. Kozu's helpful overview does not include a detailed treat-ment of the sexual-genital relation, however.

10. See John McCumber, "Commentary on [Murray Greene's] 'Natural Life and Subjectivity,'" in Peter G. Stillman, ed., *Hegel's Philosophy of Spirit* (Albany: State University of New York Press, 1987), 119. McCumber cites

Hegel's remark on the male prostate as "a likely story" in the sense of Plato's *Timaeus*. He encourages us, however, not to read the statement for its empirical verifiability but to see it in the context of Hegel's "rigorously developed" system. "I do not see why such a sentence should lose its place in the system if, for various reasons, scientists should cease to assert it" (119–20). Nor do I. Hegel's analysis of the slippage in and of the prostrate from the reproductive to the urinary system in fact encapsulates the entire story of spirit externalized as nature. Thus the statement not only belongs to "our spiritual gene pool," as McCumber avers, but is also symptomatic of the status of nature—of nature's prost(r)ation—in Hegel's system as a whole.

11. Luce Irigaray, "The Eternal Irony of the Community," in *Spéculum de l'autre femme* (Paris: Minuit, 1974), 266–81; translated as *Speculum of the Other Woman* by Gillian C. Gill (Ithaca: Cornell University Press, 1985), 214–26.

12. See the addendum to §349 of the *Encyclopedia* on the transition from the plant's ethereal oil to the warm-blooded animal (9: 429), §354, on blood as the essentially *nourishing* element and the inherent *agitation* of the animal organism (9: 440, 447), and the addendum to §356, where Hegel tries to show that blood is self-moving, that it does not depend even on the heart for its coursing through the veins (9: 461–63). There are of course other references—these hematological hints are only the beginning. The matter is important, inasmuch as heat and fluidity are positive signs of life—and health—for Hegel. On the fluidity of life, and the possible restoration of health to the individual, see Wolfgang Jacob, "Der Krankheitsbegriff in der Dialektik von Natur und Geist bei Hegel," in Gadamer, ed., *Stuttgarter Hegel-Tage 1970* (cited in note 14 to the introduction), 169. John N. Findlay, "The Hegelian Treatment of Biology and Life," in Cohen and Wartofsky, eds., *Hegel and the Sciences* (cited in note 11 to chap. 9), 87–100, offers an interesting account of Hegel on *Flüssigkeit*, fluidity or flux; see esp. 91–92.

13. Gaston Bachelard, *L'Air et les songes: Essai sur l'imagination du mouvement* (Paris: José Corti, 1943), 148: "It is one of the most infallible touchstones: only a passionate lover of the earth, only a terrestrian touched by a bit of aquatism can escape from the *automatically pejorative* character of the metaphor of the *spongy.*" Bachelard's context is Nietzsche's ostensibly "ascensional psychism," and I have replied to it, and to Irigaray's reading of Nietzsche, in the final chapter of Krell, *Infectious Nietzsche* (cited in note 9 to the introduction). Bachelard would also have been intrigued by *Schelling*'s version of the "upswelling heart": in *The Ages of the World*, Schelling describes the origins of *space* as *turgescence*. See *Die Weltalter Fragmente* (cited in note 12 to chap. 5), 85–86.

14. I have commented on this passage in Hegel's Jena *Realphilosophie* elsewhere, precisely in this respect: see David Farrell Krell, "Lucinde's Shame: Hegel, Sensuous Woman, and the Law," in *Hegel and Legal Theory*, ed. Drucilla Cornell, Michel Rosenfeld, and David Gray Carlson (New York: Routledge, 1991), 287–300; revised and reprinted under the same title in *Feminist Readings of Hegel*, ed. Patricia Jagentowicz Mills (University Park: Pennsylvania State University Press, 1995), 89–107.

## 11. Turned to the Inside:
## The Dialectic of Death

1. The squalor of the living may be viewed in terms of the relationship of biology to chemistry, inasmuch as the organic constantly threatens to regress to the level of mere chemical alteration. Dietrich von Engelhardt analyzes Hegel's conception of death, at least as a *physical* fact, in terms of such a reduction of the organic to the chemical: "Chemistry continues to work its effects in the organic realm, just as anorganic principles in general are still valid for botany and zoology; in illness and death the perdurant power of the chemical reveals itself." See von Engelhardt, *Hegel und die Chemie: Studie zur Philosophie und Wissenschaft der Natur um 1800* (Wiesbaden: Guido Pressler Verlag, 1976), 102. See also, by the same author, "Hegel on Chemistry and the Organic Sciences," in Petry, ed., *Hegel and Newtonianism* (cited in note 6 to chap. 9), 657–65. In his account of biochemistry, von Engelhardt stresses the close relation between assimilation and the account of disease in Hegel's notion of the organism: see esp. 662–63. On Hegel's understanding of illness and medicine in general, see Dietrich von Engelhardt, "Hegel's Philosophical Understanding of Illness," in Cohen and Wartofsky, eds., *Hegel and the Sciences* (cited in note 11 to chap. 9), 123–41, which gives an excellent account of Hegel's difficult position on the theories of medicine contemporary to him. To make a long and complex history short, Hegel despises both the empiricism that is devoid of philosophical principles and the Romantic *Naturphilosophie* that is too confident about prescribing such principles. Empiricism atomizes appearances, Romanticism analogizes them, and Hegel is allergic to both. If the former is always bogged down in matter, like an architecture too much in love with its materials, the second is soaring through the air without a thought to foundations. Yet Hegel's discomfiture with regard to theories of medicine may run deeper: it may well be that the squalor of the living runs so deep that Hegel despairs of a cure—life being the incurable melanomas of sea and sky.

2. For Hegel's remark, see the *Theorie Werkausgabe*, 9: 474; for Heidegger's, see *Basic Writings* (cited above in note 5 to chap. 1), 352: "Mortals dwell in that they receive the sky as sky. They leave to the sun and the moon their journey, to the stars their courses, to the seasons their blessing and their inclemency; they do not turn night into day nor day into a harassed unrest."

3. On the figures of the Phoenix, Phoenix-fire, and the burning of nature, as a theme in the alchemical and Christian-mystical traditions, see Karin Figala, "Der alchemische Begriff des Caput Mortuum in der symbolischen Terminologie Hegels," in Gadamer, ed., *Stuttgarter Hegel-Tage 1970* (cited in note 14 to the introduction), 141–51.

4. Although I will not pause to do so here, an interesting comparative study of Schelling and Hegel on *Hemmung* could be made. In addition to the sources on Schelling cited earlier, one should examine the following pages of the *Encyclopedia*, which refer in important ways to inhibition: 9: 417–19, on the growth and configuration of plants; 9: 424, on the destiny of the sexual parts of plants; 9: 428, on the scarring of plants (caprification) in order to

induce their going to seed; and 9: 520, on the inhibition of the liquid process in animal life through illness. No doubt there are other references, but these would be sufficient to get such a comparative study going.

5. Wolfgang Jacob cites a declaration in Hegel's very early Jena course on *Realphilosophie*, from the year 1803, that is most apt for this mystifying emergence of consciousness, to which we will no doubt have to return: "With illness, the animal steps beyond the boundaries of its nature; but the animal's illness is spirit's becoming." See Jacob, "Der Krankheitsbegriff in der Dialektik von Natur und Geist bei Hegel," in Gadamer, ed., *Stuttgarter Hegel-Tage 1970* (cited in note 14 to the introduction), 165.

6. See Martin Heidegger, *Sein und Zeit*, 12th ed. (Tübingen: Max Niemeyer Verlag, 1972), 283. On the question of the organic in Heidegger, see Krell, *Daimon Life: Heidegger and Life-Philosophy* (cited in note 10 to the introduction), esp. chaps. 6 and 9.

7. In the margin at this point Hegel cites a fragment of Heraclitus, which he numbers 144B, a fragment not in Diels-Kranz with regard to any of the pre-Socratic thinkers. (It is reminiscent of Empedocles more than Heraclitus, but, to repeat, it cannot be found in this form ascribed to any author anywhere in Diels-Kranz; it may appear in the Schleiermacher collection of the fragments, which I believe Hegel is using but which I have been unable to track down.) Hegel reproduces it as follows: ὅσα ἐν ἡμιν ἑκαστου κρατος νοσημα, ὑπερβολη θερμου, πυρετος, ὑπερβολη ψυχρου παραλυσις, — ὑπερβολη πνευματος, πνιγος. An approximation: "The dominion of each thing in us is illness; for excess of heat makes us feverish, excess of cold freezes us, and excess of wind suffocates us."

While the present note has us among the ancients, I should add that everything that is being said here—and has been said throughout the book—ought to be read once again in the context of Plato's *Symposium*, in at least three of its moments: 1) at the moment when Diotima is identified in one breath as the one who preserves Athens from the *plague* for ten years (201d 4–5: τῆς νόσου) and the one who teaches Socrates τὰ ἐρωτικά (ibid.); 2) in the context of Eryximachus's entire speech, in which love, opposites, and illness are interwoven; and 3) at the moment when Diotima asserts that every animal, including the mortal human, when it is hot for love, appears to be both sick and lovesick (207b 1: νοσοῦντά τε πάντα καὶ ἐρωτικῶς). It may be that where the aporias of *eros* and *morbus* are concerned, thinkers in the West have not made much progress since the good doctor and Socrates' Diotima—who is both "most wise" and "the perfect sophist"—spoke.

8. During the philosophical meeting that celebrated the two-hundredth anniversary of Hegel's birth in Stuttgart, Heinrich Schipperges presented a catalogue of the most bizarre notions in Hegel's nature philosophy, intending to show why Hegel's account of nature has for so long been neglected by philosophers. Schipperges concluded his list of Hegel's sins with a reference to what we have just now heard: ". . . to say nothing at all of his doctrine of illness as a mystical assignation *[der mystischen Beischlafslehre]*, in which the individual 'as it were, mates with itself.'" It is with this assignation of self

with self, male-self with female-self, that I am principally concerned in part three of the present book. I am pursuing the theme of self-mating as illness and death, however, not in order to cultivate the bizarre, nor to surrender Hegel to either Carl Jung or Sigmund Freud, but in order to observe Hegel at his very best. See Schipperges, in Hans-Georg Gadamer, ed., *Stuttgarter Hegel-Tage 1970* (cited in note 14 to the introduction), 105.

9. For a general discussion of Hegel's view of illness, see Werner Leibbrand, *Die spekulative Medizin der Romantik* (Hamburg: Claassen Verlag, 1956), 267–70. For a more detailed view, see Dietrich von Engelhardt, "Hegel's Philosophical Understanding of Illness," in Cohen and Wartofsky, eds., *Hegel and the Sciences* (cited in note 11 to chap. 9), 128–29. Von Engelhardt follows Hegel's "idea of illness" to the very edge of the thought of self-mating. Yet, perhaps because that thought is not as starkly developed in Michelet's addendum as it is by Hegel himself at the conclusion of his course on *Realphilosophie* at Jena in 1805/06, von Engelhardt does not see that the illness of the body contaminates the thought of spirit—in other words, that the birth of spirit is a birth by contagion. Von Engelhardt writes: "As the individual human being fundamentally cannot transfer the spiritual universality that is possible for him into his bodily individuality, cannot let it appear in sensual reality, he must die, and again and again he becomes ill. Spirit is eternal. In illness and in death, the aliveness and mental character of humankind manifest themselves; pain is the privilege of the higher developmental stages of nature. All the processes of illness ultimately pass over into a process that can no longer be recovery. . . . Illness documents the power of nature over the individual; in the sexual relationship, man relates to nature in another person, in taking nourishment he relates to external nature; but in becoming ill he has to carry out this confrontation within himself. Sexuality, as the foundation of the species, and illness are philosophically related phenomena. [Here the editors help with a note on *gatten*, which means to mate, and *Gattung*, which means species or genus.] In the perspective of Hegelian philosophy, nature and mind must necessarily fall asunder for a positive interpretation of reality; man must become estranged from his material environment and also from his own body" (128–29). Yet by the time von Engelhardt reaches his discussion of therapy (136–37), this fatal prognosis will have been forgotten and the relation of sexuality, disease, and death allowed to fall into oblivion. It will always be more attractive to conclude an account of illness with triumphant therapy and cure, even though Hegel's analysis of illness is itself fatal.

10. Matthew Arnold, *Empedocles on Etna*, written in 1852 but suppressed in 1853, Act II, lines 69–72:

> To see if we will poise our life at last,
> To see if we will now at last be true
> To our own only true, deep-buried selves,
> Being one with which we are at one with
>     the whole world.

See *The Poems of Matthew Arnold*, ed. Miriam Allott (London: Longman, 1979), 654; I cite Arnold in another context in *Postponements: Woman, Sensuality, and Death in Nietzsche* (Bloomington: Indiana University Press, 1986), 33, 110–11.

11. On fever in Hegel's account of illness, see John N. Findlay, "The Hegelian Treatment of Biology and Life," in Cohen and Wartofsky, eds., *Hegel and the Sciences* (cited in note 11 to chap. 9), 99–100, and Dietrich von Engelhardt, "Hegel's Philosophical Understanding of Illness," also in Cohen and Wartofsky, 133–34. Findlay also sees the imbrication of defecation and death in Hegel's account of organic assimilation: "If defecation is . . . the highest form of organic assimilation, death is the highest achievement of the organism's generative activities" (98). He adds the comment, "One can only regret that Freud knew nothing of these scatological passages" (ibid.), to which I would only add that, granted Hegel's understanding of death, they are as much *eschatological* as scatological passages. Von Engelhardt calls fever "this complete embarrassment of the organism by an illness," emphasizing, however, that for Hegel fever is also a sign of recuperation. He does not fail to note that in Hegel's account sweat is the excretion not only of what the ancients called "cooked morbid matter" but also of the *self* as such (135). In other words, feverish perspiration accompanies the ultimate *crisis*. Yet von Engelhardt does not take the *crisis* as the ultimate separation—which is what Hegel and Schelling too always mean by κρίσις—of spirit and body, as the proper *birth* of spirit in the *death* of the organism. He takes the "complete embarrassment" to be "at the same time the sign of overcoming it [the illness]" (134). He proceeds quickly to Hegel's notion of therapy, which means to be "humane" (136–37). Yet the humaneness of therapy is occasioned by nothing other than a sense of helplessness in the face of the Hegelian requirement for the birth of spirit—namely, the death of the patient. All this, of course, touches on the most general questions of the meaning of "life" in the Hegelian system. The two best discussions I have seen, by Jacques D'Hondt and Klaus Düsing, appear in Horstmann and Petry, eds., *Hegels Philosophie der Natur* (cited in note 8 to chap. 9); see 138–150 for the article by D'Hondt, and 276–89 for the article by Düsing.

12. Eric von der Luft notes that spirit is always being "born" in Hegel's philosophy, and that the birth takes place whenever biological science and medicine give over to speculative thought as in the instance of the "travesty" of phrenology, recounted in the *Phenomenology of Spirit*. For there, in the phenomenological account of phrenology, "spirit" first of all comes into play as a figure of the experience of consciousness. Yet von der Luft does not venture the thought that spirit, if it is dialectical, and if it is alive, must continue to bear the traces of its birth and its birthplace, must continue to show its birthmarks. See Eric von der Luft, "The Birth of Spirit for Hegel out of the Travesty of Medicine," in Stillman, ed., *Hegel's Philosophy of Spirit* (cited in note 10 to chap. 10), 25–42, esp. 35–36. Not only that. One must wonder whether, once "spirit" is "born," it will suffer the effects of "spiritual illness." Or does Hegel truly manage to convince himself that all illness is bound up with the feverish body, and that once the body is sloughed off in

death, good health is assured? Wolfgang Jacob expands the scope of our theme—illness in Hegel's philosophy of *nature*—to the "Anthropology" of Hegel's "Philosophy of Spirit," in the third part of the *Encyclopedia*. He shows that in Hegel's view *all* illness, even psychological or mental illness, is illness of the human *body*, or at least of the coupling *(Verknüpfung)* of soul and body in the human being. See Jacob, "Der Krankheitsbegriff in der Dialektik von Natur und Geist bei Hegel," in Gadamer, ed., *Stuttgarter Hegel-Tage 1970* (cited in note 14 to the introduction), 166–67. Finally, for an authoritative *and* critical account of the transition from nature (and its "naturalness") to spirit, an account once again located in the "Anthropology" of Hegel's *Philosophy of Spirit* in the *Encyclopedia*, see Hans-Christian Lucas, "The 'Sovereign Ingratitude' of Spirit toward Nature: Logical Qualities, Corporeity, Animal Magnetism, and Madness in Hegel's 'Anthropology,'" *Owl of Minerva* 23, no. 2 (Spring 1992): 131–50. Lucas emphasizes the development of Hegel's notion of the human body as "the work of art of the soul" (132), or, alternatively, as the obstacle to the "liberation struggle" of the soul (136). Particularly important for our topic are Lucas's pages on the relationship between the development of spirit and *pathology*, especially in dream life and madness (142–46). Lucas's thesis on the failure of the transition from nature to spirit in the "Anthropology," the thesis that this failure constitutes the "(perhaps secret) burden" for the later parts of the system, is sound. I would only ask whether the perhaps secret burden is already oppressing the system in its account of the origin of consciousness in the death of the animal and the holocaust of nature. Is that burden in fact expressed in the feverish exhalations of the dying manwoman, and does nature in the end release a ghostly laugh at spirit's sovereign ingratitude?

## 12. CONCLUSION: A TRIUMPH OF ASHES

1. As a way of pointing ahead to the future of this area of research, allow me to point back to an important influence on the present book. In 1990 I attended a series of lectures by Jacques Derrida at the Ecole des Hautes Etudes en Sciences Sociales, Paris, entitled "Eating the Other." Among Derrida's sources was the book by Jean Jenneret, *Les mots et les mets: Banquets et propos de table à la Renaissance* (Paris: José Corti, 1987), translated by Jeremy Whiteley and Emma Hughes as *A Feast of Words: Banquets and Table Talk in the Renaissance* (Chicago: University of Chicago Press, 1991). A second important source for Derrida was an extensive series of scientific-theoretical fragments by Novalis—many of which, no doubt, appear in part one of my own book. One of the few published sources of Derrida's views on the "system of the mouth," a phrase I borrow from him—in addition, of course, to *Glas*—is the interview with Jean-Luc Nancy, "'Il faut bien manger,' ou le calcul du sujet," *Confrontation* 20 (Winter 1989): 91–114; see esp. 108–14.

I also want to thank Ron Scapp and Brian Seitz for their forthcoming *Eating Culture*, from State University of New York Press. My own focus on the relation between eating, sexuality, and illness goes back at least as far as the following two articles: 1) "Female Parts in *Timaeus*," *Arion: A Journal of Humanities and the Classics*, New Series 2, no. 3 (Fall 1975): 400–21; 2) "Pitch: Genitality/Excrementality from Hegel to Crazy Jane," *boundary 2* 12, no. 2 (Winter 1984): 113–41. It extends, of course, up through the recent publication of *Infectious Nietzsche* (cited in note 9 to the introduction).

2. Johann Wolfgang von Goethe, *Faust*, ed. Erich Trunz (Munich: Verlag C. H. Beck, 1972), part one, lines 1338–40.

3. A final note—for the time being—on the debate among Hegelians as to whether Hegel's empirical data are worthless, or at least of dubious value, while the logical structures are productions of genius. Heinz Kimmerle argues that it is not Hegel's unfamiliarity with empirical investigations into the natural sciences that caused his philosophy of nature to be either ignored or deplored by the subsequent tradition; rather, it was Hegel's overriding need to subject all his scientific observations to the structures of his programmatic philosophy that did the damage. Hegel was never able to overcome a felt need to guarantee every fact and event in nature "a higher dignity." In the earliest Jena system (1801/02), Hegel sought that guarantee in an account of the *celestial* system—in astronomy rather than a philosophy of the organic—not yet aware that even the night sky of stars is reproduced in the slime of the sea. See Kimmerle, "Hegels Naturphilosophie in Jena," in Henrich and Düsing, eds., *Hegel in Jena* (cited in note 3 to chap. 5), 207–15, esp. 207. The debate will undoubtedly go on. My only contribution to it will be to wonder aloud whether Hegel's genius—his tutelary daimon—lies not in his obsession with structure but in his dalliance with the farthest reaches of the empirical.

Hegel's dalliance with the farthest and lowest reaches of the empirical is perhaps most manifest in his *metaphorics*. There the metaphors of health and illness in the organic realm are among the most prevalent. Allow me to appeal to the most famous and most familiar example—that of Hegel's use of organic metaphors in his *Philosophy of Right*. For such usage also corroborates the point made a moment ago, namely, that the "inadequacy" of the logical structures of Hegel's system to master or even masticate all its materials marks Hegel's greatness as a thinker. In the *Philosophy of Right*, Hegel is clear about the superiority of family, civil society, and state over nature and the merely "natural," which each stage of objective spirit's development eradicates for the sake of the next. In the addendum to section 272, which discusses the internal constitution of the state, Hegel emphasizes that the state is "the world that spirit has made for itself" and that the state is therefore as elevated over the natural and living world as god himself; for revealed religion is elevated over the created world (7: 434). It is thus all the more remarkable that a metaphorics of the living should undergird Hegel's analysis of family, civil society, and state at each stage along the way, and up to the very end. For even when one state is at war with another, and when a horrifying contingency seems to put all the works of objective spirit at risk, warfare stirs the world of objective spirit in the way that gales stir the ocean—so that the brine of world history does not stagnate and become a fetid pool (7: 493). Perhaps the most sustained metaphor (and, yes, here once again the entire meaning of *metaphor* and *metaphorics* would have to be deconstructed and rethought) is the following one, in which the structures of John Brown's nosology and physiology are brought to bear on the august state. My own long note, which ought to be infinitely longer, will end with the following long quotation from Hegel: "The state, as spirit, divides itself into the particular determinations of its concept and thus distinguishes its way to be. If we wish to adduce an example from nature *[ein Beispiel aus der Natur beibringen]*, then the nervous system is the system of sensation proper *[das eigentliche empfindende System]*: it is the abstract moment of being with oneself *[bei sich selbst zu sein]*, and one has one's identity with oneself in it. Yet if we analyze sensation *[Empfindung]* we find that it breaks down into two sides, dividing itself in such a way that the divisions appear as the entire system: the first is abstract feeling, keeping for itself *[Beisichbehalten]*, the muted movement within itself, reproduction, internal nourishment of the self, producing and digesting. The second moment occurs when being-with-self confronts the moment of difference, going to the outside *[das Nachaußengehen]*. The latter is irritability, in which sensation turns to the outside. Sentience constitutes its own system, and there are lower classes of animals that have developed this system alone, not the soulful unity of sensation in itself. If we compare these natural relations with those of spirit, then the family is to be aligned with sensibility *[Sensibilität]*, civil society with irritability. The third, of course, is the state, the nervous system for itself, organized in itself. Yet the state lives only to the extent that both moments—here the family and civil society—are developed in it. The laws that govern the two moments are the institutions of the rational element that radiates within them. But the ground and ultimate truth of these institutions is the spirit that is their universal purpose and their known object. To be sure, the family too is ethical, but the purpose is not in it as known; by contrast, in civil society separation *[die Trennung]* is determinative" (7: 411). Why the "rational element" and the "known object" need the humble metaphorics of the lowly, of the merely sentient, and why political science needs John Brown is but one facet of the burning question—the question of an idealism triumphant only in its ashes.

4. Walt Whitman, "Out of the Cradle Endlessly Rocking," in *Leaves of Grass*, ed. Sculley Bradley and Harold W. Blodgett (New York: W. W. Norton, 1973), 252–53:

> Whereto answering, the sea,
> Delaying not, hurrying not,
> Whisper'd me through the night, and very plainly before daybreak,
> Lisp'd to me the low and delicious word death,
> And again death, death, death, death,
> Hissing melodious, neither like the bird nor like my arous'd child's
>     heart,
> But edging near as privately for me rustling at my feet,
> Creeping thence steadily up to my ears and laving me softly all over,
> Death, death, death, death, death.

# ANNOTATED BIBLIOGRAPHY

The bibliography contains annotated references to 1) the primary sources and 2) the secondary literature employed in the research and writing of the present book. Even though the field of the philosophy of nature has been relatively neglected heretofore in research on German Idealism and Romanticism, including research on Novalis, Schelling, and Hegel, the relevant literature by and about these three figures is enormous. The following represents only a selection of materials. It should be supplemented by the standard philosophical and literary-historical bibliographies as well as by specialized bibliographies in monographs and journals in the history and philosophy of science and medicine.

## I. PRIMARY SOURCES

*The following abbreviations have been used in the text:*

*AE* = William Harvey, *Anatomical Exercises*
*EE* = Friedrich Wilhelm Joseph von Schelling, *Erster Entwurf*
*JS* = Georg Wilhelm Friedrich Hegel, *Jenaer Systementwürfe*
*KU* = Immanuel Kant, *Kritik der Urteilskraft*

*Full references for these works are given below.*

Aristotle. *On the Soul.* Volume 8 of the Loeb Classical Library edition of Aristotle. Translated by W. S. Hett. Cambridge: Harvard University Press, 1975. Aristotle's text is particularly relevant to our topic when it speaks of the sense of touch and of the aporia of the organ and medium of touch, that is, σάρξ, flesh.

Bataille, Georges. *L'érotisme.* Paris: Union Générale d'Editions, 1972. First published by Minuit in 1957, Bataille's meditation on eroticism, particularly with regard to its thought of *discontinuity*, is in the lineage of Novalis, of a certain Schelling, and perhaps also of a certain Hegel.

Beck, Adolf, editor. *Hölderlin's Diotima Susette Gontard: Gedichte—Briefe—Zeugnisse.* Frankfurt am Main: Insel Verlag, 1980. An excellent edition of the seventeen extant letters from Susette Gontard to Hölderlin, the volume is unfortunately no longer in print.

Blanchot, Maurice. *L'entretien infini.* Paris: Gallimard, 1969. Blanchot's notion of the exigency of discontinuity, as well as his theory and practice of "fragmentary writing," may help us to find our way back to a reading of Novalis.

Brown, John. *Elementa medicinae.* Translated by the author in *The Works of Dr. John Brown.* Edited by William Cullen Brown. London, 1804. The single

most important influence on the physiological and medical theories of
Novalis and Schelling. See the books by Henkelmann and Neubauer listed
in the secondary literature, below.

Derrida, Jacques. *La carte postale de Socrate à Freud et au-delà*. Paris: Aubier-
Flammarion, 1980. Translated by Alan Bass as *The Post Card: From Socrates to
Freud and Beyond*. Chicago: University of Chicago Press, 1987. See especially
the section entitled "Spéculer—sur 'Freud.'" While Derrida has little to say
about the Romantic background to Freud, his own reading moves in a
direction that advances our reflections on Novalis and Schelling.

———. *Dissémination*. Paris: Editions du Seuil, 1972. Translated as *Dissemination*
by Barbara Johnson. Chicago: University of Chicago Press, 1981. See especially "Plato's Pharmacy."

———. *Feu la cendre*. Paris: Des Femmes, 1987. Translated as *Cinders* by Ned
Lukacher. Lincoln: University of Nebraska Press, 1991. This work shows
Derrida's growing affinity with the thought of Novalis.

———. *Glas*. Paris: Galilée, 1974. Translated as *Glas* by John P. Leavey Jr. and
Richard Rand. Lincoln: University of Nebraska Press, 1986. This remarkable reading of Hegel focuses in part on Hegel's theory of genitality.

———. *De la grammatologie*. Paris: Editions de Minuit, 1967. Translated as *Of
Grammatology* by Gayatri Chakravorty Spivak. Baltimore: Johns Hopkins
University Press, 1974. See especially part two of the work, on Rousseau,
though even the "theoretical matrix" in part one has much to say on issues
of contaminaiton and contagion.

———. Interview with Jean-Luc Nancy, "'Il faut bien manger,' ou le calcul du
sujet." *Confrontation* 20 (Winter 1989): 91–114. The interview anticipates a
series of lectures by Jacques Derrida at the Ecole des Hautes Etudes en
Sciences Sociales, Paris, entitled "Eating the Other," in which Novalis
played a central role.

———. *Khôra*. Paris: Galilée, 1993. This text is particularly relevant for Schelling's early fascination with Plato's *Timaeus*.

Ferenczi, Sandor. *Versuch einer Genitaltheorie*. In Ferenczi, *Schriften*. Edited by
Michael Balint. Two volumes. Frankfurt am Main: Fischer Taschenbuch
Verlag, 1982, 2: 317–400. Translated as *Thalassa: A Theory of Genitality* by
Henry Alden Bunker. New York: W. W. Norton, 1968. One of the most
extraordinary speculative feats in the psychoanalytic tradition; an inspired
grandchild of Novalis, Schelling, and Hegel, Ferenczi expands on Freud's
late insights in order to develop what he calls a *bioanalysis*.

Fichte, Johann Gottlieb Fichte. *Die Bestimmung des Menschen (1800)*. Edited by
Theodor Ballauff and Ignaz Klein. Stuttgart: Philipp Reclam Verlag, 1962.
An easily accessible introduction to Fichte's formulation of his *practical*
philosophy after the 1794 *Wissenschaftslehre*.

———. *Grundlage der gesamten Wissenschaftslehre (1794)*. Hamburg: Felix Meiner
Verlag, 1961. Essential background to Novalis, Schelling, and Hegel. Their
shared starting point in philosophy of nature cannot be understood without
study of Fichte's early work.

Freud, Sigmund. *Aus den Anfängen der Psychoanalyse*. Edited by Ernst Kris. New
York: Imago, 1950. Contains the correspondence with Wilhelm Fliess and
the famous 1895 *Entwurf* of Freud's "scientific psychology." Parallels between Novalis, Schelling, and Freud emerge at many different levels.

Goethe, Johann Wolfgang von. *Faust*. Edited by Erich Trunz. Munich: Verlag
C. H. Beck, 1972. Based on the ninth edition of the historical-critical
Hamburger Ausgabe.

———. *Metamorphose der Pflanzen (1790)*. Illustrated edition. Rudolf Steiner,
editor. Sixth edition. Stuttgart: Verlag Freies Geistesleben, 1992. An inex-

pensive paperback edition, with beautiful and informative illustrations by Goethe and Goethe's contemporaries.

———. *Naturwissenschaftliche Schriften*. Edited by Rudolf Steiner. Five volumes. Dornach, Switzerland: Rudolf Steiner Verlag, 1982. An inexpensive paperback edition. Although sometimes intrusive, and always enthusiastic, the commentary by Steiner offers much useful historical information.

Harvey, William. *Anatomical Exercises on the Generation of Animals, etc.*, in *The Works of William Harvey, M.D.* Translated from the Latin by Robert Willis, M.D. London: Sydenham Society, 1847; New York: Johnson Reprint Corporation, "The Sources of Science," number 13, 1965. An important source for Schelling's *First Projection*.

Hegel, Georg Wilhelm Friedrich. *Jenaer Systementwürfe III: Naturphilosophie und Philosophie des Geistes*. Edited by Rolf-Peter Horstmann. Hamburg: Felix Meiner Verlag, 1987. This inexpensive paperback edition, volume 333 of the Meiner "Philosophische Bibliothek," is based on volume eight of the new historical-critical edition of the *Gesammelte Werke*. It supersedes the older edition by Georg Lasson published by Meiner in 1930–1932.

———. *Phänomenologie des Geistes*. Edited by Johannes Hofmeister. Sixth edition. Hamburg: Felix Meiner Verlag, 1952. Volume 114 of the Meiner "Philosophische Bibliothek," the *Phenomenology of Spirit*, is Hegel's early masterwork.

———. *Werke in zwanzig Bänden: Theorie Werkausgabe*. Twenty volumes, with index. Frankfurt am Main: Suhrkamp Verlag, 1970. Still an excellent source, despite the historical-critical edition published by Felix Meiner. Hegel's philosophy of nature, the second part of the *Encyclopedia of Philosophical Sciences*, appears in volume 9 of the *Theorie Werkausgabe*. That part has been translated in three volumes entitled *Philosophy of Nature*, with introduction and explanatory notes, by Michael John Petry. His translation is reviewed by Gerd Buchdahl in *British Journal for the Philosophy of Science* (see secondary literature, below).

Heidegger, Martin. *Basic Writings*. Edited by David Farrell Krell. Revised and expanded edition. San Francisco: HarperCollins, 1993. A useful collection.

———. *Beiträge zur Philosophie (Vom Ereignis)*. Martin Heidegger Gesamtausgabe, volume 65. Frankfurt am Main: Vittorio Klostermann, 1989. Although this is one of the most exciting of the recent publications of heretofore unpublished works by Heidegger, the account of "life" here, and specifically of the relation of the individual to its species, is disappointingly traditional—and in this case, that means *Hegelian*.

———. *Die Grundbegriffe der Metaphysik: Welt—Endlichkeit—Einsamkeit*. Martin Heidegger Gesamtausgabe, volume 29/30. Frankfurt am Main: Vittorio Klostermann, 1983. Translated as *The Fundamental Concepts of Metaphysics: World, Finitude, Solitude* by William McNeill and Nicholas Walker. Bloomington: Indiana University Press, 1996. The most important work by Heidegger on philosophy of nature.

———. *Identität und Differenz*. Pfullingen: Günter Neske, 1957. One of Heidegger's most important confrontations with Hegel, emphasizing the *Logic*.

———. *Schellings Abhandlung über das Wesen der menschlichen Freiheit (1809)*. Edited by Hildegard Feick. Tübingen: Max Niemeyer Verlag, 1971. English translation by Joan Stambaugh. Athens: Ohio University Press, 1985. Predictably, given Heidegger's resistance to life-philosophy and philosophy of nature, little is said here about Schelling's early work on *Naturphilosophie*. Yet behind Heidegger's critique of Schelling's ontotheology one sees Heidegger's admiration of Schelling as the "properly creative and most far-reaching thinker in this entire era of German philosophy" (4).

——. *Sein und Zeit*. Twelfth edition. Tübingen: Max Niemeyer Verlag, 1972. The classic source of Heidegger's fundamental ontology of finite existence, or *Dasein*, a work that shows ever greater affinities with the philosophical projects of the young Schelling and Hegel.

——. *Unterwegs zur Sprache*. Pfullingen: Günter Neske, 1959. Perhaps Heidegger will be remembered first and foremost as a philosopher of language, in which case his confessed proximity to Novalis will be assured.

——. *Was heißt Denken?* Tübingen: Max Niemeyer Verlag, 1954. A lecture course on Nietzsche and Parmenides, this book is one of Heidegger's best and most readable efforts.

Hölderlin, Friedrich. *Sämtliche Werke und Briefe*. Edited by Michael Knaupp. Three volumes. Munich: Carl Hanser Verlag, 1992. A relatively inexpensive edition, it is a welcome addition to the Stuttgart complete edition by Friedrich Beißner and the Frankfurt Hölderlin Ausgabe by D. E. Sattler. Unfortunately, the commentary in the Knaupp edition is always meager and not always reliable.

Irigaray, Luce. *Spéculum de l'autre femme*. Paris: Minuit, 1974. Translated as *Speculum of the Other Woman* by Gillian C. Gill. Ithaca: Cornell University Press, 1985. See especially "The Eternal Irony of the Community," 266–81 in the French, 214–26 in the English, on the role of woman in Hegel's *Phenomenology of Spirit* and other texts, one of Irigaray's most challenging and thought-provoking analyses.

Kant, Immanuel. *Anthropologie in pragmatischer Hinsicht (1798)*. Edited by Wolfgang Becker. Stuttgart: Philipp Reclam Verlag, 1983. An important supplement to the third *Critique*, offering insight into Kant's nontranscendental views of the human condition.

——. *Kritik der reinen Vernunft*. Edited by Raymund Schmidt. Hamburg: Felix Meiner Verlag, 1956. The "Philosophische Bibliothek" edition of Kant's classic work. Translated as *The Critique of Pure Reason* by Norman Kemp Smith. New York: St. Martin's Press, 1965.

——. *Kritik der Urteilskraft*. A reprinting of the Akademieausgabe (B edition) of 1793. Edited by Gerhard Lehmann. Stuttgart: Philipp Reclam Verlag, 1966. A reliable, inexpensive edition of Kant's text.

Merleau-Ponty, Maurice. *Le visible et l'invisible*. Paris: Gallimard, 1964. Translated as *The Visible and the Invisible* by Alphonso Lingis. Evanston, Ill.: Northwestern University Press, 1968. Chapter 4 of this work is the classic source of the touched-touching paradigm, germane to the question of contagion.

Novalis (Friedrich von Hardenberg). *Werke, Tagebücher und Briefe*. Edited by Hans-Joachim Mähl and Richard Samuel. Three volumes. Munich: Carl Hanser Verlag, 1987. I make particular reference to volume two, *Das philosophisch-theoretische Werk*. A relatively inexpensive clothbound edition, based on the historical-critical edition initiated by Paul Kluckhohn and Richard Samuel. The Hanser edition, while not complete, contains most of the material that is in volumes 2 and 3 of the larger far more expensive edition. Readers should nevertheless check important passages in volumes 2 and 3 of the larger edition: Novalis, *Schriften*. Edited by Richard Samuel et al., revised in 1981 by Richard Samuel and Hans-Joachim Mähl. Stuttgart: Kohlhammer Verlag, 1981.

Scheler, Max. *Von der Ganzheit des Menschen: Ausgewählte Schriften*. Edited by Manfred Frings. Bonn: Bouvier, 1991. See especially Scheler's *Ordo amoris*, 3–32, perhaps the most Romantic (and therefore best) of his works.

Schelling, Friedrich Wilhelm Joseph von. *Erster Entwurf eines Systems der Naturphilosophie*. Jena and Leipzig: Gabler Verlag, 1799. See *Schriften von*

*1799–1801*. Darmstadt: Wissenschaftliche Buchgesellschaft, 1975, 1–268. This is a photomechanical reprint of the 1858–1859 edition by Karl Schelling, published in Stuttgart and Augsburg by the J. G. Cotta'scher Verlag. A new historical-critical edition headed by Hartmut Buchner is now under way, but most of the texts germane to the topic have not yet been published. The *First Projection of a System of Nature Philosophy* is regarded by most interpreters, myself included, as the most significant of Schelling's major texts on philosophy of nature.

———. *Ideen zu einer Philosophie der Natur als Einleitung in das Studium dieser Wissenschaft.* First published in 1797, second edition in 1803, then in the *Sämmtliche Werke* edited by Karl Schelling. See *Schriften von 1794–1798*. Darmstadt: Wissenschaftliche Buchgesellschaft, 1980, 333–97, which unfortunately contains only the introductions and not the main body of the text. An English translation of the entire work, *Ideas for a Philosophy of Nature*, has been done by Errol E. Harris and Peter Heath. Cambridge: Cambridge University Press, 1988. The first of Schelling's major treatises in philosophy of nature, promising but not presenting a philosophy of the organic.

———. *Stuttgarter Privatvorlesungen.* See *Schriften von 1806–1813*. Darmstadt: Wissenschaftliche Buchgesellschaft, 1983, 361–428. Lectures given in 1810, on the threshold of *Die Weltalter.*

———. *System der Weltalter: Münchener Vorlesung 1827/28 in einer Nachschrift von Ernst von Lasaulx.* Edited by Siegbert Peetz. Frankfurt am Main: Vittorio Klostermann, 1990. A late formulation of Schelling's never-completed, never-published work, *Die Weltalter.*

———. *"Timaeus" (1794).* Schellingiana volume 4. Edited by Hartmut Buchner. Stuttgart: Frommann-Holzboog, 1994. A fascinating recent discovery, this volume shows that even at the moment of his adherence to Fichte's subjective idealism Schelling was drawn to the principal questions and sources of philosophy of nature.

———. *Über das Wesen der menschlichen Freiheit und die damit zusammenhängenden Gegenstände.* Edited by Horst Fuhrmans. Stuttgart: Philipp Reclam Verlag, 1964. This work, one of Schelling's most influential, introduces his "middle period," which culminates in the projected *Ages of the World.*

———. *Von der Weltseele: Eine Hypothese der höheren Physik zur Erklärung des allgemeinen Organismus.* See *Schriften von 1794–1798.* Darmstadt: Wissenschaftliche Buchgesellschaft, 1980, 399–637, which presents the entire text. First published in 1798, this text influenced Goethe and the entire Jena and Weimar circles. On the strength of this work, Schelling received his professorship at the University of Jena. In spite of its title, however, the work does not give a detailed account of the organic realm. Such an account awaited Schelling's inaugural lecture course at Jena, which would be published in 1799 as the *Erster Entwurf eines Systems der Naturphilosophie.*

———. *Die Weltalter, Erstes Buch.* Edited by Karl Schelling for the *Sämmtliche Werke* in 1861. See *Schriften von 1813–1830*. Darmstadt: Wissenschaftliche Buchgesellschaft, 1976, 1–150. This text, along with the supplement attached to it, *Über die Gottheiten von Samothrake (1815)*, while only tangentially related to the philosophy of nature, takes Schelling to the farthest reaches of his speculation—in which nature is still extremely powerful.

———. *Die Weltalter Fragmente.* Edited by Manfred Schröter. Nachlaßband to the Münchner Jubiläumsdruck. Munich: Biederstein Verlag und Leibniz Verlag, 1946. Presents the original versions of *Die Weltalter,* set in print (but not released for publication) in 1811 and 1813; the first half of the 1811 version is, I believe, of special interest. Jason Wirth, of Ogelthorpe University, is now preparing an English translation of *Die Weltalter.*

Schlegel, Friedrich. *Lucinde.* Stuttgart: Philipp Reclam Verlag, 1979. First published in 1799, *Lucinde* remains one of the finest flowers of Romantic fiction. Hegel gave it a bad review.

Selye, Hans, M.D. *The Stress of Life.* New York: McGraw Hill, 1956. Nelly Tsouyopoulos (cited in the secondary literature, below) brings Schelling's theory of illness into relation with Dr. Hans Selye's highly influential theory of, and experimental research into, stress.

Simmel, Georg. *Lebensanschauung: Vier metaphysische Kapitel.* Munich: Duncker und Humblot, 1918. Perhaps the most metaphysically astute of the *Lebensphilosophen,* his remarks in this work have particular relevance to Schelling's concept of God.

Strauss, Richard. *Vier letzte Lieder.* Sung by Jessye Norman, with Kurt Masur and the Gewandhausorchester Leipzig. Phillips compact disc 411 052-2. It may be that the music that is appropriate to Novalis, Schelling, and the young Hegel develops only many decades or even centuries after these thinkers. I had long been familiar with the Jessye Norman version when Gisela Baurmann presented me with Elisabeth Schwarzkopf's older version, with George Szell conducting the Radio-Symphonie-Orchester, Berlin, on an EMI Classics release, compact disc 7 47276 2. Now Strauss has *eight* last songs.

## II. SECONDARY LITERATURE

Baumgartner, Hans Michael. *Schelling: Einführung in seine Philosophie.* Freiburg im Breisgau: Verlag Karl Alber, 1975. An excellent collection on the early Schelling. See especially the article by Harald Holz, "Perspektive Natur," 58–74, discussed separately in this bibliography.

Bluth, Karl Theodor. *Medizingeschichtliches bei Novalis: Ein Beitrag zur Geschichte der Medizin der Romantik.* Berlin: Verlag Dr. Emil Ebering, 1934. Bluth's volume is principally of historical interest, that is, of interest with regard to the *Rezeptionsgeschichte* of Novalis's views on medicine. Yet chapter 5, which focuses on sin, illness, and death, and which draws parallels to Freudian psychoanalysis, is still of inherent interest.

Bonsiepen, Wolfgang. "Hegels kritische Auseinandersetzung mit der zeitgenössischen Evolutionstheorie." In Horstmann and Petry, editors, *Hegels Philosophie der Natur,* 151–71. Bonsiepen interprets Hegel's theory of development (which is not a theory of evolution) in terms of a "system of stages *[Stufen]*" (151). (Bonsiepen does not draw the parallel with Schelling's *First Projection.*) If there is evolution in the Hegelian system, it is not of a species but of the idea, not of biological function and morphology but of the logic of the concept. Bonsiepen offers an excellent discussion of Leibniz's great chain of being (he cites·Arthur O. Lovejoy in this context), discusses Hegel's confrontation with Buffon and Lamarck, Goethe and Herder, and concludes with a critical judgment concerning Hegel's incapacity (shared with many others, it must be noted) to imagine the evolution of species. See also the article by Olaf Breidbach, discussed below.

———. "[Über Nachschriften zu] Hegels Vorlesungen über Naturphilosophie." *Hegel-Studien* 26 (1991): 40–54. Beginning with comments on the *Jenaer Systementwürfe,* Bonsiepen discusses the eight sets of student notes still extant for Hegel's lectures on philosophy of nature in Berlin from 1819–1820 through 1828. Bonsiepen then evaluates the relevance of such notes for Hegel's reordering of his philosophy of nature in the 1827 edition (i.e., the second) of the *Encyclopedia.*

————. "Zu Hegels Auseinandersetzung mit Schellings Naturphilosophie in der 'Phänomenologie des Geistes.'" In Hasler, editor, *Schelling: Seine Bedeutung,* 167–72. Bonsiepen tests Hegel's own claim (in the letter of May 1, 1807, to Schelling) that in the *Phänomenologie* Hegel is criticizing Schelling's epigones rather than Schelling himself. The influence of John Brown on Schelling proves to be the decisive factor in this question. Bonsiepen concludes that Hegel is in fact criticizing Schelling's own "identity philosophy," which in his view does not achieve the level of a speculative logic.

Breidbach, Olaf. "Hegels Evolutionskritik." *Hegel-Studien* 22 (1987): 165–72. Breidbach offers an account of Hegel's critique of "evolution," which, of course, is not to be taken in a Darwinian sense and to which Hegel counterposes (and over which he favors) the notion of *Emanation.* See also the first article by Wolfgang Bonsiepen, discussed above, and the piece by Martin Drees, listed below.

————. *Das Organische in Hegels Denken: Studie zur Naturphilosophie und Biologie um 1800.* Würzburg: Königshausen & Neumann, 1982. Reviewed by Michael John Petry in *Hegel-Studien* 18 (1983): 411–13. A full-length study of the organic in Hegel's thinking. According to Petry, the main theme of the volume is "the complex and variegated relationship between the systematic expositions of botany and the animal sciences worked out during the Jena period, and the contemporary state of empirical research on which these expositions were based" (411). Unfortunately, Breidbach's book is plagued by organizational problems, with topics discussed several times in various places of the book—which makes it difficult to read; nevertheless, it contains much useful information, especially on the historical background, the empirical sources, etc. Unfortunately again, Breidbach's exposition does not take up in a detailed way any of the problems associated with Hegel's account of the life of the organism—problems such as illness and death.

Brinkmann, Richard, editor. *Romantik in Deutschland: Ein interdisziplinäres Symposion (Sonderband der "Deutschen Vierteljahrsschrift für Literaturwissenschaft und Geistesgeschichte").* Stuttgart: J. B. Metzlersche Verlagsbuchhandlung, 1978. A very rich text, one of the most important for the topic of dire forces in nature; see especially the articles by Dietrich von Engelhardt, John Neubauer, Henricus Adrianus Marie Snelders, Heinrich Schipperges, and Karl Eduard Rothschuh, all of them discussed separately in this bibliography. An extensive bibliography by Dietrich von Engelhardt of the topic "Romantik—im Spannungsfeld von Naturgefühl, Naturwissenschaft und Naturphilosophie," covering the years 1950–1975, appears at 307–30.

Buchdahl, Gerd. "Hegel's Philosophy of Nature." *British Journal for the Philosophy of Science* 23 (1972): 257–66. A review of Michael John Petry's translation of Hegel's *Philosophy of Nature* (see under "Hegel" in primary sources, above). Buchdahl's review also serves as an excellent introduction to the problem of the neglect of Hegel's philosophy of science in the English-speaking world—as well as to the reasons for a resurgence of interest in our own time.

Capek, Milic. "Hegel and the Organic View of Nature." In Cohen and Wartofsky, editors, *Hegel and the Sciences,* 109–21. A scathing criticism of Hegel's bad science, informed by Benedetto Croce's thesis, though not by his suppleness, and by Whitehead's organicism, though not by his elegance.

Carlsson, Anni. *Die Fragmente des Novalis.* Basel: Verlag Helbing & Lichtenhahn, 1939. Carlsson's full-length treatment, although it has little to say about our specific theme, and in spite of its age, is still to be taken quite seriously. It focuses on the *fragmentary* nature of Novalis's thinking and writing and their *ontological* import, based on Nicolai Hartmann's ontology.

Her reflections on the Novalisian fragment, along with the more recent reflections of Géza von Molnár, are, it seems to me, among the best in the literature.

Cohen, Robert S., and Marx W. Wartofsky, editors. *Hegel and the Sciences.* Dordrecht: D. Reidel, Kluwer Academic Publishers, 1984. See especially the articles by John N. Findlay, George Di Giovanni, Milic Capek, and Dietrich von Engelhardt, discussed separately in this bibliography.

D'Hondt, Jacques. "La concept de la vie chez Hegel." In Horstmann and Petry, editors, *Hegels Philosophie der Natur,* 138–50. A faithful yet critical presentation of Hegel's views of "life." D'Hondt interprets Hegel's fascination with nature throughout his long career in terms of Hegel's own citation of Pascal in *Glauben und Wissen* (1802): "Nature is everywhere marked as a forlorn God, both in man and apart from man" (138). Hegel's nature is *le cadavre de l'esprit,* but a cadaver that comes to *life.* D'Hondt focuses on the superiority of spiritual life over mere organic life, hence of "life" over the merely "living," in a word, the superiority of the concept—as the *survivor* in Hegel's system. This article, along with the piece by Klaus Düsing, "Die Idee des Lebens in Hegel's Logik," cited below, is one of the best on the topic.

Diepgen, Paul. "Novalis und die romantische Medizin." *Mitteilungen zur Geschichte der Medizin, der Naturwissenschaft und der Technik* 33 (1934): 349ff. A standard source listed in all the bibliographies, but one that I have been unable to track down; I include a listing of it so that others may have better luck. At least *some* of Diepgen's views on Novalis and Romantic medicine in general are saved in the second volume of his comprehensive two-volume *Geschichte der Medizin: Die historische Entwicklung der Heilkunde und des ärztlichen Lebens.* Berlin: Walter de Gruyter, 1949.

Di Giovanni, George. "More Comments on the Place of the Organic in Hegel's Philosophy of Nature." In Cohen and Wartofsky, editors, *Hegel and the Sciences,* 101–107. A commentary on John N. Findlay's paper, cited below, Di Giovanni's response places greater stress than Findlay's on the essentially *reflective, speculative* character of Hegel's *Logic.* It also scolds Findlay for spending so much time on Hegel's philosophy of nature, which Di Giovanni reduces to "an illegitimate extrapolation" of the *Logic.* Di Giovanni's position, along with Capek's, is perhaps the farthest from my own. Any Hegelian who regards Hegel as a speculative genius and an empirical fool is less an Hegelian than even I.

Drees, Martin. "Evolution and Emanation of Spirit in Hegel's *Philosophy of Nature.*" *Bulletin of the Hegel Society of Great Britain* 26 (Autumn–Winter 1992): 52–61. Drees argues convincingly against Wolfgang Bonsiepen that Hegel is essentially an emanationist, rather than an evolutionist, in spite of his commitment to the development of spirit. In Bonsiepen's defense (see his article, listed above), one must note that Bonsiepen himself argues that Hegel is essentially incapable of imagining the evolution of species; for Bonsiepen, too, Hegelian "evolution" is the unfolding of spirit and idea. On this topic, see also the piece by Olaf Breidbach, discussed above.

———. "The Logic of Hegel's Philosophy of Nature." In Petry, *Hegel and Newtonianism,* 91–101. Drees discusses the difficult relation between *logic* and *philosophy of nature* in Hegel's system in terms of 1) the *transition* from logic to nature and 2) logic and contingency. Drees concludes that Hegel "did not always remember that 'it is an error on the part of the philosophy of nature to attempt to face up to all phenomena'" (*Encyclopedia,* §270, Addendum [9: 106]).

Durner, Manfred, Francesco Moiso, and Jörg Jantzen. "Wissenschaftlicher

Bericht zu Schellings naturphilosophischen Schriften, 1797–1800." In F. W. J. Schelling, *Historisch-kritische Ausgabe: Ergänzungsband zu Werke Band 5 bis 9*. Edited by Hans Michael Baumgartner, Wilhelm G. Jacobs, and Hermann Krings. Stuttgart: Frommann-Holzboog, 1994. This 850-page volume, with a bibliography of 1,544 items, presents in extraordinary detail the *background* to Schelling's theories of chemistry, electromagnetism/galvanism, and physiology, in particular the physiology of reproduction and regeneration. The volume is, to repeat, not an exposition of Schelling's own views but an invaluable compendium of the principal scientific views inherited by Schelling. The authors succeed in the monumental task of opening up the world of science as it stood precisely at the moment when the young Schelling began his scientific studies. For our immediate purposes, the contribution by Jörg Jantzen, "Physiologische Theorien," 373–668, is of special value.

Düsing, Klaus. "Idealistische Substanzmetaphysik: Probleme der Systementwicklung bei Schelling und Hegel in Jena." In Henrich and Düsing, editors, *Hegel in Jena*, 25–44. Düsing focuses on the year 1801 and on the project, common to Hegel and Schelling, "of an absolute metaphysics, that is, a theory of complete, rational knowledge and systematic explication of the absolute" (25). The article stresses the importance of the reversion of both thinkers to Spinoza's concept of substance.

———. "Die Idee des Lebens in Hegels Logik." In Horstmann and Petry, editors, *Hegels Philosophie der Natur*, 276–89. Düsing reviews the importance of "life" in conceptions of being from Greek antiquity (especially Aristotelian οὐσία) through modernity. He treats Hegel's conception of life principally in terms of the speculative-logical idea, the absolute in Schelling's and Hölderlin's sense. Yet this view of life is complicated by three other conceptions: life is also viewed variously as 1) the Platonic-Aristotelian relation of body and soul, 2) the painful contradiction between individual and genus, and 3) a prefiguring of subjectivity and self-consciousness. Along with the article by Jacques D'Hondt, discussed above, Düsing's is one of the most thought-provoking reflections on the topic.

———. "Spekulation und Reflexion: Zur Zusammenarbeit Schellings und Hegels in Jena." *Hegel-Studien* 5 (1969): 95–128. Düsing's is an authoritative account of the mutual influence and cooperative labors of Hegel and Schelling in Jena during the years 1801–1803. The article emphasizes the importance of Hegel for Schelling's "identity philosophy," developed during these years, and the primary importance of Schelling for the philosophy of nature in Hegel's early lectures (1801/02) in Jena.

———. "Teleologie der Natur: Eine Kant-Interpretation mit Ausblicken auf Schelling." In Heckmann et al., editors, *Natur und Subjektivität*, 187–210. A discussion of Kant's and Schelling's shared project of an overcoming of the mechanistic conception of nature.

Dyck, Martin. *Novalis and Mathematics: A Study of Friedrich von Hardenberg's Fragments on Mathematics and Its Relation to Magic, Music, Religion, Philosophy, Language, and Literature*. Chapel Hill: University of North Carolina Press, 1960. Chapter 4, on the extension of mathematical thinking into other apparently unrelated fields, is of particular interest for our topic.

Engelhardt, Dietrich von. "Die biologischen Wissenschaften in Hegels Naturphilosophie." In Horstmann and Petry, editors, *Hegels Philosophie der Natur*, 121–37. Von Engelhardt, a professor at the Lübeck Medical College, is clearly one of the most important researchers on the topic of the present book. The article in question offers a detailed account of the eighteenth-century background in biology, for example, Linnaeus's classificatory system (1735),

Buffon's natural history (1749), Haller's physiology of sensibility and irritability (1752), Blumenbach's account of the *Bildungstrieb* or formative drive (1779), and so on. Von Engelhardt offers an excellent discussion of Hegel's lifelong fascination with botany and anatomy, along with a reliable account of the principal features of the biological sciences in Hegel's thought. Unfortunately, his study stops short of posing *philosophical* questions, such as that concerning the relation of sexuality to death in Hegel.

———. "Das chemische System der Stoffe, Kräfte und Prozesse in Hegels Naturphilosophie und der Wissenschaft seiner Zeit." In Gadamer, editor, *Stuttgarter Hegel-Tage 1970*, 125–39. Von Engelhardt shows that chemistry occupies a mediating position between physics and organics in Hegel's philosophy of nature: "As organics realizes a concept that arises from chemistry, so chemistry actualizes a concept that originates in magnetism and electricity" (134).

———. "Einführendes Referat." In Brinkmann, editor, *Romantik in Deutschland*, 167–73. A sympathetic introduction to the role of reflections on science, and especially medicine, in German Romanticism. See also von Engelhardt's excellent bibliography, 307–30.

———. "Hegel on Chemistry and the Organic Sciences." In Petry, editor, *Hegel and Newtonianism*, 657–65. Von Engelhardt's remarks on of organism in terms of the eighteenth-century antiphlogistical movement, and especially on chemistry and *disease* (662–63), are germane to our topic.

———. *Hegel und die Chemie: Studie zur Philosophie und Wissenschaft der Natur um 1800*. Wiesbaden: Guido Pressler Verlag, 1976. Reviewed quite positively by Michael John Petry in *Hegel-Studien* 14 (1979): 333–40. Von Engelhardt's is a full-length study containing much historical background (e.g., on the theory of phlogiston). The book is clearly organized, lucidly presented, and has an extensive bibliography. See especially section 3.3, "Chemistry between Physics and Organics." The appendix contains useful information on 1) Hegel's empirical sources in chemistry, 2) Hegel's chemistry as developed in the three editions of the *Encyclopedia*, and 3) translations of the *Encyclopedia* into other languages.

———. "Hegels Organismusverständnis und Krankheitsbegriff." In Petry, editor, *Hegel und die Naturwissenschaften*, 423–30 (Discussion, 430–41). This brief résumé of von Engelhardt's views is reluctant to engage with the problems. Even the remarks on illness and healing, and on the Hegelian paradox of life as the seed of death, are schematic. Von Engelhardt's importance in this area of research is indicated more by the discussion than by the article itself; Vittorio Hösle's question to von Engelhardt (on figuration, assimilation, and reproduction: 432–33) is the most notable moment in this exchange. A far more detailed account of von Engelhardt's views is to be found in the article cited next.

———. "Hegel's Philosophical Understanding of Illness." In Cohen and Wartofsky, editors, *Hegel and the Sciences*, 123–41. An English translation of the following essay, this is one of the most important for our topic.

———. "Hegels philosophisches Verständnis der Krankheit." *Südhoffs Archiv* 59, number 3 (1975): 225–46. Although Hegel's early Jena lectures do not play a role in Von Engelhardt's account, except insofar as they are salvaged by Michelet's addenda to the *Encyclopedia*, this account is one of the best for our topic with regard to Hegel. It stops short of posing the questions of the relation of genitality to illness and physical death and of the relation of fever and death-by-disease to the putatively healthy birth of spirit.

———. "Die organische Natur und die Lebenswissenschaften in Schellings Naturphilosophie." In Heckmann et al., editors, *Natur und Subjektivität*, 39–

57. An excellent account of the empirical research in biology and medicine that went into Schelling's *Naturphilosophie*.

———. "Prinzipien und Ziele der Naturphilosophie Schellings—Situation um 1800 und spätere Wirkungsgeschichte." In Hasler, editor, *Schelling: Seine Bedeutung*, 77–98. Von Engelhardt emphasizes Schelling's importance for the development of Fichte's transcendental conception of nature into a metaphysical and ontological conception. An excellent, lucid summary of Schelling's nature philosophy opens the article; in the final three sections, 84–94, von Engelhardt expresses doubts concerning the fruitfulness of that philosophy's influence on later scientific research. See the replies by Toellner and Tsouyopoulos, also contained in Hasler, cited below.

———. "Schellings philosophische Grundlegung der Medizin." In Sandkühler, editor, *Natur und geschichtlicher Prozess: Studien zur Naturphilosophie Schellings*, 305–25. A remarkably clear account of the context and scope of Schelling's foundations of medicine and notion of the organic. Along with the essays of Nelly Tsouyopoulos, one of the outstanding contributions to the field.

Erdmann, Johann Eduard. *Philosophie der Neuzeit: Der deutsche Idealismus.* Reinbek bei Hamburg: Rowohlt, 1971. A useful survey, especially for Schelling's relation to Fichte.

Esposito, Joseph L. *Schelling's Idealism and Philosophy of Nature.* Lewisburg, Pa: Bucknell University Press, 1977. A helpful introduction, especially with regard to Schelling's relation to Fichtean thought, the influence on Schelling of Kant's 1786 *Metaphysische Anfangsgründe der Naturwissenschaft*, and the circle of Schelling's friends and followers during the *Naturphilosophie* period. Esposito's defense of Schelling against Hegel's attacks is eloquent.

Figala, Karin. "Der alchemische Begriff des Caput Mortuum in der symbolischen Terminologie Hegels." In Gadamer, editor, *Stuttgarter Hegel-Tage 1970*, 141–51. An excellent account of Hegel's alchemical and Christian-mystical rhetoric and vocabulary from the early years through the *Phenomenology of Spirit*.

Findlay, John N. "The Hegelian Treatment of Biology and Life." In Cohen and Wartofsky, editors, *Hegel and the Sciences*, 87–100. A paper that is fortunately unfaithful to its intention to perform "a sort of reduction to a logical skeleton in which the empirical flesh vanishes altogether" (88). Findlay's *aperçus* are far more interesting than his logical skeleton.

Fischer, Hans. "Die Krankheitsauffassung Friedrich von Hardenbergs (Novalis), 1772–1801: Ein Beitrag zur Medizin der Romantik." *Verhandlungen der Naturforschenden Gesellschaft* 56 (1945): 390–410. Fischer demonstrates that already by the late 1930s and early 1940s interpreters were attributing to the Romantic school—above all, to Novalis and Schelling—considerable influence on the theory and practice of contemporary medicine. Fischer takes Novalis's idea of a *macroanthropus* in contact—or in contagious proximity— with the world soul as the pervasive idea of Romantic medicine: "Thus the world has to some degree become a sense organ of human beings, and the macroanthropus has become the counterpart of the world" (401).

Frank, Manfred. "Die Philosophie des sogenannten 'magischen Idealismus.'" *Euphorion* 63 (1969): 88–116. Frank defends Novalis's theoretical reflections against the charge of *Phantasterei*. However, as Frank admits, that defense was already made quite ably before him by Anni Carlsson, Theodor Haering, and others. Frank's starting point is the question of finitude as defined by Schleiermacher, with reference to the dependence of finite creatures on an infinite Creator. Frank focuses on the human desire for thaumaturgic powers, that is, powers derived from some form of absolute. Illness becomes crucial for Frank's understanding of the Novalisian finitude or "lack" that prevents Novalis's magic idealism from becoming a bemused trafficking with the supernatural (110–11).

Frank, Manfred, and Gerhard Kurz, editors. *Materialien zu Schellings philosophischen Anfängen*. Frankfurt am Main: Suhrkamp Verlag, 1975. Valuable materials on Schelling's early education and formation. See especially the articles by Harald Holz and Wolfgang Wieland, discussed separately in this bibliography.

Fridell, Egon. *Novalis als Philosoph*. Munich: Verlagsanstalt Bruckmann, 1904. A brief introduction to Novalis's theoretical interests, largely supplanted by more recent and more detailed studies.

Gadamer, Hans-Georg, editor. *Stuttgarter Hegel-Tage 1970: Vorträge und Kolloquien des Internationalen Hegel-Jubiläumskongresses*. Hegel-Studien, supplement 11 (1974). One of the best collections of material on our topic. See especially Colloquium I on Hegel and the natural sciences, noting the articles by Heinrich Schipperges, Dietrich von Engelhardt, Karin Figala, Hans Querner, and Wolfgang Jacob, all of them discussed separately in this bibliography.

Gaier, Ulrich. *Krumme Regel: Novalis' "Konstruktionslehre des schaffenden Geistes" und ihre Tradition*. Tübingen: Max Niemeyer Verlag, 1970. A structuralist interpretation of Novalis's literary and theoretical work, all-too-confident of its disclosive and emancipatory power and therefore largely dated; yet it remains noteworthy because of Novalis's own logarithmic method, which is itself everywhere engaged with structures and constructions—admittedly, the more elevated the structure, the more crooked the rule that governs it. Especially valuable is the second half of Gaier's book, on Novalis's historical sources. It culminates in a fascinating comparison between Novalis on the one hand and Goethe and Hölderlin on the other, with regard to what the author calls "indirect construction."

Gies, Manfred. "Naturphilosophie und Naturwissenschaft bei Hegel." In Petry, editor, *Hegel und die Naturwissenschaften*, 65–83 (Discussion, 83–88). Gies focuses on Hegel's 1819/20 lectures on the philosophy of nature at Berlin, in which nature is invoked as a *problem* for spirit, inasmuch as spirit is both "drawn to" and "repulsed by" nature (70). Gies's attention to this course shows that all those who try to show why and how spirit *must* externalize itself in nature, or fall into it, as though off a log, always have Hegel working against them.

Greene, Murray. "Natural Life and Subjectivity." In Stillman, editor, *Hegel's Philosophy of Spirit*, 94–117. Beginning with an account of desire *(Begierde)* in the *Phenomenology of Spirit*, Greene argues for the hierarchy of knowing over living. He provides a comparison of Hegel with Aristotle in this regard, concluding that the mating process in Hegel's philosophy of nature is superseded by the "noetic life." The "spurious infinity" of natural generation is replaced by the Real Thing—the circles of the same, located in the head—which, again, only leaves the question as to why and how spirit could ever have sunk so low.

Haering, Theodor. *Novalis als Philosoph*. Stuttgart: Verlag W. Kohlhammer, 1954. A massive (650-page), detailed, impassioned, and authoritative account of Novalis's scientific and philosophical fragments. Chapters 12 and 13, which include analyses of Novalis's views on medicine and organism, respectively, are the most useful for the present project.

Harris, Errol E. "The *Naturphilosophie* Updated." *Owl of Minerva* 10, number 2 (December 1978): 2–7. Harris attempts to show that contemporary biological and physiological science (including the very different directions represented by Sir Arthur Eddington and Jacques Monod) can be accommodated by the major theoretical structures of Hegel's philosophy of nature.

————. "The Philosophy of Nature in Hegel's System." *Review of Metaphysics* 3, number 2 (December 1949): 213–28. An early attempt to awaken interest in the English-speaking world for Hegel's philosophy of nature and science, though not by following Bradley's (and other English Hegelians') rejection of the role of nature philosophy in the Hegelian system.

Hartkopf, Werner. *Studien zur Entwicklung der modernen Dialektik: Die Dialektik in Schellings Ansätzen zu einer Naturphilosophie.* Monographien zur philosophischen Forschung, volume 102. Meisenheim am Glan: Anton Hain Verlag, 1972. A reading of Schelling's nature philosophy as an important achievement of dialectical thinking after Fichte and before Hegel. Contains many pages of helpful analysis of the *Erster Entwurf* and the *Einleitung zur Erster Entwurf,* though little on our topic.

Hasler, Ludwig, editor. *Schelling: Seine Bedeutung für eine Philosophie der Natur und der Geschichte (Referate und Kolloquien der Internationalen Schelling-Tagung Zürich 1979.* Problemata 91. Stuttgart: Frommann-Holzboog, 1981. Because it contains a series of colloquia on Schelling's natural science and theories of medicine, Hasler's is one of the most significant collections of studies on Schelling with regard to the theme of dire forces in nature. See especially the articles by Hermann Krings, Dietrich von Engelhardt, Reinhard Löw, Nelly Tsouyopoulos, Richard Toellner, Hans Querner, Karl E. Rothschuh, Detlev von Uslar, and Wolfgang Bonsiepen, all of them discussed separately in this bibliography.

Heckmann, Reinhard, Hermann Krings, and Rudolf W. Meyer, editors. *Natur und Subjektivität: Zur Auseinandersetzung mit der Naturphilosophie des jungen Schelling (Referate, Voten und Protokolle der II. Internationalen Schelling-Tagung Zürich 1983.* Stuttgart: Friedrich Frommann Verlag, 1985. Along with Brinkmann, Gadamer, and Hasler, this is one of the most important collections of essays on our topic. See especially the contributions by Dietrich von Engelhardt, Klaus Düsing, Reinhard Lauth, and, above all, Nelly Tsouyopoulos. Each of these articles is cited separately in this bibliography.

Heftrich, Eckhard. *Novalis: Vom Logos der Poesie.* Frankfurt am Main: Vittorio Klostermann Verlag, 1969. Heftrich's focus is on Novalis as poet-thinker, that is, as a figure who accomplishes the Romantic task of integrating poetic creativity, literary and historical learning, and scientific rigor. See especially chapter 2, "Orphic Science: Encyclopedics and Experiment," which offers an informed and insightful discussion of Novalis's *Universal Sketchbook.*

Hegener, Johannes. *Die Poetisierung der Wissenschaften bei Novalis, dargestellt am Prozeß der Entwicklung von Welt und Menschheit: Studien zum Problem enzyklopädischen Welterfahrens.* Bonn: Bouvier Verlag Herbert Grundmann, 1975. A full-length study of Novalis's drive to compose a scientific encyclopedia. Hegener takes "development to a higher stage" to be the driving impetus in all of Novalis's work. Especially valuable are chapters 9 and 10, on the nature of the organism, on illness and death as means to higher development, and on the practice of medicine.

Henkelmann, Thomas. *Zur Geschichte des pathophysiologischen Denkens: John Brown (1735–1788) und sein System der Medizin.* Berlin: Springer-Verlag, 1981. The most detailed treatment available of John Brown's system, which was influential throughout the period of German Idealism and Romanticism. Henkelmann's account, clearly inspired by Michel Foucault's *The Birth of the Clinic,* focuses on Brown's physiological analysis of pathology; it also measures the distance between Brown's pathophysiological thought and the anatomically based diagnostic skills of modern medicine.

Henrich, Dieter, and Klaus Düsing, editors. *Hegel in Jena. Hegel-Studien*, supplement 20 (1980). This collection focuses on the development of a speculative philosophy in the Jena period, a philosophy that considers itself adequate to an account of the absolute—of what religions call *God.* See especially the articles by Xavier Tilliette, Klaus Düsing, and Jean-Louis Vieillard-Baron, discussed separately in this bibliography.

Holz, Harald. "Die Beziehungen zwischen Schellings 'Naturphilosophie' und dem Identitätssystem in den Jahren 1801/02." *Philosophisches Jahrbuch* 78 (1971): 260–94. A discussion of Schelling's dialectical method with reference to 1) Plato and Plotinus, 2) Spinoza, and 3) Hegel.

———. "Perspektive Natur." In Baumgartner, editor, *Schelling: Einführung in seine Philosophie,* 58–74. Holz regards Schelling's texts on nature philosophy as early formulations of the transcendental-philosophical system of 1800 and the "identity philosophy" of 1801–1804. He concludes with a critique of Schelling's lack of sophistication in mathematics and metatheory, both in Holz's view essential to contemporary science.

———. "Die Struktur der Dialektik in den Frühschriften von Fichte und Schelling." In Frank and Kurz, editors, *Materialien zu Schellings philosophischen Anfängen,* 215–36. A useful discussion of Schelling's response to Fichte, but with little specific reference to Schelling's writings in the philosophy of nature.

Horstmann, Rolf-Peter. Introduction to G. W. F. Hegel, *Jena Systementwürfe III: Naturphilosophie und Philosophie des Geistes.* Hamburg: Felix Meiner Verlag, 1987, ix–xxxvii. An excellent introduction to the 1805/06 Jena materials, particularly important for information concerning the manuscript itself. Horstmann also adds a brief bibliography.

———. "Logifizierte Natur oder naturalisierte Logik? Bemerkungen zu Schellings Hegel-Kritik." In Horstmann and Petry, editors, *Hegels Philosophie der Natur,* 290–308. Horstmann takes as his main text Schelling's chapter on Hegel in the 1827 Munich lectures on the history of modern philosophy. He reviews Schelling's critique of Hegel's philosophy of nature as (1) a distortion of Schelling's own early views and (2) an imbroglio in terms of the Hegelian system's own demands. Horstmann places greater emphasis on the second point. Schelling argues that Hegel is incapable of properly integrating nature into an account of the speculative idea—so that Hegel's nature is in the end "logicized." Although Horstmann ultimately finds Schelling's critique to rest on a misunderstanding of the *Logic,* he concludes by emphasizing his own doubts as to whether nature can indeed be effectively integrated into a system of spirit—whether logic can truly be "naturalized."

Horstmann, Rolf-Peter, and Michael John Petry, editors. *Hegels Philosophie der Natur: Beziehungen zwischen empirischer und spekulativer Naturerkenntnis.* Veröffentlichungen der Internationalen Hegel-Vereinigung, volume 15. Stuttgart: Klett-Cotta, 1986. A particularly valuable collection of papers. See especially the pieces by the following authors, discussed separately in the present bibliography: Francesco Moiso, Trevor H. Levere, Dietrich von Engelhardt, Jacques D'Hondt, Wolfgang Bonsiepen, Klaus Düsing, and Rolf-Peter Horstmann.

Hösle, Vittorio. "Pflanze und Tier." In Petry, editor, *Hegel und die Naturwissenschaften,* 377–416 (Discussion, 416–22). Hösle begins with the final phase of Hegel's account of electrical process and magnetism (that is, one might say, with Hegel's Schellingian heritage) and proceeds to an account of the organic the plant and animal realms—in Hegel's system. He relates Hegel's account of chemical process to the contemporary microbiological notion of "the hypercycle" as a principle of self-organization and to the phenomenon of DNA replication, interpreting both of the latter as modes of *reflexivity*. At the same time, he views Hegel's speculative venture in the philosophy of nature as more modest and more defensible than that of contemporary theoretical biologists such as Jacques Monod.

Hühn, Lore. *Fichte und Schelling, oder: Über die Grenze menschlichen Wissens.* Stuttgart: Verlag J. B. Metzler, 1994. Hühn's focus is not on the natural philosophical writings but on Schelling's 1820/21 Erlangen lectures, which pertain to the *Weltalter* period. Yet her thesis is thought-provoking, lending itself to the conclusions of the present book; for Hühn argues that precisely in the most positive fulgurations of the self-positing subject, in the early work of Schelling and Fichte, we can see traces of an inevitable "depotentiation of the subject" (vii).

———. "Das Schweben der Einbildungskraft: Zur frühromantischen Überbietung Fichtes." *Deutsche Vierteljahrsschrift für Literaturwissenschaft und Geistesgeschichte* 70, number 4 (December 1996): 569–99. Hühn investigates the metaphor of the "hovering imagination," *schwebende Einbildungskraft,* in Fichte, Novalis, and other early Romantics. She argues convincingly that Novalis and others, such as Friedrich Schlegel, follow and even surpass Fichte in establishing the imagination as the faculty that more than any other engages actuality. Moreover, the actuality engaged by the imagination, hovering between being and nonbeing, is precisely *life* (593). Hühn's study is both wide-ranging in scope and precise in detail; it is essential background for our topic.

Ilting, Karl-Heinz. "Hegels Philosophie des Organischen." In Petry, editor, *Hegel und die Naturwissenschaften,* 349–68 (Discussion, 368–76). Ilting argues for the centrality of the living, the organism, in Hegel's speculative system as a whole, especially for the "idea" as developed in the third part of the *Science of Logic.* Ilting's is a lucid introduction to the problem of the relation between logic and philosophy of nature; however, it stops short of a discussion of the specifics of plant and animal figuration, assimilation, and reproduction, and does not take up the issues of health and illness, etc.

Jacob, Wolfgang. "Der Krankheitsbegriff in der Dialektik von Natur und Geist bei Hegel." In Gadamer, editor, *Stuttgarter Hegel-Tage 1970,* 165–72. One of the very best articles available on our theme, it attempts to identify the central function of illness throughout the Hegelian system, both for the philosophy of nature and the philosophy of subjective spirit.

Jähnig, Dieter. "On Schelling's Philosophy of Nature." *Idealistic Studies* 19, number 3 (September 1989): 222–30. A brief general introduction to Schelling's philosophy of nature, against the backdrop of Kant and Fichte, and focusing on the 1809 *Treatise on Human Freedom.*

———. *Schelling: Die Kunst in der Philosophie.* Two volumes. Pfullingen: Günter Neske Verlag, 1966–69. See especially volume 1, *Schellings Begründung von Natur und Geschichte.* Chapter 2 of part 1 of this volume, "The Intuition of Nature," discusses the 1800 *System;* no detailed presentation of the writings in Schelling's philosophy of nature appears.

Jaspers, Karl. *Schelling: Größe und Verhängnis.* Munich: Piper Verlag, 1955. Practically nothing of Schelling's early philosophy of nature appears here; the focus is on Schelling's philosophy of freedom and the late thought on myth and religion. Yet Jaspers's account of Schelling's life, especially on the importance of Caroline Schlegel-Schelling, is intriguing.

Jenneret, Jean. *Les mots et les mets: Banquets et propos de table à la Renaissance.* Paris: José Corti, 1987. Translated as *A Feast of Words: Banquets and Table Talk in the Renaissance* by Jeremy Whiteley and Emma Hughes. Chicago: University of Chicago Press, 1991. Provides historical background on what will become Novalis's theory of ingestion and on the relations of eating to speech in what one might call the "system of the mouth."

Kimmerle, Heinz. "Dokumente zu Hegels Jenaer Dozententätigkeit (1801–1807)." *Hegel-Studien* 4 (1967): 21–99. An important collection of documents pertaining not only to Hegel but also to Schelling during this turbulent period of Jena University history—where the French Revolution had a direct impact on student and professorial life.

———. "Hegels Naturphilosophie in Jena." In Henrich and Düsing, editors, *Hegel in Jena*, 207–15. Kimmerle here focuses on Hegel's earliest lectures on the philosophy of nature in Jena at the turn of the century; those lectures are principally devoted to astronomy, that is, to "the system of the sun" and "absolute matter."

———. "Zur Chronologie von Hegels Jenaer Schriften." *Hegel-Studien* 4 (1967): 125–76. An essential source, not only for the chronology of Hegel's courses and writings at Jena, but also for insight into the *Privatdozent's* formative years there.

Kirchhoff, Jochen. *Schelling in Selbstzeugnissen und Bilddokumenten.* Reinbek bei Hamburg: Rowohlt, 1982. An excellent introduction to Schelling's life and thought, one of the best volumes in an excellent series. Kirchhoff's own interests lead him to focus on Schelling's philosophy of nature. Excellent bibliography.

Kozu, Konio. *Das Bedürfnis der Philosophie: Ein Überblick über die Entwicklung des Begriffskomplexes "Bedürfnis," "Trieb," "Streben" und "Begierde" bei Hegel. Hegel-Studien,* supplement 30 (1988). A full-length study that traces the development of a crucial series of terms or "conceptual complexes" in Hegel's philosophy of life: need, drive, striving, and craving or desire. See chapter 3, on the Jena period up to and including Hegel's *Phenomenology,* especially 154–67, on Hegel's *Realphilosophie.*

Krell, David Farrell. "The Crisis of Reason in the Nineteenth Century: Schelling's Treatise on Human Freedom (1809)." In John Sallis, Giuseppina Moneta, and Jacques Taminiaux, *The Collegium Phaenomenologicum: The First Ten Years.* Dordrecht: Kluwer Academic Publishers, 1988, 13–32. A study of *Sehnsucht,* "longing," "languor," or "languishing," in Schelling's conception of the ground of God's existence.

———. *Daimon Life: Heidegger and Life-Philosophy.* Bloomington: Indiana University Press, 1992. Heidegger's proximity to Hegel on the issue of the genus *[Gattung]* is noteworthy.

———. "Eating Out: Voluptuosity for Dessert." In *Eating Culture.* Edited by Ron Scapp and Brian Seitz. Albany: State University of New York Press, forthcoming. A Nietzschean and Ferenczian reading of Novalis's system of the mouth.

———. "Female Parts in *Timaeus." Arion: A Journal of Humanities and the Classics,* New Series 2, number 3 (Fall 1975): 400–21. Relevant to the Platonic background of Schelling.

———. "Lucinde's Shame: Hegel, Sensuous Woman, and the Law." In *Hegel and Legal Theory.* Edited by Drucilla Cornell, Michel Rosenfeld, and David Gray Carlson. New York: Routledge, 1991, 287–300. Revised and reprinted in *Feminist Readings of Hegel.* Edited by Patricia Jagentowicz Mills. University Park: Pennsylvania State University Press, 1995, 89–107. A reading of Hegel's diatribe in the *Philosophy of Right* against Schlegel's *Lucinde,* with reference to the material on genitality in Hegel's Jena philosophy of nature.

———. "Der Maulwurf: Philosophische Wühlarbeit bei Kant, Hegel und Nietzsche." In David Farrell Krell, *Infectious Nietzsche.* Bloomington: Indiana University Press, 1996, chapter 5. A discussion of the subversive action of the mole—a figure opposed by Kant in his *Critique of Pure Reason* but actively embraced by Hegel as a metaphor for spirit.

————. *Of Memory, Reminiscence, and Writing: On the Verge.* Bloomington: Indiana University Press, 1990. See especially chapters 1, 3, and 5 on Hegel.

————. "The Oldest Program toward a System in German Idealism." *Owl of Minerva* 17, number 1 (Fall 1985): 5–19. A presentation of this basic document of German Idealism. The document, which presents a program in ethics, metaphysics, and philosophy of nature for the generation of thinkers after Kant, has been variously attributed to Hegel, Schelling, and Hölderlin. The accompanying commentary develops an idea about further possibilities of attribution.

————. "Pitch: Genitality/Excrementality from Hegel to Crazy Jane." *boundary 2* 9, number 3, and 10, number 1 (Winter 1984): 113–41. An attempt to read Hegel's account of assimilation and sexuality in the Jena lectures—with reference to William Butler Yeats's "Crazy Jane Talks to the Bishop."

————. *Postponements: Woman, Sensuality, and Death in Nietzsche.* Bloomington: Indiana University Press, 1986. Useful in relation to Hölderlin.

Krings, Hermann. "Vorbemerkungen zu Schellings Naturphilosophie." In Hasler, editor, *Schelling: Seine Bedeutung,* 73–76. Krings places special emphasis on Schelling's *Erster Entwurf eines Systems der Naturphilosophie* in these introductory remarks.

Lauth, Reinhard. "Der Unterschied zwischen der Naturphilosophie der Wissenschaftslehre und Schellings von zwei charakteristischen Ansatzpunkten des letzteren aus erläutert." In Heckmann et al., editors, *Natur und Subjektivität,* 211–28. An excellent discussion of the bases in Fichte's philosophy of Schelling's early philosophy of nature.

Lawrence, Joseph P. "Schelling: A New Beginning." *Idealistic Studies* 19, number 3 (September 1989): 189–201. Lawrence focuses in this piece mainly on Schelling's philosophy of religion.

————. *Schellings Philosophie des ewigen Anfangs: Die Natur als Quelle der Geschichte.* Würzburg: Königshausen & Neumann, 1987. Lawrence argues persuasively that Schelling, like Aristotle, grounds his conception of history on his view of nature. Lawrence suggests that Schelling's use of nature, even in *Die Weltalter,* derives from his early treatment of nature in the 1790s.

Leibbrand, Werner. *Romantische Medizin.* Hamburg: H. Goverts Verlag, 1937. Also in Italian translation: *Medicina Romantica.* Translated by Giovanna Frederici Ajroldi. Bari: Gius, Laterza & Figli, 1939. An excellent early attempt to systematize our fragmentary knowledge concerning medicine during the Romantic era. Leibbrand emphasizes surgical practice, the theoretical presuppositions of medicine (especially Haller's concept of physiological stimulation, Galvanism, polarity, Brownianism, etc.), the major philosophical contributions to medical theory (by, among others, Novalis, Schelling, and Hegel), and the impact of all these developments on the doctor-patient relationship.

————. *Die spekulative Medizin der Romantik.* Hamburg: Claassen Verlag, 1956. The first major study early in the second half of the twentieth century. Leibbrand's elegant and eloquent study contains much information on *Naturphilosophie,* including physiology, theories of animal magnetism, and theories of illness during the Romantic period. Because it is a general study, organized by topic rather than figure, it is sometimes difficult to locate discussions of specific figures. That said, this is still an excellent introduction to the topic.

Levere, Trevor H. "Hegel and the Earth Sciences." In Horstmann and Petry, editors, *Hegels Philosophie der Natur,* 103–20. A useful account of the first stage of Hegel's "organics" or "organic physics," which comprises geology and oryctognosy (i.e., the science of mining). After an initial account of

Hegel's library in the area of the natural sciences, Levere treats the important topic of crystallization. He then proceeds to Hegel's account of the earliest stages of vegetable life, on land (lichens), and in the sea (phosphorescent seaweeds).

Löw, Reinhard. "Qualitätenlehre und Materiekonstruktion: Zur systematischen Aktualität von Schellings Naturphilosophie." In Hasler, editor, *Schelling: Seine Bedeutung*, 99–106. Löw inquires into the central problem of the construction of matter as elaborated in Schelling's *Erster Entwurf.*

Lucas, George. "A Re-Interpretation of Hegel's Philosophy of Nature." *Journal of the History of Philosophy* 22, number 1 (January 1984): 103–13. Lucas affirms Errol E. Harris's attempt to revive interest in Hegel's philosophy of nature and science. Lucas offers a Whiteheadian reinterpretation of Hegel's *Naturphilosophie*, understanding Whitehead's "organic mechanism," at least in terms of its intentions, as a response to Hegel's discomfiture in the face of the Cartesian and Kantian dualisms. Hegel's treatment of teleology in the organic realm is therefore regarded as the key to the reinterpretation.

Lucas, Hans-Christian. "The 'Sovereign Ingratitude' of Spirit toward Nature: Logical Qualities, Corporeity, Animal Magnetism, and Madness in Hegel's 'Anthropology.'" *Owl of Minerva* 23, number 2 (Spring 1992): 131–50. Lucas provides an excellent expository and critical close reading of the "Anthropology" in the three editions of the *Encyclopedia*, focusing on the highly problematic transition from philosophy of nature to philosophy of spirit in the system. Even though Lucas locates his inquiry in the philosophy of spirit, his aim is to show that nature is neither left behind nor successfully sublated in the philosophy of spirit. One of the very best articles available on our topic.

von der Luft, Eric. "The Birth of Spirit for Hegel out of the Travesty of Medicine." In Stillman, editor, *Hegel's Philosophy of Spirit*, 25–42. Starting from an analysis of the section on phrenology in the *Phenomenology of Spirit*, which is spirit's proper—if embarrassing—birthplace in the *Phenomenology*, von der Luft argues that biology and medicine play a crucial role throughout Hegel's philosophy, namely, whenever spirit is about to be born (see esp. 35–36). The article stops short of an account of the role of *crisis* in Hegel's early account of illness. It rescues the Hegelian analysis with the help of the traditional hierarchy—spirit being "higher than" nature and matter—without noting that this hierarchy may itself be the travesty that troubles Hegel most.

McCumber, John. "Commentary on [Murray Greene's] 'Natural Life and Subjectivity.'" In Stillman, editor, *Hegel's Philosophy of Spirit*, 118–23. In his response to Murray Greene, McCumber refers to Hegel's analysis of genitality (in particular, the prostate) in an interesting way.

Mende, Erich. "Die Entwicklungsgeschichte der Faktoren Irritabilität und Sensibilität in deren Einfluß auf Schellings 'Prinzip' als Ursache des Lebens." *Philosophia naturalis* 17 (1979): 327–48. Mende offers a detailed account of the Haller-Brown theory of irritability-sensibility, and shows that this theory becomes the very principle of life for Schelling by the time of the 1797 *Ideen.*

Miller, Arnold Vincent. "Defending Hegel's Philosophy of Nature." In Petry, *Hegel and Newtonianism*, 103–13. With regard to the question of the relation of *logic* to philosophy of nature, Miller (as opposed to Martin Drees), is a "tight constructionist"; that is, he insists that the categories of both logic and philosophy of nature must function in precisely the same way, no matter how the exigencies of the empirical may influence the finite sciences.

Moiso, Francesco. "Die Hegelsche Theorie der Physik und der Chemie in ihrer Beziehung zu Schellings Naturphilosophie." In Horstmann and Petry, editors, *Hegels Philosophie der Natur,* 54–87. Moiso focuses on the period of Schelling's *Von der Weltseele* and *Erster Entwurf* (1798/99) and Hegel's 1803/04 lectures on physics and chemistry. Although Moiso largely neglects the organic realm that is our primary concern, he does take up the problem of "individuals" and their "discontinuous existence" (55); he also sheds light on the importance of magnetism and polarized matter in general for both Schelling and Hegel (81–82).

———. "Zur Quellenforschung der Schellingschen Naturphilosophie." In Hasler, editor, *Schelling: Seine Bedeutung,* 153–59. A complement to the study by Dietrich von Engelhardt, "Die organische Natur und die Lebenswissenschaften in Schellings Naturphilosophie." Moiso focuses on the sources of Schelling's theory of caloric, principally in *Ideen* and *Von der Weltseele.*

Molnár, Géza von. *Novalis' "Fichte Studies": The Foundations of His Aesthetics.* The Hague: Mouton, 1970. An excellent account of Novalis's formation of his basic theoretical position vis-à-vis Fichte in 1795/96. Especially useful are the pages on "Novalis' Concept of Unity" and "The Concept of Limitation and the Unifying Function of the Imagination."

———. *Romantic Vision, Ethical Context: Novalis and Artistic Autonomy.* Minneapolis: University of Minnesota Press, 1987. Von Molnár focuses on the importance of theory and philosophy (especially the "Fichte Studies") for Novalis's major creative works. He also provides very useful background and biographical material. Unfortunately, the theoretical sketches after 1796 receive no detailed treatment; even so, this is clearly one of the very best books on Novalis in any language.

Neubauer, John. *Bifocal Vision: Novalis' Philosophy of Nature and Disease.* Chapel Hill: University of North Carolina Press, 1971. The definitive study of our theme in relation to Novalis. Neubauer's full-length study is clearly organized and presented, is lucid in its style and its argument, and offers excellent background information on Schelling, John Brown, and Novalis.

———. "Zwischen Natur und mathematischer Abstraktion: der Potenzbegriff in der Frühromantik." In Brinkmann, editor, *Romantik in Deutschland,* 175–86. An authoritative account of the theory of "powers" or "potencies," focusing on Novalis but applying Novalis's theory of potencies and his combinatorics to other figures and aspects of Romanticism—including William Wordsworth.

Neuser, Wolfgang. "Die naturphilosophische und naturwissenschaftliche Literatur aus Hegels privater Bibliothek." In Petry, editor, *Hegel und die Naturwissenschaften,* 479–99. An important resource for tracking down precisely which volumes and journals Hegel had at his disposal. One finds, for example, Jakob Ackermann's study (discussed in chapter 10 of the present book) cited there.

———. "Sekundärliteratur zu Hegels Naturphilosophie (1802–1985)." In Petry, editor, *Hegel und die Naturwissenschaften,* 501–42. A massive bibliographical undertaking—in spite of the fact that Hegel's philosophy of nature has long been neglected!

Oldenburg, Dieter. *Romantische Naturphilosophie und Arzneimittellehre.* Braunschweig: Pharmaziegeschichtliches Seminar der Technischen Universität Braunschweig, doctoral dissertation, 1979. A detailed discussion of the pharmaceutical doctrines of the key Romantic philosophers of nature, including Schelling and Hegel, but unfortunately with only scant references to Novalis. Oldenburg does discuss the matter of poisons, but perhaps for professional reasons does not give this theme due weight in his discussions.

Olshausen, Waldemar. *Friedrich von Hardenbergs (Novalis) Beziehungen zur Naturwissenschaft seiner Zeit.* Leipzig: Philosophische Fakultät der Universität Leipzig, doctoral dissertation, 1905. Olshausen emphasizes the influence of Jakob Böhme—specifically, Böhme's prevailing mood of cheerful-ness or *heitere Fröhlichkeit*—on Novalis's relation to all the sciences. Most useful to us today is the second of the three chapters, concerning the influence on Novalis of the science contemporary to him, especially the examples of Werner and Ritter.

Peterson, Mark C. E. "Animals Eating Empiricists: Assimilation and Subjectiv-ity in Hegel's *Philosophy of Nature.*" *Owl of Minerva* 23, number 1 (Fall 1991): 49–62. An account of assimilation in Hegel's *Encyclopedia* that tries to outline the logical categories reflected in Hegel's account. It stops short of posing critical questions on the proximity of theoretical and alimentary ingestion in Hegel, and on the admitted proximity of both types of ingestion to poison-ing.

Petry, Michael John. "Hegel's Philosophy of Nature: Recent Developments." *Hegel-Studien* 23 (1988): 303–26. Reviews the collections by Heckmann and Cohen-Wartofsky, along with the *Jenaer Systementwürfe* in the new histori-cal-critical edition.

———, editor. *Hegel and Newtonianism.* Dordrecht: Kluwer Academic Publish-ers, 1993. See especially the articles by M. Drees, A. V. Miller, and Dietrich von Engelhardt, discussed separately in this bibliography.

———. *Hegel und die Naturwissenschaften.* Stuttgart: Frommann-Holzboog, 1987. This useful collection, in which each paper is followed by extensive discussion, is reviewed by Stefan Büttner in *Hegel-Studien* 29 (1994): 198–202. See especially the two articles by Dieter Wandschneider, along with the articles by Manfred Gies, Karl-Heinz Ilting, Vittorio Hösle, and Dietrich von Engelhardt, which are discussed separately in this bibliography. See also the excellent bibliographical materials collected by Wolfgang Neuser.

Pixberg, Hermann. *Novalis als Naturphilosoph.* Gütersloh: C. Bertelsmann, 1928. Pixberg's clearly written study is still an excellent introduction to some of the most important lesser-known influences on Novalis—Hemsterhuis, Ritter, Baader, and Böhme—as well as the more familiar influences, such as Fichte, Kant, Goethe, and Schelling.

Querner, Hans. "Das Phänomen der Zweigeschlechtlichkeit im System der Naturphilosophie von Schelling." In Hasler, editor, *Schelling: Seine Bedeu-tung,* 139–43. As its title suggests, Querner's is one of the most important studies in the area investigated by the present volume, largely corroborating the theses argued for here. Querner shows that the fundamental presuppo-sitions of Schelling's nature philosophy, especially the duplicity of infinite activity and inhibition, necessitate the *Entgegensetzung der Geschlechter,* the bipolar sexual opposition. He also demonstrates that such a duplicity poses unresolvable problems for Schelling's account of the *individual.* Unfortu-nately, Querner stops just short of acknowledging that the absolute itself—the original, divine *monas*—is such a problematic individual; he also fails to observe that the place where Schelling discusses the fate of the individual is the appendix on *illness* in the *Erster Entwurf;* he therefore misses the essential complicity of sexuality and illness in Schelling's philosophy of nature. Even so, Querner's brief study is a most valuable contribution to the literature.

———. "Die Stufenfolge der Organismen in Hegels Philosophie der Natur." In Gadamer, editor, *Stuttgarter Hegel-Tage 1970,* 153–63. Although we may be accustomed to identifying *Schelling*'s philosophy of organism in terms of a system or sequence of stages *(Stufen),* Querner shows that Hegel's system is also dominated by this developmental, progressivist structure. An excellent account, beginning with the logical structures of Hegel's system as a whole, it nevertheless stops short (see 159) of an account of illness in the *Stufenfolge.*

Risse, Günter B. "Schelling, 'Naturphilosophie' and John Brown's System of

Medicine." *Bulletin of the History of Medicine* 50 (1976): 321–34. An excellent introduction to the influence of John Brown's theories on the early Schelling, on Goethe's importance for Schelling at Jena, and on the details of Schelling's appreciation—and critique—of Brown.

Rothschuh, Karl Eduard. "Deutsche Medizin im Zeitalter der Romantik: Vielheit statt Einheit." In Hasler, editor, *Schelling: Seine Bedeutung*, 145–51. A brief history of the concepts of "Romantic medicine" and "Romantic physiology." Rothschuh argues that these categories have to be more finely differentiated into four distinct groups, with Schelling as the most important figure in the second group, the "nature-philosophical stream."

———. *Konzepte der Medizin in Vergangenheit und Gegenwart*. Stuttgart: Hippokrates Verlag, 1978. A full-length account of the history of medicine in the West, with excellent background—from antiquity through modernity—on the dominant conceptions of illness and of the practice of medicine. Especially useful for our topic are the section on John Brown (342–52) and the chapter (12) on Schelling and Romantic medicine (385–416).

———. "Naturphilosophische Konzepte der Medizin aus der Zeit der deutschen Romantik." In Brinkmann, editor, *Romantik in Deutschland*, 243–66. Rothschuh shows the extensive influence Schelling's theory and practice of medicine had on practitioners during the nineteenth century—comparing that influence to contagion (251)!

Sallis, John. *Spacings—of Reason and Imagination in Texts of Kant, Fichte, Hegel*. Chicago: University of Chicago Press, 1987. Although it makes little reference to the philosophy of nature as such, Sallis's work presents a number of *ontological* analyses—especially touching the Kant of the first and third *Critiques*—that underlie my own work and are formative for it.

Sandkühler, Hans J. *Natur und geschichtlicher Prozess: Studien zur Naturphilosophie Schellings*. Frankfurt am Main: Suhrkamp Verlag, 1984. See especially the articles by Jiri Cerny and Wolfgang Förster for accounts of Schelling's importance for a dialectical-materialist account of nature; for the present topic, see above all Dietrich von Engelhardt's article (discussed above) on Schelling's theoretical foundations of medicine.

Scheier, Claus-Artur. "Die Bedeutung der Naturphilosophie im deutschen Idealismus." *Philosophia naturalis* 23 (1986): 389–98. Scheier offers a broad-based discussion of the topic: he provides an overview of German Idealism as a whole from the time of Kant's 1786 *Metaphysische Anfangsgründe der Naturwissenschaft* onward, seeing in Schelling's philosophy of nature the decisive departure from Fichte's emphasis on practical philosophy.

Schipperges, Heinrich. "Hegel und die Naturwissenschaften: Einleitende Vorbemerkung." In Gadamer, editor, *Stuttgarter Hegel-Tage 1970*, 105–10. In a dialogue with Ernst Bloch and Nietzsche, Schipperges shows precisely how daring a colloquium on Hegel and the natural sciences had to appear in 1970. An excellent brief introduction to the topic.

———. "Krankwerden und Gesundsein bei Novalis." In Brinkmann, editor, *Romantik in Deutschland*, 226–42. One of the very best discussions of the topic, beautifully organized and lucidly presented. Unfortunately, the importance of sexuality in Novalis's philosophy of nature in general and theory of illness in particular is not recognized.

Schulz, Gerhard. *Novalis in Selbstzeugnissen und Bilddokumenten*. Reinbek bei Hamburg: Rowohlt, 1969. An excellent introductory account, with a brief yet insightful discussion of "magical idealism," and a useful bibliography.

Simon, Heinrich. *Der magische Idealismus: Studien zur Philosophie des Novalis*. Heidelberg: Carl Winter's Universitätsbuchhandlung, 1906. Perhaps because of the nature of the earlier editions of Novalis's works, in which the theoretical and scientific writings played a minor role, this work concentrates on Novalis's literary work; it discusses the literary production in terms of the magical ego, knowledge, experience, forms, and belief. It is no doubt important for Novalis's *Rezeptionsgeschichte*, but it is otherwise of little value for our topic.

Snelders, Henricus Adrianus Marie. "Atomismus und Dynamismus im Zeitalter der Deutschen Romantischen Naturphilosophie." In Brinkmann, editor, *Romantik in Deutschland*, 187–201. An account of atomism in the eighteenth century, emphasizing Dalton but with good discussion of Schelling at 190–91.

Sohni, Hans. *Die Medizin der Frühromantik: Novalis' Bedeutung für den Versuch einer Umwertung der "Romantischen Medizin."* Freiburg im Breisgau: Hans Ferdinand Schulz Verlag, 1973. Sohni's is an important contribution to our topic, especially with regard to Novalis but also because it makes extensive reference to Schelling. Sohni offers a detailed reading of Novalis's concept of illness, a concept based on various phenomena under the heading of *polarity*. According to Sohni, the importance of polarity in medical theory and practice is common to Romanticism as a whole.

Stieghahn, Joachim. *Magisches Denken in den Fragmenten Friedrichs von Hardenberg*. Berlin: Philosophische Fakultät der Freien Universität, doctoral dissertation, 1964. Stieghahn interprets magical idealism in terms of the principal cultural-anthropological categories of "animism," with particular attention to the alchemical tradition. With regard to our topic, see especially section 5 of chapter 2, "Methods of Healing Our Current Condition" (80–101). Unfortunately, the work is insufficiently articulated into self-contained sections, a lack that makes the reading difficult.

Stillman, Peter G., editor. *Hegel's Philosophy of Spirit*. Albany: State University of New York Press, 1987. See the articles by Eric von der Luft and Murray Greene, both cited above.

Tilliette, Xavier. "Hegel in Jena als Mitarbeiter Schellings." In Henrich and Düsing, editors, *Hegel in Jena*, 11–24. An excellent and entertaining account of the cooperation between Hegel and Schelling on the *Critical Journal* in Jena, 1801–1803.

Toellner, Richard. "Randbedingungen zu Schellings Konzeption der Medizin als Wissenschaft." In Hasler, editor, *Schelling: Seine Bedeutung*, 117–28. Toellner confirms Nelly Tsouyopoulos's and Karl Eduard Rothschuh's argument (against a suspicion expressed by Dietrich von Engelhardt) that Schelling's influence on the history of medical science is, on balance, a positive and very extensive one. He refers to Schelling's positive influence on later scientists and medical researchers, including Jan Purkyne (1787–1868) and Karl Ernst von Baer (1792–1876), the cofounders of modern comparative embryology.

Tsouyopoulos, Nelly. "Schellings Konzeption der Medizin als Wissenschaft und die 'Wissenschaftlichkeit' der modernen Medizin." In Hasler, editor, *Schelling: Seine Bedeutung*, 107–16. Nelly Tsouyopoulos, of the Institute for the Theory and History of Medicine, University of Münster, is one of the most important researchers on Schelling in this area. Tsouyopoulos argues, against Dietrich von Engelhardt, that Schelling's nature philosophy had a positive impact not only on the history of speculative philosophy (as von Engelhardt too affirms) but also on the scientific-medical tradition as such, "that the influence of Schelling's philosophy played a decisive role in the origins and development of modern medicine" (108).

———. "Schellings Krankheitsbegriff und die Begriffsbildung der Modernen Medizin." In Heckmann et al., editors, *Natur und Subjektivität*, 265–90. Tsouyopoulos offers here one of our most detailed and penetrating discussions of Schelling's conception of medicine, demonstrating the decisive influence Schelling had on the theory and practice of medicine in the nineteenth century.

————. "Der Streit zwischen Friedrich Wilhelm Joseph Schelling und Andreas Röschlaub über die Grundlagen der Medizin." *Medizinhistorisches Journal* 13 (1978): 229–46. A meticulous account of Schelling's close work during the years 1799–1802 with the most famous physician and adherent of the Brownian system of his time. Tsouyopoulos also recounts their eventual split, which weakened the influence of *Naturphilosophie* on the further development of medicine in Germany.

von Uslar, Detlev. "Die Aktualität Schellings für Tiefenpsychologie und Psychotherapie." In Hasler, editor, *Schelling: Seine Bedeutung*, 163–66. A brief comparison of C. G. Jung's notion of identity with that of Schelling in the 1800 *System* and later "identity philosophy." Von Uslar argues that Schelling offers new resources to a psychology that must struggle against philosophy's tendency to cut off the subject from the world—and also against psychology's own tendency to psychologize that subject.

Vieilliard-Baron, Jean-Louis. "L'interprétation hégélienne du *Timée*, ou la philosophie de la nature." *Revue de Métaphysique et de Morale* 81, number 3 (July–September 1976): 376–95. A careful, philologically informed, and erudite reading of Hegel's account of the most famous Platonic dialogue on the philosophy of nature. Vieilliard-Baron focuses on the Christian-theological (and Jakob Böhmean) problematic of the world as the Son of the creator God. Most interesting for our topic are those pages (392–93) that contrast Hegel's and Schelling's responses to the "mother and nurse of becoming" in *Timaeus*—the famous problem of the receptacle or χώρα.

————. "La notion de matière et le matérialisme vrai selon Hegel et Schelling à l'époque d'Iéna." In Henrich and Düsing, editors, *Hegel in Jena*, 197–206. A critical historical account of the dual conception of matter held by both Schelling and Hegel during the Jena period: matter may be an object of chemistry, thus being matter in the usual sense; or it may be an object of ontology and theology—it may be "ethereal" matter, in which case it is the stuff of spirit and life.

Volkmann-Schluck, Karl Heinz. "Die Entäußerung der Idee zur Natur." In Gadamer, editor, *Heidelberger Hegel-Tage 1962. Hegel-Studien*, supplement 1 (1964): 37–44. Volkmann-Schluck devotes himself here to the problem of the transition from *logic* to *philosophy of nature* in Hegel's system, conceived of as a system of and by "the absolute idea." He focuses on the dilemma of the movement of the idea into nature as both *necessary* and *free*, seeing in this dilemma the key to the most problematic writings in Hegel's corpus, the *Phenomenology of Spirit*, *Science of Logic*, and *Encyclopedia of Philosophical Sciences*.

————. "Novalis' magischer Idealismus." In Hans Steffen, editor, *Die deutsche Romantik: Poetik, Formen und Motive*. Göttingen: Vandenhoeck & Ruprecht, 1967, 45–53. Volkmann-Schluck discusses the relation of Novalis's scientific fragments to the poetic work and argues that Novalis's magical idealism is "metaphysics itself become poetry" (52).

Wagner, Lydia Elizabeth. *The Scientific Interest of Friedrich von Hardenberg (Novalis)*. Ph.D. dissertation. Ann Arbor, Mich.: Edwards Brothers, 1937. In spite of its age, Wagner's dissertation offers a readable and reliable biographical account of Novalis's scientific interests and achievements; it is also excellent on the scientific influences on Novalis, especially in the areas of biology and medicine.

Wandschneider, Dieter. "Anfänge des Seelischen in der Natur." In Petry, editor,

*Hegel und die Naturwissenschaften*, 443–67 (Discussion, 467–75). Wandschneider emphasizes the character of the organism as a *system*, hence as an analog of the reflexive philosophical system that tries to understand the organism. This systematic chiasm would be the *soul*. Wandschneider takes sensibility or sensation *(Empfindung)* as his guideline to the question of the soul, interiority, and subjectivity in nature. An excellent introduction to the fundamental problem of life as infinite process (466–67), Wandschneider's article stops short of a clear and full discussion of the *corporeality* of the soul that wants to be immortal and infinite.

———. "Nature and the Dialectic of Nature in Hegel's Objective Idealism." *Bulletin of the Hegel Society of Great Britain* 26 (Autumn–Winter 1992): 30–51. An effort to confront the monumentally difficult question of spirit's move— or fall—into the externality of nature. The argument is difficult to follow, and it leaves the mystery of spirit's plunge intact.

———. "Die Stellung der Natur im Gesamtentwurf der hegelschen Philosophie." In Petry, editor, *Hegel und die Naturwissenschaften*, 33–58 (Discussion 58–64). Wandschneider identifies the ontology of nature as the Achilles' heel of modern philosophy from Descartes onward, and recommends Hegel's as the most detailed and empirically rich (and also most logically grounded) engagement with nature.

Wandschneider, Dieter, and Vittorio Hösle. "Die Entäußerung der Idee zur Natur und ihre zeitliche Entfaltung als Geist bei Hegel." *Hegel-Studien* 18 (1983): 173–99. A *systemimmanente* attempt to explain why spirit and idea must externalize themselves as nature and reality, thus "falling into time" and then *returning to themselves* from out of nature. Wandschneider and Hösle do not underestimate the difficulty of their task, and yet their lucubrations leave the mystery of spirit's externalization unresolved.

White, Alan. *Schelling: An Introduction to the System of Freedom*. New Haven: Yale University Press, 1983. A sparse account of Schelling's philosophy of nature (see 50–54) as prelude to a "system of freedom"; White's discussion stops short of sexuality, illness, or other expressions of duplicity and bipolarity in Schelling's system.

Wiedmann, Franz. *Hegel in Selbstzeugnissen und Bilddokumenten*. Reinbek bei Hamburg: Rowohlt, 1965. Wiedmann's is still a useful introductory account of the life and work, although Hegel's philosophy of nature, early and late, receives little comment. For a biting critique of Wiedmann's neglect of recently discovered sources, however, see Günther Nicolin's review in *Hegel-Studien* 4 (1967): 286–88.

Wieland, Wolfgang. "Die Anfänge der Philosophie Schellings und die Frage nach der Natur." In Manfred Frank and Gerhard Kurz, editors, *Materialien zu Schellings philosophischen Anfängen*. Frankfurt am Main: Suhrkamp, 1975, 237–79. An excellent general introduction to the main topics under discussion today, although it falls short of a detailed reading of Schelling's texts, especially the *First Projection*.

Zizek, Slavoj. *The Indivisible Remainder: An Essay on Schelling and Related Matters*. London: Verso, 1996. The first part of Zizek's three-part essay offers a real-imaginary-symbolic (i.e., Lacanian–Neo-Marxian) account of Schelling's system of freedom, with reference to the 1809 *Treatise on Human Freedom* and the 1811–1815 *Ages of the World*. Nothing is said about Schelling's philosophy of nature, but then what other critic could bring Schelling into vital contact with Keanu Reeves and *The Flintstones?*

# INDEX

*Authors of books and articles in the secondary literature, along with authors of primary literature who are cited only once in the text, have been omitted from the index for reasons of space. All authors of secondary literature cited in the book are listed in the Annotated Bibliography. The names of the three principal philosophers studied in the book—Novalis, Schelling, and Hegel—have not been included in the index, since they appear on virtually every page.*

**David Farrell Krell** is Professor of Philosophy at DePaul University. He is author of *The Good European: Nietzsche's Work Sites in Word and Image; Archeticture: Ecstasies of Space, Time, and the Human Body; Daimon Life: Heidegger and Life-Philosophy; Infectious Nietzsche; Of Memory, Reminiscence, and Writing: On the Verge; Postponements: Woman, Sensuality, and Death in Nietzsche,* and other works.